Youth Work Process, Product and Practice

Creating an Authentic Curriculum in Work With Young People

RHP

Russell House Publishing

D1427047

Russell House Publishing
Published in 2007 by:
Russell House Publishing Ltd.
4 St. George's House
Uplyme Road
Lyme Regis
Dorset DT7 3LS

Tel: 01297-443948
Fax: 01297-442722
e-mail: help@russellhouse.co.uk
www.russellhouse.co.uk

British Library Cataloguing-in-publication Data:

A catalogue record for this book is available from the British Library.

ISBN: 978-1-905541-11-9

Typeset by TW Typesetting, Plymouth, Devon

Printed by Biddles, King's Lynn

Russell House Publishing

Russell House Publishing aims to publish innovative and valuable materials to
help managers, practitioners, trainers, educators and students.

Our full catalogue covers: social policy, working with young people, helping
children and families, care of older people, social care, combating social
exclusion, revitalising communities and working with offenders.

Full details can be found at www.russellhouse.co.uk and we are pleased to send
out information to you by post. Our contact details are on this page.

We are always keen to receive feedback on publications and new ideas for
future projects.

Contents

Section Five: Curriculum in Context

Dedication

Dedicated to Jim Hewitt
who died on 6th August, 1991, aged 43.
A youth worker
whose energy, passion and commitment
live on
in those he inspired

Acknowledgements

I would like to express my gratitude to all those who have helped in no small way to the writing of this book.

Firstly to Bernard Davies for his 'critical friendship' throughout the writing process, for his detailed comments on earlier drafts, and for agreeing to write a foreword to the book.

To all those who took the time to read the draft manuscript in its entirety, Michael O'Haodain, Prof. John O'Neill, Gillian Hall, Jan Stockings, Pete Jolly, Prof. John Pitts, Sue Cooper, or parts thereof, including Mike Ireland, Sue Wayman, Ruth Hubbard and Trevor Hamilton.

To all my colleagues at the College of St Mark and St John, in particular to Ruth Hubbard and Colin Dawson for ensuring that I had some relief from other commitments to gain some time to write to Dr Will Large for his encouragement and advice on the proposal for this book, and to Sue Wayman for her encouragement and support.

To the late Ron Kirby who had the foresight to request a lecture on curriculum, the research for which led to my initial paper, and who encouraged me to write it. To Tony Jeffs for his realisation that this was a pertinent issue and his corresponding call for a debate on the subject, without which the seed for this book would never have been planted.

In addition, I would like to thank those people who provided me with their curriculum documents, without which a large part of this book would not have been possible.

And last but by no means least: to my wife Sue for her unstinting support and without whom this book would never have been written and for my two sons Nathan and Evan, who never fail to remind me of what is really important in life.

Preface

As someone who, many years ago experienced the benefit of youth work, I know first hand the power of youth workers intentions, aspirations, challenge, support and guidance; as well as how this process of engagement enables growth. I also suspect that it is unlikely that projects I had the benefit of being involved in would be either given the funding or the managerial support in the current climate of youth work. As they were holistic and embraced both the circumstances of the individual and their potential for change, but were not tied, and could not easily be tied to specific, short term outcomes.

As a professional with nearly two decades of experience of undertaking youth work I have noticed profound changes. This is exemplified by a shift from a practice which embraced youth workers' freedom to develop creative responses to individual and group needs (though admittedly often with limited resources) to a situation where short termism, accountability, and the ever present demand for outcomes predominate.

Buffeted by successive policies which do little to help and much to hinder the development of effective youth work practice, this book is motivated by dismay at the current climate affecting youth work. Importantly, however, this is not a pessimistic book, one which carps from the sidelines about the ills of the (youth work) world. It is critical and points out weaknesses, particularly of contemporary policy; but its primary purpose is to offer solutions. The book is based on the premise that youth work cannot defend itself against erroneous and rival conceptions of practice unless it can sufficiently articulate its own. Through offering a viable curriculum for youth work it is hoped that this offers one of the means by which individual workers, services and the profession as a whole can promote its unique educational practice.

Jon Ord, August 2006

Foreword

Bernard Davies

Jon Ord's book, like his earlier articles (Ord, 2004a, 2004b) steps into a controversy which goes right to the heart of youth work. Some of the protagonists within this have argued that youth work cannot have a curriculum – indeed, that for youth work such a notion is a contradiction in terms. For Jon these arguments are rooted in fundamental misconceptions – particularly about the meaning of the term and how it is applied. Though at times testy, this is a debate which has been healthy – indeed essential. It has encouraged reflection (and self-reflection) on what youth workers do and should do and how they should go about it. In the process it has provided (for youth work) much needed indications that searching intellectual work is under way. To this work, Jon's book now makes a substantial new contribution.

As he makes clear, youth work is not a practice which allows for confident prior prescriptions of what any particular young person or – more significantly for youth work – group of young people will require of its practitioners. It does not lend itself to outcomes determined in advance according to hard-and-fast targets for dealing with some adult-defined adolescent condition or category of teenager. A distinctive characteristic of the work is a responsiveness to young people as they are encountered – to who they are; what they want, demand, need; and, to a significant degree, how *they* judge the 'outcomes' once they have experienced them.

In their pursuit of this responsiveness, and indeed of the spontaneity and creativity this requires, youth workers have too often in the past resorted to flying by the seat of their pants – and then justifying this on the grounds that it displays them as true prophets of the youth work mission. Hard analysis shaped by well defined concepts has not always been a prized principle in youth work circles. If 'curriculum' can help bring some of this intellectual rigour to youth work practice, it is surely to be welcomed.

However – and this is a crucial caveat – any such concept does need to be explicitly and clearly defined. For much of its history, youth work – then called youth leadership – was in effect working to unacknowledged curriculi: pre-defined programmes of work which did not just set out content but also posited outcomes often expressed as ideal models of what young people should be and should become (see Davies, 2004). Even when the term 'curriculum' did formally enter the youth work discourse, what was meant by it too often lacked clarity or an articulated definition. As has happened recurrently in youth work's history, it had the air of the latest fad which practitioners, their managers and especially their political masters and mistresses have been prone to embrace. In this it is of a piece with, for example, the glib accretion of 'community' in the 1970s and, more recently, the knee-jerk welcomes given to 'volunteering' and even 'participation' – to say nothing of the all-pervasive *Every Child Matters*' 'five outcomes' (DfES, 2003) now required of all government-inspired (and funded) youth policies. As Gilchrist, Jeffs and Spence have pointed out (Gilchrist et al., 2001: 2–3) such 'bandwaggoning' is rooted in an historical blindness which has repeatedly left youth work open to external imposition of deeply flawed policy initiatives.

This has been true, too, of 'curriculum'. On and off for at least a quarter of a century, youth workers have reached for the term when they have felt the need to demonstrate that they do as important a job as teachers; or because ministers have told them they need it; or to explain to the uninitiated a practice too often described in mystifying (not to say mystical) terms; or because they have convinced themselves that it can act as a simple tool for satisfying that need, once recognised, to plan and guide their work. The result has been a resort to notions of 'curriculum' which have been under-defined and therefore misleading and confusing.

This situation has been exacerbated further by the way the curriculum debate in youth work has been carried on, with the term itself often being used as if it had only one handed-down-from-above meaning. Yet this is a human construct to which we can (and do) attach whatever meaning or meanings we choose. As a range of protagonists (knowingly or 'intuitively', and often without making them explicit) have settled for different and sometimes quite contradictory interpretations, confusion has been deepened. Worse still, risky hostages to (especially political) fortune have been offered up as powerful interests have seized on the term for their own diversionary ends. In the process youth workers ostensibly operating from quite different value bases have found themselves dragged into alien practice territory.

This book represents a significant contribution to redressing these intellectual and conceptual imbalances in youth work thinking and practice. No doubt some of his readers will disagree with or be discomforted by points in his analysis or conclusions he draws from this – a further sign, surely, that that healthy dialogue is continuing? (I, for example, will want to go on probing the perspective he presents on young people's voluntary participation in youth work.) Such reactions cannot, however, be allowed to detract from the book's important strengths – in particular, following its relentless unpacking of the notion of 'curriculum', its exposition of an extended definition of the concept which articulates convincingly with youth work's core concept of 'process'. In working his way through these arguments, Jon Ord, head-on, systematically confronts the historic and current controversies, not least by engaging critically with some of youth work's academic and policy-making big hitters.

In doing this, the book is also extremely timely. It appears just as the only institution which for sixty-plus years has had an explicit mandate to develop youth work – local authority youth services – is being merged into new 'trust' structures which identify themselves primarily as 'for children' though not necessarily for 'young people'. This coincides with other policy 'drivers' – particularly *Transforming Youth Work* (DfES, 2001) *Resourcing Excellent Youth Services* (DfES, 2002) and *Youth*

Matters (DfES, 2005a, 2006a) which, as Jon Ord points out, are resulting in 'a shift from traditional youth work which is based around relationships to a more formalised "delivery" emphasising outcomes and accreditation'. Among the consequences he highlights is 'an ever more stringent attempt to restrict and curtail the expansive "universal" aspect of youth work into ever more specifically predetermined responses to perceived "individual" need'. The result is 'a model which over-emphasises young people as problematic . . .' and 'the promotion of a targeted response to the perceived problems.' Not since the late 1950s and the establishment of the Albemarle Committee has the need been so pressing for youth workers and their allies to make the case for youth work in accessible, rigorous and coherent ways.

Impressive though Jon Ord's contribution is to meeting this challenge, his book will not ultimately be judged on how far it has helped deal with these current threats: if that is all it does, as these recede and others surge in to take their place, the book could easily find itself stranded on a deserted policy shore. The more demanding test must surely be: will it contribute in a substantive and sustained way to that intellectual work which youth workers need to do to underpin their claims to be making valued impacts on young people's development and welfare as *they* perceive these?

For me the clear answer to this question is: yes. For one thing, the book's arguments are consistently advanced and supported not just by use of sources from within youth work but also by reference to a wide and authoritative literature from outside it: from philosophy, educational psychology and educational sociology, management theory, politics. Without being gratuitous – quoted simply for academic effect – this material is itself, as appropriate, set within relevant historical perspectives which make clear its own sometimes controversial evolution.

All this serves to remind youth workers that, distinctive though in key respects their skills and methods may be, they cannot seal themselves off from wider policy worlds or related practice disciplines. Many of these, with strong intellectual track records, have confronted the same or similar questions, have struggled their way to some credible answers – and so can provide lessons which are transferable. Here Jon Ord's deconstruction of 'curriculum' does not only offer youth work planners and practitioners tools for clarifying whether they are talking about this as content, as product and/or as process. Given that one of the defining features of youth workers' practice is a negotiation with the young people they actually meet of a content and product which the young people can own and utilise, Jon Ord's analysis also challenges youth workers to see curriculum-as-process as the essential construct.

Secondly, the book undertakes an examination of the curriculum documents produced by local authority youth services over the last decade or so which, to my knowledge, has not been attempted before. This gives it an evidence base which takes many of its interpretations and conclusions beyond the rhetoric which has often characterised previous discussion in this area.

Thirdly, this exercise helps to keep the book closer than many such texts to practice and the realities of engaging purposefully with young people who initially may not see themselves, or wish to see themselves, as in an educational relationship. This of course does not mean that what Jon Ord has produced is a hints-and-tips manual: far from it. Indeed, precisely because its prescriptions are contextualised in a wider discourse on, in particular, educational theory and practice, it asks its readers also to undertake some of that intellectual work which has not always been fashionable in youth work. The promise it offers in return is that, if they do this, they will end up implementing youth work curricula which are credible and relevant – and will do this in ways which will strengthen rather than subvert the practice to which they are committed.

Bernard Davies, August 2006

Introduction

One of the contexts for this book is the ever widening gap between youth work theory and youth work practice, in which practice continues to be ever more informed and delivered according to a curriculum, and yet the dominant philosophy of informal education, which for many underpins youth work, continues to claim curriculum is anathema to it.

The gap between theory and practice means practitioners deliver their curriculum in a theoretical vacuum with little or no support in formulating an authentic curriculum. As a result there is an ever increasing danger that such curriculum will be buffeted by demands of policy and deviate from the essential elements of youth work.

This book sets out to solve this dilemma by formulating a viable theoretical base for curriculum in youth work. It analyses curriculum theory from the formal educational sector, and assesses its suitability for a youth work curriculum. It also draws on existing curriculum documents produced in the field, assessing their appropriateness. Ultimately utilising a combination of relevant theory and examples from curriculum in practice a framework for an authentic curriculum for youth work is established.

The other context for this book is the policy framework with which youth work currently operates, one which increasingly formalises the educational practice of youth work and which either appears to be unaware of the dynamics of youth work practice or chooses to ignore it.

Not that existing theory has been particularly helpful in defending youth work against such policy threats. Very good critiques have been written, for example by Smith (2003a). But they tend to focus on what is wrong with the policy and fail to fully articulate what it is about youth work which is so different and what is being undermined by the recent developments. Beyond that is talk of the demise of 'the relationship'. Many questions remain unanswered: Why are relationships so important? Do youth work relationships differ from the relationships other professionals have with young people and if so how? What is the process of youth work, what is it based upon and how does an educational practice based upon it operate? Why are demands for outcomes so contentious, and why are outcomes so difficult to establish? This book offers some answers to these and many other related questions about the uniqueness of youth work practice.

Youth work has never needed a viable curriculum more than it needs it now. Youth work's values, purposes and methods are under threat and an authentic curriculum can both protect and promote its practices. However, readers unfamiliar with the development of curriculum in youth work should bracket their assumptions and preconceptions about what is meant by curriculum. This is not the curriculum of the school. Youth work's curriculum is based upon and articulates its unique educational practice; one which emphasises the process of education as much as the products of it.

Structure of the book

The book is divided into five sections, and further subdivided by additional chapters therein. The section titles and subsequent chapter headings are self-explanatory and to a large extent, readers should be guided by these. The book is written with a consistent argument and thread which runs throughout it and the chapters follow on accordingly. Although the chapters can also be read in isolation if readers wish to address the specific issues raised within them.

The first Section, *Curriculum in Youth Work*, contains three chapters which focus, in turn, on an historical exploration of the emergence of curriculum through the ministerial conferences of the early 90s. It is proposed within this first chapter that during this time the curriculum passed from implicit to explicit in its formulation. Chapter 2 looks at the meaning of curriculum and begins to look at the competing theories of curriculum, as well as offering a 'working' definition. The third and last chapter in this section confronts the objections to curriculum in youth work, primarily from Jeffs (2004) and Jeffs and Smith (2005).

The second Section contains four chapters which introduce curriculum theory from three distinct perspectives, that of curriculum as content, product and process. The chapters introduce the theory and assess its relevance to a curriculum for youth work. The problems of a curriculum based around content and product are established and the benefits of a curriculum for youth work based around process are explored. The final chapter in this section looks at the process curriculum in youth work practice.

The third Section establishes the essential elements of an authentic youth work curriculum, including *Participation and Power* which includes a focus on empowerment, equality of opportunity and anti-discriminatory practice, together with *Relationships and Group Work* which explores in depth the dynamics of the youth work relationship as well as the importance of groups and group work in youth work. The third chapter looks at *Choice and Voluntary Participation* which includes a look at the importance of informed decision making in youth work, as well as an analysis of the principle of voluntary participation.

Chapter 4 in this section focuses on methodology, making a distinction between methods as 'modes of delivery' such as detached work, and methods as 'specific means of facilitating learning' such as an arts project or a quiz. It explores these distinct but related youth work methods and how they form the basis of a process approach to curriculum. The final chapter in this section critically analyses Kolb's experiential learning, perhaps one of, if not the, most misunderstood and inappropriately applied educational theories, and one which is often inappropriately applied in youth work.

The penultimate section *Policy and Practice*, analyses the current policy climate in youth work and its resulting impact on the development of curriculum. This section begins with a critical examination of the curriculum framework presented by Merton and Wylie (2002) and that latterly utilised within the *Transforming Youth Work* agenda (DfES, 2002). The two subsequent chapters explore two important and related issues to that agenda which continue to have an impact on youth work practice, that of 'targets' and 'outcomes' respectively. Chapter 4 in this section looks at the importance of progression and looks at why 'time' is an important concept which both underpins youth work practice, and is significant by its absence from current formulations of practice. Finally, this section concludes with an examination of the implications of more recent policy for youth work, addressing issues raised by *Every Child Matters* (DfES, 2003) and *Youth Matters* (DfES, 2005a).

The final section looks in turn at the *Use of Curriculum* and *Curriculum and Culture*. The first chapter challenges those who design and develop curriculum to utilise its potential as an educational vehicle for developing a 'community of practice' in their locality and for it not to be reduced to a document to appease the policy makers and inspectors. The final chapter assesses curriculum and its relationship with culture, asking ultimately what is youth works' relationship to society. Is it a vehicle for change or a method of maintaining the status quo? It concludes with a challenge to workers not to break with the tradition of 'critical social education' and work towards a 'critical curriculum' and one which is embedded within the process of youth work.

This is a book that is long overdue. It is not perfect and does not claim to exhaustively deal with the enormous range of subject matter it attempts to cover, but it can and will challenge all readers, whether advocates of curriculum or not, to think again about how they conceive of both youth work and its curriculum.

Section One
Curriculum in Youth Work

The Emergence of the Youth Work Curriculum

History of curriculum

The explicit use of the concept of curriculum in youth and community work does not have a long history. It does not appear in any detail, if at all, in the major government reports of Albemarle (Ministry of Education, 1960) Fairbairn-Milson (DES, 1969) or Thompson (DES, 1982). There was also a widespread consensus amongst the youth work profession from the early 1950s through to the late 1980s that 'curriculum' was the preserve of schools, and had little use or place in youth work (Ord, 2004a). The first explicit reference to curriculum was made by John Ewen, the then director of the National Youth Bureau (NYB) who wrote a paper entitled *Curriculum Development in the Youth Club* (Ewen, 1975). In this interesting and thought provoking paper he introduced the proposal that curriculum is a credible term to use to answer the question 'What are we doing in the youth club?' He was generally referring to the activities, such as sports, arts and some issue based work which took place in the average youth club. Thereby Ewen attempts to firmly distinguish between the purely recreational activities of leisure facilities, and the educational foundations of youth work activities.

Little appears to have been subsequently written either by Ewen or by those commenting on his idea, to continue this line of enquiry, although his paper was published as a second edition in 1983. Curriculum then, as an explicit concept in youth work, to a large extent lay dormant until it was introduced by the then, Parliamentary Under-secretary of State for Education and Science Alan Howarth MP, who launched the first of three ministerial conferences, auspiciously titled 'Towards a Core Curriculum'!

The context for what would become a radical change in the conception of curriculum in youth work was the Education Reform Act of 1988. This Act saw the introduction, or 'imposition', of the national curriculum in schools. The teachers' relative autonomy over their classroom delivery had gone. They were told what they would teach, what outcomes they would produce and testing regimes were introduced to measure those

outcomes. This radical shake up of the school curriculum set the scene for an application of curriculum to youth work, hence the first ministerial conference. Although some 'consultation' was undertaken prior to the conference most involved saw the process as a 'top down' attempt to introduce what was regarded at the time as an unwanted and unmerited concept – the curriculum.

Howarth gave the keynote address, which was later published along with the accompanying conference papers as NYB (1990) *Danger or Opportunity: Towards a Core Curriculum for the Youth Service?* In the address he made it quite clear that he was aware of the controversial nature of curriculum in youth work but he maintained that the aims of the conference were:

1. Clarification on core business of youth work;
2. Priority outcomes of youth work;
3. Agreement on concept of 'Core Curriculum' for youth work.

Howarth was very specific about what he meant by '... core curriculum – that is the priority outcomes which the youth service should seek to provide', NYB (1990: 34).

He was also keen to distinguish clearly between other aspects of youth work, which he thought might be incorporated:

> ... by curriculum I mean not the aims of the youth service ... Nor do I mean the detailed activities or methods of delivery ... but the outcomes ...
>
> NYB (1990: 34)

It is important to note at this point that though Howarth's attempt to introduce a concept of curriculum is recounted uncritically, it is because we are concerned at the moment with its historical importance in terms of the emergence of the concept in youth work. However, it must be noted that the concept of curriculum conceived of by Howarth which focuses exclusively on 'outcomes' is a particular notion of curriculum which it is argued (Davies, 1991; Ord, 2004a) is not appropriate for youth work.

Moreover, the curriculum that has gained a currency in the field in the period following the ministerial conferences was significantly different to that which was narrowly defined by Howarth. Not least, because it incorporated the element of process in the curriculum.

Despite Howarth's bold intentions at the first conference he did not achieve much of his ambitious plan. Needless to say the antipathy from the field to what was perceived to be an imposition of a concept of curriculum was considerable and 'evaluation forms' from the conference reiterated the need for 'ownership' by the field of any 'core curriculum' (NYB, 1990: 80).

This whole affair was described by Tom Wylie (2001: 244), currently chief executive of the National Youth Agency, in his *Memoir of HM Inspectorate and Youth Work in the Thatcher Era*, as:

> . . . the attempt to produce a consensus across such a wide field of endeavour – both statutory and voluntary sector – and in a form which would be genuinely useful was doomed from the start. It was made worse, in the view of the HMI, by the failure to offer clarity about the meaning of the very word 'curriculum'. . . The department's great project was also handicapped by the generally ham-fisted management of the tortuous process of a series of minister-ial conferences . . . The result pleased no one.

The second ministerial conference (NYB, 1991) took 165 written submissions as part of its pre-conference consultation. This, according to Bernard Davies, 'offered a revealing insight into the youth service's collective and highly pluralistic view of itself, its mission and its methods' (1999b: 133). As a result the task was redefined to the production of a statement of purpose. The 'new' minister did not attend the conference in person, choosing instead to address the audience by video link. However, perhaps because of this lack of prescription from government as to what to focus on, the field was able to discuss and agree its own 'statement of purpose':

> . . . to redress all forms of inequality and to ensure equality of opportunity for all young people to fulfil their potential as empowered individuals and members of groups and communities and to support young people during their transition to adulthood.
>
> (NYB, 1991)

The conference also recommended therefore that youth work should:

- Offer opportunities which are *'educative'*;
- Promote *'equality of opportunity'*;
- Be *'participative'* and *empowering'*.

(NYB, 1991)

It was also recommended that any future curriculum would be based upon this agreed statement of purpose. The fact that the statement of purpose was largely ignored by government ministers did not matter in the respect of its influence in the production of future curriculum documents. The statement became embedded in the field of youth work and began to inform what was the most important implication of the ministerial conferences; that individual youth services began to produce their own 'locally specific' curriculum documents. Indeed many of the documents to date, as will be seen in the chapters on the essential elements, retain a commitment to these 'cornerstones'.

By the time the third ministerial conference (NYA, 1992) had been completed, which achieved some discussion and partial agreement around the notion of performance indicators (Davies, 1999b) it was evident the 'curriculum project' as originally conceived by Howarth, had withered on the vine. As Davies puts it the third conference 'proved to be the final resting place for the ministerial bandwagon' (1999b: 135). However, it would be quite wrong to conclude that the status quo, therefore, prevailed and that it was very much 'normal service resumed'! Although Janet Pareskeva, the then chief executive of the NYA, was right, she acknowledged 'There was to be no core curriculum or even published common learning outcomes' (Davies, 1999b: 136). The 'state of play' in the field of youth work had changed and curriculum emerged as a concept which would in the coming years be applied to youth work.

Newman and Ingram curriculum research

In the absence of significant writing on youth work curriculum there is in fact a very thoughtful and interesting publication called *The Youth Work Curriculum* by Eileen Newman and Gina Ingram. This was published in 1989, and was an action research project with four statutory youth services in the north west of England. As stated 'The purpose of the project was to discover and record the youth work curriculum' (1989: 1).

The timing of the project is interesting as although it preceded the first, now infamous, ministerial conference, as the research commenced in 1988, it was set up quite explicitly by the Further Education Unit in response to the Education Reform Act of 1988. It should clearly be seen therefore not as an original attempt to innovatively develop notions of curriculum in youth work, as Ewen had, but as a direct response to policy shifts within education. As the authors confess: 'Following the 1988 Education Reform Act, it is essential that the Youth Service is able to defend successfully its existing role and mark out clearly its contribution to work with young people within the education service and with other agencies' (1989: vii).

That said, however, in many ways this is a gem. There is a lot one could be critical about but as the authors say themselves 'the project should be no more than a first stage in describing the youth work curriculum' (Newman and Ingram, 1989: 3). It is in fact disappointing that despite the authenticity of the youth work which is at the heart of the authors' attempts to describe the youth work curriculum, this document appears to have been largely ignored. For example it is absent from the NYA's *Planning the Way* (1995), their later published guidance on curriculum.

Newman and Ingram demonstrate that it is perfectly possible to apply notions of curriculum 'unproblematically' to youth work. They conducted an action research project, with four authorities, Liverpool, Knowsley, Thameside and Cheshire and produced a consensus on key curricular concepts, like open and voluntary access, and the importance of micro learning cycles. What is most noteworthy about their formulation of curriculum is its commitment to an incorporation of 'process'. They propose that: 'Curriculum is an organic process. It is not a list of subject areas, syllabus or a statement of aims or objectives' (1989: 1). Importantly, it is this commitment to process which is becoming increasingly more undermined with recent formulations as we will see in Chapter 4.5 on the recent policy.

Curriculum is embedded in youth work

What resulted from the ministerial conferences and occurred throughout the 1990s was an acceptance by youth workers of the task of

articulating their work in terms of curriculum – 'on their terms'. The NYA was tasked with the job of facilitating this process. Importantly the responsibility for the production of the subsequent curriculum documents was undertaken by youth workers in their respective services, autonomously and without prescription. As summarised in the NYA guidance on curriculum *Planning the Way* (1995):

> *The concept of a core curriculum for the service as a result [of the ministerial conferences] shifted to a framework for fundamental principles in order to facilitate flexibility and to take account of the social factors which have an impact on young people at the local level. The importance of local determination and the freedom for each organisation to define its own values, goals and priorities was a major feature . . .*
>
> (NYA, 1995: 6–7)

By the mid 1990s many local authority youth services did produce their own locally agreed curriculum documents. Kingston Youth Service had their first document in 1990, West Sussex in 1989, Hampshire 1991 and Gloucestershire 1992. The fact that so many local authority youth services were able to make a shift from what appears to be animosity and antipathy, to acceptance of the concept and production of their own documents appears to need some explanation. There were very real concerns expressed by a large majority over the introduction of curriculum. The NYB's own consultation in 1989 'revealed profound concerns about the term curriculum and whether its definition in relation to youth work could indeed encapsulate and do justice to the nature of youth work' (1990: 5). What this concern alludes to, is not however a fundamental inability of youth work to be articulated by curriculum, or a fundamental inappropriateness of an application of curricular concepts to the principles and practices of youth work, rather what underpins these concerns is a lack of control in the application of the concept of curriculum to youth work; is evidenced by the request for 'ownership' from the delegates at the first ministerial conference (NYB, 1990).

That curriculum can be integrated into articulations of youth work was shown quite clearly by Newman and Ingram (1989). The four local authorities they worked with in their participative action research project produced a consensus on many important features of a youth

A number of 'working definitions' are therefore provided below. They are taken from writers who are very critical of the restricted concept of curriculum in formal education and argue for a more holistic notion of curriculum to be applied to education in schools. On this basis it does therefore to some extent encapsulate what is meant by curriculum in youth work.

Firstly, two definitions are presented from Lawrence Stenhouse. He was an innovative educationalist who advocated a formulation of curriculum which was both critical of and opposed to restrictive notions of curriculum, which are only concerned with the products:

- A curriculum is an attempt to communicate the essential principles and features of an educational proposal in such a form that it is open to critical scrutiny and capable of effective translation into practice (1975: 4).
- A curriculum is a means by which the experience of attempting to put an educational proposal into practice is made publicly available. It involves both content and method, and in its widest application takes account of the problem of implementation in the institutions of the educational system (1975: 5).

In Stenhouse's definitions he clearly focuses on the 'how' of educational practice as opposed to the 'what': that is he focuses on the 'translations of educational principles into practice' and on the 'methods and their implementation' rather than the products and their attainment.

Similarly Grundy (1987: 5) states that curriculum '. . . is a way of organising a set of educational practices'.

A further definition which is also worthy of consideration is offered by Kelly as he alludes to another important feature of what is meant by curriculum in youth work. That curriculum is a holistic concept:

- 'curriculum is the totality of the experiences the pupil has as a result of the provision made' (2004: 8).

What Kelly implicitly includes in his definition is both the planned and unplanned aspect of our educational practice, the overt and the hidden curriculum. Importantly, he also encapsulates the overall 'values' that underpin the educational practices, as well as its purposes, which is clearly very important for a youth work curriculum:

- Any definition of curriculum, if it is to be practically effective and productive, must offer more than a statement about the knowledge-content or merely the subjects which schooling is to 'teach' or transmit or 'deliver'. It must go far beyond this to an explanation, and indeed a justification, of the purposes of such transmission and an exploration of the effects that exposure to such knowledge and such subjects is likely to have . . . indeed it is from these deeper concerns that . . . any curriculum planning worthy of its name must start.

(Kelly, 2004: 4)

It can be clearly seen with reference to many of the curriculum documents in use in the field that it is in fact the case that curriculum in youth work is 'a total curriculum'. Many of them include the kind of features which Kelly recommends: the underlying values, methods, processes and products, indeed they are very often referred to as 'curriculum frameworks' because they are over arching conceptualisations of the educational practice of youth work which 'frame it' in its totality.

To conclude then with the caveat that any attempt to offer an exhaustive definition is inevitably problematic, the working definition of a youth work curriculum proposed here is: the means by which the educational values, purposes, methods, processes, as well as possible outcomes are made explicit.

Objections to Curriculum in Youth Work

Opposition to curriculum is most often expressed by advocates of 'informal education' (Smith, 1988; Jeffs and Smith, 1990; 2005). There are many instances from these writers of quite explicit opposition to the notion of curriculum, and below are some examples:

> Where a national curriculum exists for schools it is tempting to imagine that what is essential for formal educational settings is also needed for the informal. In fact it is the very absence of curriculum that is a key defining feature.
>
> (Jeffs and Smith, 2005: 81)

> The problem with the term curriculum in my view is . . . workers have got taken in by it. Somehow we thought it would make us more important like teachers! . . . I would argue for a return to first principles, voluntary participation, association and fun, and let those who want to teach have a curriculum.
>
> (Robertson, 2004: 78)

> I cannot comprehend why youth work needs a curriculum any more than a house needs wings.
>
> (Jeffs, 2004: 57)

Stanton even goes so far as to say:

> . . . the youth work curriculum is an oxymoron. Curriculum is restrictive whereas informal education is not. It is a high priority of informal educators to reject curriculum.
>
> (Stanton, 2004: 84)

These objections raise very important issues for the practice of youth work. Given that many youth workers consider themselves to be exponents of informal education, and that many statutory youth services have been applying notions of curriculum to their youth work, and producing locally agreed curriculum documents, for approaching two decades, these very challenging assertions *beg some important questions*.

Have youth services stopped applying the principles of 'informal education' in their youth work, and if, as Jeffs and Smith claim, informal education values underpin youth work does this in turn mean that youth workers have now divorced themselves from their value base? Have

they merely become a branch of the formal education system?

On the contrary, as will be shown throughout this book, with a detailed critical examination of curriculum in youth work, the protagonists of informal education have fundamentally misunderstood the concept of curriculum and unnecessarily taken objection to its incorporation into youth work. In addition, they have failed to see any of the advantages that the incorporation of the concept has brought to the articulation of youth work.

The explicit rejections of curriculum from within informal education appear quite clear, as the above quotes show, informal education is in total opposition to curriculum and it is anathema to it. However, beneath these protestations of antipathy are some complexities and contradictions, which raise important questions for the coherence of informal education as a basis for youth work.

Jeffs and Smith's attitude to curriculum is not straight forward, and as I previously intimated there appears to be some inconsistency and contradiction. Their book *Informal Education: Conversation, Democracy and Learning*, contains on the one hand clear opposition to the idea: 'it is the very absence of curriculum that is a key defining feature (of informal education)' (Jeffs and Smith, 2005: 81). However, at other times importantly they fail to dismiss it outright and indeed insist curriculum must be used:

> Informal educators can and **must** employ more formal approaches from time to time.
>
> (my bold) (Jeffs and Smith, 2005: 81)

Let us be quite clear that by 'more formal approaches' they mean quite explicitly both what they refer to as the 'negotiated curriculum' which 'entails educators and learners sitting down in advance and working out what the curriculum will be' (2005: 80); as well as what they refer to as 'set curriculum' where 'they (the workers) decide on the content and the process' (2005: 81).

This is quite inconsistent. Informal education is on the one hand opposed in both principle and

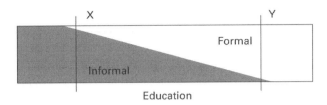

Figure 1.3.1 Informal/formal education continuum (Jeffs and Smith, 2005: 24)

practice to curriculum. Curriculum is described as its antithesis, the defining feature of informal education being the absence of curriculum. Yet at the same time informal educators propose that they 'can and must' employ formal curriculum. This certainly appears nonsensical, thereby raising concerns about the educational validity of 'informal education', which at the very least requires some explanation.

An informal/formal education continuum?

Although seemingly unaware of this contradiction within their rationale, there is an implicit justification for it, in their proposal that formal and informal education are not mutually exclusive and in fact a continuum exists between them.

This diagram, originally conceived by John Ellis (1990) is utilised by Jeffs and Smith 2005, who argue that:

> *Those that work in everyday social situations need to define themselves primarily by conversation. They may at times use formal settings and have a curriculum to follow, but the balance of their work names them as informal educators.*
> (Jeffs and Smith, 2005: 25)

It is evident that the strong opposition and antipathy is reduced merely to an issue of *balance.* However, this balance is in itself contradictory –

it cannot be that informal educators, at the same time, both utilise and are opposed to curriculum.

Moreover, despite the contradictory attitude towards curriculum the creation of a formal/informal continuum is itself problematic. It is incorrect to describe youth workers (whether as informal educators or not) as formal educators, like school teachers. Youth workers rarely if ever deliver formal education. One of the few examples of this would be perhaps where a youth worker delivers a Personal Health And Social Education (PHSE) session on drugs or sexual health in a school. But even then the reason they would be brought in would not just be because they had knowledge that the teacher did not have, but because the discursive style and approach the youth worker would take would be more conducive to the topic in question. Furthermore, that style reflects their methodology and curriculum, which is distinctly different to that of a school teacher. It is on this basis, that teaching (formal education) and youth work (whether described as informal education or not) are in fact more mutually exclusive than Jeffs and Smith would have us believe. There is a clear distinction between the teacher as formal educator in a school and the youth worker. The relationship between the two is best described, not as a continuum but, as two overlapping circles of distinctive practice, see Fig. 1.3.2.

The shaded area of practice contains examples like that of the PHSE lesson delivered by the

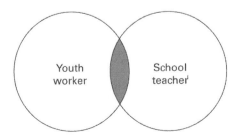

Figure 1.3.2 Distinct but overlapping domains of practice

youth worker or perhaps the teacher undertaking a pastoral role outside class, in addition and distinct from their normal teaching role. But the majority of their time, and the key defining features of their practice, are distinct. This is in no small part due to the distinctly different relationship which the youth worker fosters, as a result of which they do not engage in formal education, which by definition has more 'formal' relationships.

Jeffs and Smith's conception of formal education is an idealistic one. It follows Dewey (1966, 1997) and contains a very different view of the role and the relationship of a teacher. It is a progressive view of education which is far from the current reality. Until the sort of radical changes to the education system, which are required to make this become a reality, the comparisons between youth work and formal education need to be based on the current situation; one which situates youth work and formal education as separate forms of educational practice rather than mere variations on a continuum.

There are two further justifications for their opposition to curriculum offered by Jeffs and Smith which are encapsulated within the following quote:

> *Informal education is, thus, not curriculum based. It is driven by conversation and informed by certain values.*
> (Jeffs and Smith, 2005: 78)

We will therefore look at conversation and values in turn.

Curriculum and conversation

Jeffs and Smith's premise that informal 'education is not curriculum based, because it is driven by conversation', needs careful examination. For it begs important questions:

- Are conversation and curriculum fundamentally opposed?
- Is conversational based learning not present in curriculum based education?
- If so, is the distinction proposed between conversation and curriculum valid?

Jeffs and Smith use an illustration of the role of conversation in a comparison between a formal and an informal educator, to elucidate their point:

> *Imagine yourself entering a classroom as an educator. Often the conversation of students will fade and they will turn to look to the front and you. They will be usually waiting for you to take the lead. Indeed they may be irritated if you do not do so.*
> (Jeffs and Smith, 2005: 77–8)

This is distinguished from the role of an informal educator:

> *Compare this (the above example) with joining a group of residents in a community lounge. Our presence may be acknowledged; it may not. It could be that the conversation turns to something that involves us. Equally we may find ourselves on the fringe awaiting a suitable opportunity to engage with the group. We are far less likely to be the centre of attention. In such settings we cannot carry a curriculum with us and hope to employ it (or impose it).*
> (Jeffs and Smith, 2005: 77–8)

Whilst both scenarios are perfectly plausible, and may be accurate descriptions of events which may occur in practice, the problem is that they are used out of context to imply a distinction which is problematic. The problem is that no one would question the teacher whose students stop talking when they enter the room and look to them to communicate the focus of the learning for the particular lesson. However, there certainly would be a problem if every time the informal educator entered the room their presence was not acknowledged and they found themselves on the fringe. At least this is certainly true of a youth worker working with young people, whether employed or volunteering, and this is a session that they are working in.

This is because it is the responsibility of the youth worker to engage with the group. One would quite rightly question their role if they were consistently peripheral. They have a responsibility for the education or learning of the young people during the time they are with them. An important part of that responsibility is to be **pro-active**. It is not sufficient to consistently sit and wait for opportunities to intervene in existing conversations, to attempt to steer the existing focus, or make comments on what is prescient to the young people. Part of the curriculum of youth work is generated from an awareness of the needs of the young people they are working with, which may well not be present in the conversations being had by the young people. They must provide vehicles for dialogue. This aspect is absent in the descriptions of the role of the informal educator characterised by Jeffs and

Smith above. In short, the above description of the relatively passive or reactive worker only makes sense if it is conceived of in respect of a new worker or an existing worker meeting a new group: in both situations the 'pro-active role' of the worker has (rightly) not yet been developed.

It is no coincidence that there is a lack of emphasis on, what is for youth work, an integral element. That is a belief that the educator has knowledge above and beyond that of those being educated, and that they have a responsibility to be pro-active and 'input' into the educational setting based on that knowledge. There is a tradition in informal education to deny or be opposed to the very notion of educational expertise. This can be seen to follow from a belief that as informal education is learning in life and for life – we are all experts in our own lives, and also it is a philosophy which is based on the principles of democracy where each individual is equal and to be respected as such. Therefore we are either all experts or no one is an expert. Educational authority as such is therefore seen as oppressive.

The problems of Paulo Freire

This denial of educational input and the questioning of the assumption that the educators have authority to educate can be seen to derive from the criticisms of education by Paulo Freire. Freire is very critical of what he refers to as 'the banking concept of education, in which the scope of action allowed to students extends as far as receiving, filing and storing the deposits' (1972: 45).The deposits being the knowledge and information which the teacher or educator has deemed to be worthy of knowing and decides to 'transmit' to them. He claims this approach is typical of traditional forms of education, which he claims are oppressive. However, he contrasts this approach with 'the problem posing concept of education' which by contrast is education for liberation and emancipation. 'In problem posing education, men develop their power to perceive critically *the way they exist* in the world *with which* and *in which* they find themselves; they come to see the world not as a static reality, but as a reality in process, in transformation (1972: 56) (authors italics).

Thus according to Freire:

The two educational concepts and practices under analysis come into conflict. Banking education (for obvious reasons)
attempts, by mythicising reality, to conceal certain facts which explain the way men exist in the world; problem-posing education sets itself the task of de-mythologising. Banking education resists dialogue; problem-posing education regards dialogue as indispensable to the act of cognition which unveils reality.

(1972: 56)

One can see why Freire is an important thinker underpinning informal education. On a personal level he sees the importance of the developmental nature of human growth, claiming that: 'Problem-posing education affirms men as beings in the process of becoming' (1972: 56). Importantly, he also maintains a critical eye on the social world when he suggests 'Problem posing education is revolutionary' (1972: 57).

There is much that is relevant to youth work in Freire's conception of problem solving education, particularly his emphasis on dialogue and his awareness of the power relations between the educator and those being educated. However, whilst attempting to equalise the relationship between educator and student, Freire (1972: 53) eradicates the distinction totally:

Through dialogue, the teacher-of-the-students and the students-of-the-teacher cease to exist and a new term emerges: teacher-students with students-teachers. The teacher is no longer merely the-one-who-teaches, but one who is himself taught in dialogue with the student, who in their turn while being taught, also teach. They become jointly responsible for a process in which they all grow. In this process arguments based on authority are no longer valid.

Thus we can see that this emasculation of the teacher's authority which is inherent in Freire and which is implicit in Jeffs and Smith, is problematic for youth work. Whilst it is paramount for a youth worker to foster mutuality and to be aware of the power relations that exist, to devolve power where possible and exercise what power they retain justly, it would appear to be untenable to suggest that this power and authority, together with their knowledge and expertise can be eradicated completely.

Radical adult and community educators such as Lovett, Clarke and Kilmurray agree and question Freire suggesting that 'When he goes on to call for a virtual elimination of the distinction between teachers and taught, he goes altogether too far' (1983: 143).

Importantly, it can be seen how it follows from a belief that there is no difference between the educator and the educated, that the educator no longer has an educational responsibility for being proactive in the educational environment. Everyone or no one would have that right or responsibility. It is quite easy to see how following the Freirian tradition Jeffs and Smith are committed to devaluing or dismissing the notion of educational input.

It is not inconsistent with the important youth work principle of respecting individual's rights to self-determination, to believe that as a youth worker you also have knowledge above and beyond the experiential horizons of the young people you are working with. This can clearly be seen in relation to any number of issues the youth workers would be engaging in, whether it be sex or sexuality, drugs or crime and the police. Youth workers are in a position to both appreciate where the young people are, at the present time, consider their needs and offer suitable support, advise or challenge as appropriate in relation to where they want to go or what they want to do. This is, in part, because of their reflection on their own experience, but also their knowledge and experience of working with other young people in similar situations. It is what is best termed the 'educational responsibility' underpinning pro-active youth work, and is one of the defining differences between informal education and youth work. Indeed as Lawton et al. rightly assert 'The teacher (or youth worker) who has nothing to offer the child by way of knowledge or interesting experiences is not justifying his existence' (1978: 3).

Clearly any notion of educational input or educational authority that is exercised by youth workers is done so with a critical and reflective edge. It must be, and always is, open to challenge, through a mutual relationship, engaged in through dialogue. But to deny this pro-active aspect of youth work would be denying an important part of its educational raison d'être.

The negotiated curriculum?

Jeffs and Smith may want to argue that in fact the 'proactive role' is encompassed within what they refer to as the negotiated curriculum, where the content or programme is discussed and agreed beforehand with the participants. This however does not fully account for the pro-active responsibility of youth workers, because the input of the youth workers is not necessarily negotiated; it could be a judgement of what is

deemed appropriate at the time. For example, if the workers were aware of an issue of bullying in the club, they would not have had to ask the young people if they would agree to them raising the issue. They may want to show the group a newspaper article describing the suicide of a young person who had been bullied. The workers would make a judgement, based on their 'educational responsibility' that they needed to address the issue.

Also, Jeffs and Smith maintain that the negotiated curriculum is not the primary focus of informal educators, and that those who consistently operate within a negotiated curriculum are more legitimately 'labelled non-formal educators' (2005: 68).

Any preordained educational input is, according to Jeffs and Smith, associated with the 'set curriculum' and this they claim is the remit of schools. So again we see the mistake being made that an educational input which is organised and constructed by teachers or youth workers prior to the educational engagement is associated with formal education.

Perhaps then we should stop considering youth workers as informal educators at all and just talk about 'youth work'. This is not necessarily advocated as there are important aspects of informal education which firmly locate education in the community in terms of building association and fostering democracy which need to be retained. But there are questions to be answered, however, by anyone who promotes informal education as a rationale for youth work, in relation to curriculum and the pro-active responsibility of workers.

Conversation as unpredictable or predicating relevant conversations

Jeffs and Smith use the fact that informal education is conversation based as a justification as to why they claim workers cannot be proactive and why conversational based educative practices cannot be curriculum based because: '. . . in conversation everything is so unpredictable. Talk can lead anywhere. In this sense it is difficult to be so specific about outcome or aim. Content cannot be sequenced in any meaningful way beforehand' (Jeffs and Smith, 2005: 77).

However, conversation is not 'totally unpredictable', and Jeffs and Smith overstate the case. Conversation is anything but random. If a youth worker has a good relationship with the group they are working with and they would have a good idea of the sort of issues that are pertinent to that group. Not least because they know what kind of conversations they have had before, they would have a good idea of current issues for that group. This knowledge will form part of the basis for the pro-active response the worker would take: the points of interest the worker thinks the group need to return to, the issues which were left unresolved from the previous week or what has been bubbling under for this group which the worker would like to bring to the surface. The conversation may take a turn away from the focus the worker had prepared for and it would be legitimate and correct to 'go with that flow' but equally it may not. The fact that a worker shows the group a newspaper cutting of a suicide pact of a group of bullied teenagers could be the catalyst for the group to talk about their experience of being bullied for the first time or for a group to disclose their ambivalence to their own bullying.

It is the knowledge that the workers hold which is in their judgement pertinent to the young people and can be injected into the learning environment in an appealing and acceptable way which in part informs the curriculum.

Educative conversation

It is important to be clear about what is meant by conversation as an educational activity, both to assess Jeffs and Smith's premise that conversation is opposed to curriculum as well as for the youth work curriculum as a whole, as conversation is equally important as a youth work method. Conversation is not necessarily educational. Idle conversation is not educational. Importantly, what makes conversation educational is its purpose, its intent, combined with a commitment to facilitate learning. Williamson makes this point very well:

> Youth work should be about the capability to engage young people (as individuals or in groups) in **serious** conversation and discussion on key issues affecting their lives. Sensitised and sensitive reactions to experiences, incidents and comments always provide a learning opportunity. Cursory and fleeting banter is clearly not enough (though it may be a launching cornerstone of positive relationships).
>
> (Williamson, 2005: 77)

One should not be seduced into thinking this provides all the answers. This merely begs more questions: 'What purpose? What intent? What learning?' Ultimately it is a value judgement which is required to ascertain if one regards a conversation as being educational or not. Ascertaining whether or not learning has or is likely to have taken place is a contentious issue for youth work, and the profession in the past has shied away from attempts to grasp this nettle. But it does go to the heart of the curriculum debate: what is the educational basis of learning in youth work? A key theme in answering that question, and one we will return to throughout, is that in order to sufficiently account for the learning in youth work one must provide details of both the product and the process of the work. And it is a curriculum that can provide a framework for this.

Curriculum and values

The second part of the justification of an opposition to curriculum now needs careful examination: 'Informal education is, thus, not curriculum based. It is . . . informed by certain values' (Jeffs and Smith, 2005: 78).

That informal education is explicitly value laden education is not open to question, as the following quote exemplifies:

> Informal education is a moral craft. Because we are concerned with fostering learning in life as it is lived, we often have to make difficult choices. The people we are, and the values we hold, are fundamental to how we deal with these . . . The complex personal and social choices others, and we, make are not external to our work but sit at the very heart of it.
>
> (Jeffs and Smith, 2005: 94)

The fact that youth work is similarly underpinned by values is also not contended, as Young identifies:

> A youth worker's values are important not only because they impact directly on the work . . . but because the worker's values both underpin the work and form the basis for the young people's moral reflections and exploration.
>
> (1999: 99–100)

However, no argument is offered as to why it follows that value based education necessitates a lack of curriculum; this is merely asserted by Jeffs and Smith. The fact that youth work is driven by values would (and does) fundamentally affect the concept of curriculum. But there is nothing integral to an explicit incorporation of values within an educational proposal that obviates curriculum. It makes sense to conclude as youth work is explicitly driven by values, the resulting youth work curriculum must therefore be informed and driven by those values. Perhaps the nature and type of curriculum utilised by youth work would be significantly different to that which is associated with traditional formal education, which is either less explicit about its value base or is driven by a different set of values. Either way it would certainly appear to be fallacious to conclude, as Jeffs and Smith do, that as informal education is value driven it is not, and cannot, be curriculum based.

The need for specific (not general) values

There is a counter argument that suggests that, on the contrary, because informal education is quite explicit about its values it should therefore be clearer about its curriculum. That is, it should be clearer about what is derived from those values in terms of the implications for its practice. Jeffs and Smith avoid this and this is one of the problems of informal educator's descriptions, or incorporation, of values. They are only at the holistic, general and non-specific level. Jeffs and Smith (2005: 95) describe the core values as: *Respect for persons, The promotion of well being, Truth, Democracy and Fairness and Equality.*

Whilst there are few youth workers, or indeed members of the general public, who would disagree with these statements 'in principle', however, as is so often said, 'the devil is in the detail'. What do youth workers or informal educators 'actually do' as a result of holding these values? Again Jeffs and Smith are rather vague. They maintain that the values 'inform commitments' and 'develop responses in relation to human flourishing'.

> *. . . rather than using a curriculum we are guided in our actions by our role as educators and by certain commitments. These commitments should be related to ideas about what may make for human flourishing.*
>
> (2005: 78–9)

Ultimately, it is a holistic notion of human well being or human flourishing that is the guiding principle of informal education. It is this principle

that guides their interactions and interventions and it is this generality which is ultimately problematic. Banks concurs, concluding that ultimately 'these values are very general, they not only fail to distinguish a youth worker from a school teacher, but could equally apply to a social worker, nurse, or even a police officer. In fact they could be said to be the fundamental values of any liberal democracy' (2001: 64).

In addition, one should remember that we live in a pluralist society, one which accepts that differing and competing values coexist. Therefore as soon as one begins to make specific the general values of informal education, or any values for that matter, one is bound to reach disagreement and potential conflict, or at the very least have a disagreement over competing priorities. Jeffs and Smith agree that even their 'core values are . . . debated' (2005: 94). Banks (1999, 2001) also expands in depth on the inevitability of conflict in both personal and professional values, describing how moral dilemmas, where two or more values irreconcilably conflict, are an inevitable aspect of youth work practice.

So what is true for wider society is also the case for youth work. Moral debate is rife with controversy over issues such as abortion, animal rights, even something as central to youth work values as sexuality. So the question is not whether individual youth workers hold the value of fairness and equality, or any of the other general values of informal education, but what they do in relation to fairness and equality is the question. Furthermore they could, and probably would, do very different things.

Thus youth workers argue over the relative priority of work with young women, young men, young black and minority ethnic young people, disabled young people etc. This is not problematic in itself. However, given that this is true, the fact that values underpin informal education and values are pluralistic and inevitably conflictual, results in an onus on the informal educator to make their values more specific. How do organisations and individual workers within them interpret the general values; what do they mean by them and what implications does this have for their practice? If these questions are not specifically addressed there is the danger that individual practice is at the whim of the individual and their personal, rather than professional, values inform their work. It is only on the basis that values are made specific that individual workers can be accountable and practice is not the consequence of personal bias.

The example of gender

This precise point is illustrated clearly in relation to gender. Jean Spence, writing in 1990, rightly argues that:

> *It has taken over a decade and more of determined effort to establish the comprehensive validity of gender questions within youth work. Practice and analysis which initially emerged as a feminist inspired response to the lack of involvement of girls in the Youth Service have grown into a movement which asserts that the issue of sexism affects both female and male managers, workers and young people.*
>
> (1990:69)

That the issue of gender is indeed an area of debate, and that a commitment to it does not necessarily follow from a belief in more general values of, for example, fairness and equality, is further evidenced by Bessant and Evans (1996). They argue from their experience in Australia that there is a need for a formal commitment to, and inclusion of, gender within the curriculum of trainee youth workers. Arguing that if this were the case: 'Graduates will be familiar with, and be able to specify and critically evaluate the way issues relating to gender impact on professional practice and ethical issues youth workers confront' (1996:34).

In relation to the practice of youth work Spence is quite clear that not only was a debate necessary (and probably still is necessary) to establish this important and legitimate area of practice, but that: 'It has become apparent that gender questions cannot be fully addressed unless they become part of an integrated (youth work) curriculum' (1990: 69).

Values in the curriculum

The questions of values are directly confronted by the youth work curriculum. It is in the production of the youth work curriculum, that the more general values are applied to practice and made more specific. One can see what it is youth workers in a given locality or organisation mean by fairness and equality, or the promotion of well being, and more importantly, what they intend to do about it.

Values do have distinct implications for the practice of youth work, and importantly its values do not preclude specifying content. Rather they imply it and it is the 'content' which results from those values that should be made more explicit. This in part is what makes up the youth work curriculum. This criticism of informal educators for their lack of specification regarding the educational content is not confined to the realms of youth work. Radical adult and community educators such as Lovett, Clarke and Kilmurray similarly argue:

> *Education aiming to promote the eradication of class division must include, at the very least, some old-fashioned instruction, set into an ordered curriculum, which includes basic information and skills required to execute necessary management tasks.*
>
> (Lovett et al., 1983: 144)

Finally, we must concern ourselves with the end products of informal education. Jeffs and Smith admit informal education is explicitly concerned with ends as well as the means to achieve those ends:

> *Process is important but it can never be divorced from ends. All educational interventions relate in some way to either the sort of individual or world that those undertaking the work wish to achieve. Interventions that do not pay attention to ends, but merely process, cease to be educational in intent.*
>
> (1998/99: 50)

On this basis therefore informal educationalists must explain their refusal to frame those ends in a 'curriculum' as most if not all, other educationalists do. Their response is simply to inadequately specify 'one end product' of informal education:– the open and contentious 'human flourishing or well being'.

Section Two
Theory and Practice

Curriculum as Content

Introduction to curriculum theory

Readers will note that the theory relating to curriculum is almost exclusively related to formal educational settings whether that be primary, secondary, further or higher education. However, just because the theories of curriculum have been independently generated this is not necessarily problematic for youth work. As the theories formulated within formal education are transferable and can be used to analyse the youth work setting. In addition, certain ideas, beliefs and assumptions which underlie curriculum in practice can be seen to have emerged from, and be located within, specific theories. Therefore to enable readers to acquire an informed knowledge of curriculum it is necessary to familiarise ourselves with formal curriculum theory. However, one must take a critical view of the application of educational theory to youth work, and be wary, for example, of simply applying the dominant theories.

The emergence of curriculum in youth work has to some extent been developed independently of the influence of mainstream curriculum theory, and therefore must be viewed in its own right. However despite this an understanding of curriculum theory can better inform the development of curriculum in practice, not least, because certain less favourable aspects of curriculum theory are beginning to take hold in current youth work policy (Ord, 2004a, 2004b).

Curriculum theory is divided into a number of different categories. For example Eisner and Vallance (1974) divided curriculum theory into five categories – cognitive processing, technology, self-actualisation, social reconstruction, and academic rationalism. Lawton et al. (1978) proposes three categories of subject centred, child centred and society centred curriculum. For the purpose of this analysis, curriculum theory will be divided into three distinct categories of curriculum – content, product and process. These are the categories utilised by Kelly (2004) as well as those now adopted by Lawton (though he does offer a fourth model of curriculum as assessment

but as he himself notes: 'It is doubtful whether this is a model in its own right' (1996: 7). The division of curriculum into the categories of content, product and process is the most relevant to the youth work curriculum.

Theory of curriculum as content

Curriculum as content or, as it is sometimes commonly known, curriculum as syllabus, is the traditional conception of curriculum. It is concerned with the identification and transmission of knowledge. Curriculum as syllabus or content is associated with formal education and with the transmission of specified content or subject matter. There is an emphasis on the delivery by the teacher to pupils who receive the information passively. Focus on the syllabus has been common since the earliest examples of organised formal education from the Greeks between the 5th and 7th centuries BC (Pope, 1983: 14), through to the 'Victorian principles' of passive pupils, rote learning and regurgitation of facts. Clearly in this, its crudest sense, curriculum as content has little relevance to youth work. Likewise the sterility of the national curriculum with its emphasis on the authority of the teacher's knowledge, set syllabi and education underpinned by the analogy of 'the filling up of empty vessels' is also of little relevance to the dynamic learning environment of youth work.

Curriculum as content cannot be dismissed outright however, as Kelly points out, 'For many curriculum is still a syllabus . . .' (Kelly, 2004: 46). In addition, the notion of content appears in many of the curriculum documents produced by statutory youth services. On this basis we must therefore critically analyse 'curriculum as content', consider its merits and expose any deficiencies.

Problems with the theory of curriculum as content

There are fundamental problems with the organisation of curriculum on the basis of content alone, which Kelly identifies below, and although he is offering a critique of the national curriculum the same warnings apply to a youth work curriculum:

> *To frame a national curriculum in terms of its constituent subjects and worse, the content to be transmitted under those subject headings, on the other hand, is to put at risk every principle of democracy and of democratic education we have identified . . . and thus of the denial of genuine empowerment.*
>
> (Kelly, 1995: 153)

The problems with curriculum as content can be summarised as firstly the 'problem of knowledge' itself and secondly the problem of 'education as transmission'. These will be looked at in turn.

The problem of 'knowledge'

The philosophical basis of knowledge is in itself problematic for curriculum as specified content. This objection (Kelly, 2004; Carr, 1995) claims that theories of curriculum as content conceive of knowledge as absolute, and unchallengeable. They argue that in the post-modern world all knowledge is relative. Knowledge should therefore be seen as a consequence of its 'social and ideological roots' (Carr, 1995:115) and cannot therefore provide an absolute and unchallengeable foundation for a curriculum.

This claim can be interpreted in two ways. Firstly, a strong claim, that what counts as knowledge is 'in itself' a value choice, or a weaker claim that what knowledge is thought to be worth including in the curriculum is a value choice, but that what 'actually counts as knowledge' is in itself unquestionable.

The strong claim, that there are no philosophical foundations to knowledge appears untenable, especially if one considers that criteria for what counts as knowledge would no doubt include consistency, explanatory power, reliability etc. This stronger claim would also lead to an indefensible form of relativism. It is not entirely clear which of the two claims is being made by Carr or by Kelly. However, the second claim is sufficient to support their argument, that the choice of content is not objective but normative. That is, a value judgement is made in deciding what knowledge is, or is not, important and worthy of inclusion in the curriculum.

Knowledge does not provide a value free basis to the curriculum, and therefore, as Kelly (2005)

proposes, democratic principles suggest that knowledge specified by the educator 'as content' does not provide a tenable basis for a curriculum.

Education as transmission

When education is framed as transmission it views the educational process as passive. The learning environment is one which explicitly defines the authority of the teacher. The content is communicated uncritically and the learners are also seen as passive in this process, accepting and learning uncritically. Clearly this passive educational process is anathema to youth work's dynamic learning environment.

Freire (1972) was rightly critical of this conception of teaching and learning, describing it as: 'the 'banking' concept of education in which the scope of action allowed to the student extends only as far as receiving, filing, and storing the deposits . . .' (1972: 46) and 'In the banking concept of education, knowledge is a gift bestowed by those who consider themselves knowledgeable upon those whom they consider to know nothing' (ibid.). As we saw earlier Freire takes this criticism too far, with his recommendation to eradicate altogether the distinction between learner and educator, as it denies the responsibility of the educator to input into the learning environment. In order to overcome the problems of transmission one does not need to eradicate the teacher, merely for the teacher (and the learners) to adopt what Carr (1995) calls a 'critique' of educational practice. Which would be '. . . a democratic, rather than an elitist, community committed to the formation and development of common educational purposes through critical reflection on existing policies and practice. It would thus be a community in which all participants were treated equally; in which there were no barriers to open and free communication' (1995: 188). To overcome the problem of education as transmission one does not need to abolish the teacher but to replace the authority of the teacher with the humility of the teacher.

Another problem with education as transmission is it merely focuses on 'what is being taught'. As Kelly points out, 'what is important is not merely *what* knowledge we present via our curricular, but more so, *how* we present it' (Kelly, 2004: 48). The discursive methods of youth work, with an emphasis on conversation, negotiation and challenge are clearly contrary to any notion of education as transmission.

Given that curriculum as content is therefore inherently problematic one must be cautious about how content is utilised in the youth work curriculum.

Curriculum as content in youth work practice

Curriculum as content (or syllabus): 'can be seen to be analogous to the content areas prevalent in the curriculum documents produced by local authority youth services'. (Ord, 2004a: 48). Indeed, a great many curriculum documents conceptualise content in respect of areas, some explicitly referring to them as such, including Wiltshire (2005) Gloucestershire (circa 1992) and Havering (2004)

Many documents use different terms, but with a similar intention, of categorising content, e.g. Herefordshire (2002) use a list of 20 'delivery topics', which include independent living, sexuality, citizenship and health. St Helens (undated) and Devon (2002) use the notion 'curriculum categories' both having, amongst others, categories of justice and equality, and relationships. Hampshire conceives of content as a way of identifying 'The priority areas of skills, knowledge and understanding' (2003: 11) which include personal and social skills, and healthy lifestyles. For others like Plymouth (1999) it is a mechanism for communicating what are regarded as the key issues for young people in their curriculum framework.

It would certainly appear that the majority wish to categorise content in one form or another, apart from a couple of notable exceptions including Cumbria (undated) and Shropshire (2001). The fact that so many youth work curricula in practice have incorporated a reference to content should not be interpreted as a tacit acknowledgement of the legitimacy of the model of 'curriculum as content'. There is clearly an important distinction between 'framing the curriculum' of youth work through overarching areas or categories etc. and the conception of curriculum as the specific transmission of knowledge. The documents do not approximate to a syllabus indeed some make this explicit: 'The Shropshire Youth Work Curriculum is not seen as a list of subjects, a syllabus . . .' (2001: 4) and

similarly Torbay state: 'It is not a list of activities you have to provide and which they have to learn' (2006:1)

The distinction offered by Curzon (1990) is useful, between a specific syllabus which defines content in considerable detail with a 'general or outline syllabus' which he regards as a 'summary of course content headings' (1990: 166). Clearly if youth work curriculum are going to specify content it ought to be of the general kind and clearly content 'areas' do that.

Content areas are a legitimate way of 'framing' content without incorporating a view of education which involves passive transmission or is committed to a view of the knowledge, contained within those content areas, as absolute, unquestionable or unchallengeable. It is a balance between on the one hand the need to be specific about the identification of content, to enable clarity of purpose and on the other being open enough to allow for flexibility and not be too prescriptive; whilst at the same time not being so open as to appear vague. West Sussex (2000) have one of the most detailed of content specifications and so for example, rather than the more open title of 'equality of opportunity' (Plymouth, 1999) they have the more detailed 'Anti-Racist Work' and 'Gender Issues'. This has the added advantage of reputedly making it easier to undertake such work (Ord, 2004b).

It is not necessarily the case that just because a particular youth work curriculum frames its content in this acceptable manner that it is immune from the above criticisms. It does not mean that the interpretation of the curriculum document, or more importantly its application, is not in a manner which is tantamount to curriculum as 'specific' content, and therefore becoming a syllabus. That is, do youth workers begin to plan sessions to communicate what they regard as the essential knowledge about for example healthy eating, or the dangers of drugs, in a sense which implicitly assumes a relatively passive group of young people, and, it is deemed by the workers that this is essential knowledge that they need to acquire. Whether or not this will be the case will be determined by the manner in which the curriculum is applied in practice, and to what extent other aspects of the curriculum such as 'curriculum as process', which is more consistent with youth work principles and practices, are utilised and applied. We will shortly take a look at other aspects of curriculum and the more important 'curriculum as process', but first let us consider an example of where curriculum as content may actually apply, at least in theory.

Information as 'content'?

Before leaving curriculum as content it is worth considering a possible application of this aspect of curriculum theory to youth work: Is the providing of information an application of curriculum as content?

For curriculum as content to be legitimately applied it must overcome the two former objections: that it is legitimate for the content to be received passively by the young person and that there is at least a high degree of assurance that the knowledge is well grounded (absolute) or at least what Kelly (2004: 47) calls 'intrinsically valuable'. In youth work it could be argued that the concept of 'information' fits this bill and the communication of information as 'essential facts' (which have for example, considerable scientific validity) to young people alludes to this notion of curriculum as content.

One should be cautious, however, before accepting the simplicity of this argument. There are examples in youth work of the need to communicate basic information, for example in relation to sexual health and the 'facts' about sexually transmitted diseases or contraception; or information about the effects of specific drugs. However, the manner in which this information is delivered rarely approximates to notions of mere 'transmission' which is integral to curriculum as content.

The information required by young people is often of a sensitive nature and is therefore often best communicated through a trusting relationship between the learner and the educator (or in our case the young person and the youth worker), the importance of which is an integral feature of the process approach to the youth work curriculum. Even if a request for 'the facts' is made and the information is provided, the decisions made in relation to the information given, as well as the resulting actions, will very often require discussion and deliberation. In addition decisions about what young people will actually do with the information may also take time to be made. Information exchange in youth work is therefore rarely passive. We can conclude therefore that 'information', even when it

approximates to 'justifiably specific content', is problematic in the educational environment of youth work. It should not be seen as a legitimate application of the content theory of curriculum.

Content curriculum and outcomes

A further problem which Kelly identifies with the content model is that content curricula '. . . often framed in terms of subjects and knowledge-content, are also laden with references to the 'aims and objectives' of these subjects and this content' (2004: 56). That is, although claiming the curriculum is justified solely in terms of its content, it is actually the result of acquiring the knowledge in terms of its objectives or outcomes that is implicit within it and is actually regarded as more important. So, in our example of the essential sexual health information and the content relating to facts about contraception, although it could be argued that these represent legitimate curricular content, in reality the educational justification is actually more likely to be found in the objectives that relate to the communication of this information. For example, in the reduction of sexually transmitted diseases or in the reduction of teenage pregnancies. It would therefore be more legitimate to view the information as a form of curriculum as product.

So we can see then that the notion of a syllabus, and the content based curriculum, is problematic on two counts. Firstly in terms of what constitutes that syllabus that the subject matter is itself necessarily contentious. Secondly, it is problematic because the educational relationship is conceived of as a passive process of transmission.

As Kelly proposes:

The idea of education as transmission or curriculum as content is simplistic and unsophisticated because it leaves out of the reckoning major dimensions of the curriculum debate. In particular, it does not encourage or help us take any account of the children who are the recipients of this content, or the objects of the process of transmission, or of the impact of this content or process on them, and especially their right to emancipation and empowerment.
(2004: 52)

It is therefore to the curricula based around outcomes: curriculum as product that we must now look.

Curriculum as Product

Theory of curriculum as product

Curriculum as product is the dominant theory of curriculum. Kelly (2004) refers to it as being characterised by a conception of education as 'instrumental', that is, a primary concern for what it is that education leads to or brings about. It is primarily concerned with ends not means. Its first question is one of purpose, but a purpose articulated in terms of end products. However, it is not satisfied with generality. In contrast, according to the rationale of curriculum as product, the more detailed and specific the explanations of educational products the better.

The pioneer of this approach to curriculum is Franklin Bobbitt. His first book *The Curriculum* (1918) published in America, was the first formal text on curriculum. It had considerable influence in his native land and later in the UK and his influence is still in evidence today. His approach is a highly technical approach to curriculum which involves the pre-specification of educational objectives. Taylor and Richards describe Bobbitt's rationale as:

A scientific approach to planning school curricula by the systematic analysis of those human activities which the curriculum was intended to develop. The activities to be focused on were those which made for efficiency in living as a healthy, gainfully employed citizen. Those activities, analysed in detail, would be the intended outcomes of the curriculum.

(1985: 13)

This product based approach to curriculum was advanced by Ralph Tyler (1949) in his seminal text *Basic Principles of Curriculum and Instruction*. Tyler's rationale 'begins with identifying four fundamental questions which must be answered in developing any curriculum . . .' These are:

1. What educational purposes should the school seek to attain?
2. What educational experiences can be provided that are likely to attain these purposes?
3. How can these educational experiences be effectively organised?
4. How can we determine whether these purposes have been attained? (1949: 1)

Essentially, what Tyler is proposing is a sequence which begins with 'aims', then identifies 'content', from which it establishes the necessary 'methods' and then finally this leads to 'evaluation'. However, it is important to note that it is the educational aims that are given the most prominence in his schema. These aims are not general but specific and are probably more clearly identified as objectives or goals. As Taylor and Richards point out:

. . . according to his (Tyler's) view, if such goals are to be formulated, vaguely stated aims are not sufficient. Statements of goals need to indicate both the kind of behaviour to be developed in the pupil (or young person) and the area of content in which the behaviour is to be applied. Such closely formulated statements of intent are termed objectives. It is very important to note here that such objectives are to be specified before the remaining components of the design model are considered (i.e. the objectives are to be pre-specified).

(1985: 58)

Benjamin Bloom, who was a student of Tyler's, continued the work to develop the product based curriculum, and produced *The Taxonomy of Educational Objectives. Handbook 1, Cognitive Domain* in 1956. This work follows a distinction between the cognitive, affective and psychomotor domains and was a systematic attempt to categorise both the general and specific 'behavioural' objectives of the first domain: the cognitive realm. Though latterly criticised for a flawed distinction between cognitive and affective aspects of learning (Curzon, 1990: 150) the work of Bloom does show the considerable extent to which educationalists advocating a product approach to curriculum were prepared to go in pre-specifying the behavioural objectives.

What is meant by 'objectives' in the Tylerian, and many of the subsequent 'product' models of curriculum, are behavioural objectives: that is the specific and measurable changes in the learners behaviour. As Tyler describes:

Since the real purpose of education is not to have the instructor perform certain activities but to bring about significant changes in the students' patterns of behaviour, it becomes important to recognise that any statement of objectives by the school should be a statement of changes to take place in students.

(1949: 44)

This insistence on behavioural objectives is problematic as not all outcomes are reducible to behavioural objectives. A significant criticism of the product based approach to curriculum is that it was exclusively, and to some extent still is, concerned with behavioural objectives. For example, Ross argues that '. . . in higher order learning it is not likely to be the case that behavioural evidence alone will be either the only or sufficient evidence of learning' (2000: 119); and he goes on to suggest that 'many intellectual and aesthetic activities involve imagination and other qualities that are difficult to describe in behavioural terms' (2000: 120).

Paul Hirst, an influential advocate of the product curriculum, in his article *The Logic of Curriculum* (1969; 1974) accepted this criticism, admitting: 'Most of the central objectives we are interested in, in education' are not themselves reducible to observable states' (1974: 21). Instead he advocated the development of the 'rational mind' as the central purpose and suggested that objectives could result from this. He therefore advocated an objectives based 'product' curriculum, which is based on the first principle of the detailed specification of the end product, as both the starting point and defining principle of curriculum; but one that was not based on behavioural objectives:

> *If what it is we want to achieve is first indicated in expressions of great generality, these need to be unpacked into much more specific terms or little positive guidance is provided for educational purpose. To be of value we must eventually analyse these ends down to particular achieve-ments we wish pupils to reach, detailed enough for us to be able to judge how to promote these.*
>
> (1974: 16)

So it is as Kelly identifies that with the establishment of the Schools Council in 1964: 'the concept of curriculum planning by objectives finally entered into the consciousness of the practicing teacher' (2004: 58). By the late 1980s with the politicisation of curriculum (Ross, 2000; Kelly, 2004) one could be forgiven for thinking that curriculum as product was the only notion of curriculum.

Problems with the theory of curriculum as product

Curriculum is often still based on behavioural objectives. These 'competency led' approaches are often overly concerned with specifying the resulting behavioural end products. Education becomes concerned with measuring what students can and cannot do. Whilst this is not problematic for some traditional school subjects, like the basic skills of literacy and numeracy, where behavioural changes are measurable, there are however problems with this approach for other academic subjects, and similarly it is problematic for a curriculum in youth work, as many of the changes will not be either behavioural or measurable. Even one of the principle advocates of a product based curriculum, Hirst, (1969; 1973; 1974) concedes behavioural objectives are problematic.

However, whether behavioural or not the product based curriculum is itself problematic for the following reasons:

The lack of justification of objectives

'No account is given of the source and origins of curriculum objectives in the beliefs, values and conceptions of those engaged in planning and those influencing the planners' (Taylor and Richards, 1985: 63). There is a distinct lack of justification of the objectives or end products within a product based approach to curriculum. The desirability of the objectives in Tyler's scheme, for example, like many others, are taken for granted. They are the starting point, but the question why choose one particular behaviour or set of behaviours, or one curriculum objective over another is never asked. There is circularity implicit in its rationale in that it both starts and ends with the objective which in itself has no way of justifying itself. There is a sense in which, as Kelly puts it, 'The aims and objectives approach to curriculum planning, like all pseudo scientific approaches to the study and planning of human activity, endeavours to be value neutral' (2004: 65). There is perhaps an assumption that they are intrinsically valuable. But this assumption is highly questionable and the fact that it is not addressed undermines the approach's validity.

Controversial issues and the problem of objectives

As previously identified, in relation to the problem of selecting content, similarly for the specification of objectives, the fact that the focus of much of our education is on controversial issues and contentious areas, and that knowledge itself is not absolute, the product approach becomes problematic. Judgements are required on conflicting arguments, as are aspects of taste and style in the appreciation, or not, of a piece of music. How can, therefore, objectives be set for what will be the end point of a process of analysis? Should we be telling people what the outcome of reflections and analysis of a debate on abortion should be? Where is the role of insight, intuition and the creative development of students own thoughts and ideas? As Stenhouse observes:

> *Controversial issues are defined empirically as issues which do in fact divide people in our society. Given divergence among students, parents and teachers, demo-cratic principles are evoked to suggest that teachers may wish to ensure that they do not use their position of authority in the classroom to advance their own opinions or perspectives, and that the teaching process does not determine the outcome, opinions and perspectives of the students . . . given a dispute in society about the truth of a matter the teacher in a state school might wish to teach the dispute rather than the truth as he knows it.*
>
> (1975: 93)

Education as production is 'training not education'

It is claimed that the product approach in many senses is more akin to training than education. It is technocratic and conceives of education as if it were a production line with a clear idea of what it is that is to be produced. For many 'the terminology of the production line is inappropriate' (Curzon, 1990: 137). Indeed as Kelly points out, 'as we have seen (in product based approaches) any conceptual distinction between education and training, instruction or teaching is ignored, or even simply rejected' (2004: 54) and Ross concurs that 'systematic technical evaluation of a learning programme is not possible in anything of a higher order than training' (2000: 120). Youth work is by its nature more complex and dynamic than the production analogy implies.

Linear concept of learning

Linked to the criticism of education as a production line, is one of the most important criticisms of the product approach to a youth work curriculum; that it contains a linear conception of learning (Ord, 2004b; Kelly, 2004). Learning is conceived as the conversion of specific input into a definable output the end product. Learning in terms of output is both reducible to, and derived from, specific input. It is presumed therefore that a one-to-one causal relationship exists between input and output, between specific educational interactions and the eventual learning. This is problematic for the curriculum per se but particularly problematic for a youth work curriculum. This is a point which will be returned to later when the process approach to learning and the curriculum is expanded upon.

Indoctrination not emancipation

In a product based curriculum all the desired educational ends are established by the teacher in advance, and likewise the methods, and the means of assessing their attainment. This places the teacher in a position of absolute authority. Also implicit in this approach is an underlying domination of behaviourism. Kelly rightly describes this as 'assum(ing) that it is legitimate to mould human beings, to modify their behaviour according to certain clear cut intentions without making any allowance for their individual wishes, desires or interests . . . (is tantamount to indoctrination) and is fundamentally at odds with a notion of education for emancipation or empowerment' (2004: 60). This doctrinaire approach to curriculum is not appropriate for a youth work curriculum if it is to be consistent with its emancipatory principles of young people's empowerment.

Curriculum as product in youth work practice

Given these problems associated with curriculum as product, even when relating it to formal education, it would be all too easy to dismiss it out of hand. Also, in its strictest sense, and when formulated in its crude behavioural terms, perhaps it is not immediately recognisable to youth workers, and it does not appear entirely relevant. It would be all too easy to conclude that it is not immediately applicable to youth work. Indeed for many youth workers this technocratic formulation of curriculum may have been one of the main reasons why they rejected curriculum in the first place, because it did not concur with the dynamic and fluid nature of the youth work process.

Curriculum as product is, however, the dominant view of curriculum and therefore rightly or wrongly it underlies many of the rationales and underlying assumptions of curriculum, whether in youth work or in formal education. It is worth remembering that it was this approach that Alan Howarth MP took when he tried to impose his notion of curriculum as outcomes at the first ministerial conference (NYB, 1990). Also outcomes, the products of youth work, loom large in much of the contemporary debate about youth work, whether they are communicated through curriculum documents or not. A recollection of a conversation with an experienced Ofsted inspector illustrates this point. The first question he asked the youth workers on arrival at a particular club or project on an inspection would be, 'What are the young people learning tonight?' Make no mistake, this was a clear request for clarity about what the objectives of the session were. This question was asked at the outset, it was his starting point prior to any knowledge of the context, process or any other factors influencing the circumstances, educational or otherwise, of the project. He was not concerned with what emerged out of the session but what were the 'intended learning outcomes'. A clear commitment to an objectives (product based) approach to youth work, and therefore the curriculum.

It is necessary, therefore, to take a closer look at 'outcomes' and see how they are incorporated into the youth work curriculum produced in the field, and see whether the conceptualisation of them is guilty of some of the criticisms of the product approach to curriculum.

'Outcomes' in youth work and product models of curriculum?

Planning by objectives may not be immediately recognisable to many youth workers but planning by outcomes certainly is. The most easily recognisable application of 'curriculum as product' to youth work would be the way in which it develops its articulation of its outcomes. Many, though by no means all, of the curriculum documents developed in the field include a focus on outcomes. The extent to which it is a problem is dependant on how these outcomes approximate to objectives and more importantly where they fit in the rationale for the organisation and justification of the work, and therefore the curriculum. This is an important question. How far have youth workers in their incorporation of outcomes in the curriculum adopted methods which are akin to curriculum as product?

The role of outcomes and how they are articulated is of crucial importance in the extent to which they undermine the processes of youth work. If the pre-specification of outcomes is both expected of workers and utilised to plan and deliver youth work it has the potential to undermine that process.

In early formulations of youth work curriculum outcomes were not given significance. This is evidenced by the first major piece of documentation to be produced for guidance on curriculum in youth work by Ofsted (1993) entitled *The Youth Work Curriculum*. Ord notes that:

> . . . *importantly the document is not prescriptive and does not attempt to impose a predetermined concept of curriculum. Also significantly it does not emphasise 'outcomes' as being integral to the youth work curriculum and it certainly does not equate the two concepts . . . the document focuses on descriptions of the educative principles of youth work.*
>
> (2004a: 46)

Importantly: 'Educative means introducing young people to ideas and areas of experience from which they can learn new skills and knowledge and develop understanding' (Ofsted, 1993: 5). What is apparent is that at least in the early formulations of curriculum in youth work there is no particular emphasis placed on outcomes and there is nothing within it that would lead one to believe that a model of curriculum as product was being applied.

What Ofsted (1993) also did was attempt to reflect and comment on how the curriculum was being developed in the field 'post Howarth' and it is to some of those documents that we must look to answer the question of whether a product based approach is being adopted in youth work or not?

It is probably true that most curriculum documents produced by statutory youth services feature outcomes in some respect. Some notable exceptions include Leicestershire (2000) and Milton Keynes (2003). Some did not, for example, Hampshire (1991) but have subsequently included them (Hampshire, 2003). The question remains for those that do. In so doing, to what extent are they adopting a model of curriculum as product? The answer can be found in how the particular outcomes are stated; whether they pertain to objectives and how specific or general they are. Are they general and intended to act as guidelines for identification of outcomes through an evaluation process, and to communicate to those who have an interest, the kind of outcomes one may expect, or are they specific, often behavioural, outcomes which could be used to inform a planning process and thus be incorporated into a strict product based approach?

For some it is quite clear that they do not approximate to objectives. For example Cumbria's (undated) outcomes are articulated in a way which makes it quite clear that they are general and non-specific. For example: 'develop sense of belonging, express feelings, develop sense of personal identity'. These are not objectives, nor do they approximate to them, and they could not be used in an objectives style planning process; to do that they must be able to be pre-specified. They act more as overarching concepts which can make workers more aware of the kinds of things to focus on when evaluating and analysing their work and for guidance when considering the outcomes of the process. Similarly Havering (2003) have what can best be described as broad aims for their outcomes – 'Function independently and effectively at home, school/college, at work and in the community' and 'Make and keep good relationships with peers and family, respecting the lifestyles and values of others'. These general outcomes communicate the broad benefits for the young people and illustrate the key purposes of youth work.

However, other curriculum documents appear to approximate much more to a product model in their incorporation of outcomes. For example, West Sussex (2000) Devon (2002) and Kingston (2002) incorporate a statement of desirable outcomes which is to be utilised in a planning process. This planning process is what Ingram and Harris (2001) call NAOMIE:

- Identification of *Need*
- Set *Aims*
- Set *Objectives*
- Establish *Methods*
- *Implement*
- *Evaluate*

This model is clearly a version of 'curriculum as product' which includes the pre-specification of objectives as their starting point. The extent to which this matters is dependant on how well the criticisms of the curriculum as product are countered. Also whether this is a viable model of curriculum depends on what the implications are for youth work practice.

The problems of curriculum as product in youth work practice

The criticism that the product models of curriculum *lack a justification for their objectives* appears to be answered with reference to the 'needs identification', that is, a particular objective is justified or legitimate because it is presumed to be meeting a particular need. One should, however, be wary of accepting the simplicity of this argument. Whose needs are we talking about? Which particular needs? Who has the final say on what needs the objectives will be based upon? How do we distinguish between the 'real' needs and mere wants, given the majority of needs are at least to some extent culturally determined? The notion of 'needs analysis' rolls off the tongue of many professionals without them actually being at all clear about the validity of the need: As Hirst points out, 'saying what children need is only a cloaked way of saying what we judge they ought to have' (1974: 17).

Even if one turns to theorists like Maslow (1954) and his hierarchy of needs, or to developmental theorists like Kellmer Pringle (1980) as indeed Ingram and Harris do (2001) it is not clear how we can effectively translate Maslow's 'need for belonging' or Mia Pringle's 'need for security' for example, into pre-specifiable objectives in a planning process. The needs articulated in both theories might be valid, but they are broad and general and are not easily translated into specific objectives for practice. Also the youth work process encapsulates both work with individuals and work with those individuals as part of a group. Is the needs analysis based on group needs or individual needs? What happens if there is a difference or a conflict of needs, both between individuals or between individuals and the group?

Part of the problem with needs is, as Woods and Barrow point out: 'Estimating children's needs requires consideration of evaluative assumptions . . .' (1975: 119), that is, a judgement is required as to the worth of a need. 'We may disagree as to whether a particular person does need something because we have different values' (ibid.). Christians believe they have a need to pray, atheists believe they have no such need and this is merely providing false succour. A regular drug taker fervently believes they have a need to satisfy. The moralist may see them as an addict and believe they only think they have a need.

A further problem related to needs is the assumption which underlies much of the debate about needs: That individuals in fact are aware of what they need and that their expressed needs are therefore always valid. A heavy smoker actually needs to cut down or give up in many people's eyes. They do not 'need to smoke'. If someone says they need to enter a pub on a Friday night and need a drink that would appear to be perfectly legitimate, in order for them to relax after a long week. However, if they are 16 or 17 years old, you might fervently disagree, and say that they certainly do not have a need to drink. Then again you may not, you may think the law is wrong, and suggest that a 17-year-old ought to be able to drink?

This raises another question about the controversial nature of needs. What do you actually do about the needs once they have been identified, and even agreed, because nothing follows from the fact that two people have agreed about a particular need, that they actually agree about what to do about it. Detached youth workers, when coming across young people who are drinking on a Friday night, might agree that they are legitimately meeting a need, but differ as to their approach. Some may think they have no role or responsibility, some that they have certain health and safety responsibilities but no more, or alternatively have a responsibility to the young people to articulate their needs to relevant others like residents, police, etc. or even encourage them to campaign for the rights that result from that need.

It is not being denied that the meeting of young people's needs is an important part of youth work, but needs are complex and are not easily translated into a simplistic model proposed through a planning framework and within a notion of curriculum as product. It may well be that some pieces of work can legitimately overcome the problems and criticisms identified,

and work can therefore, be planned based upon articulated, negotiated and agreed needs. However, equally, the 'real' needs may well emerge out of the process of engagement, through dialogue and discussion. It would appear fallacious to found the whole of the youth work curriculum on needs based pre-specified objectives. It is, therefore more authentic, and indeed empowering to young people to incorporate *a critical reflection on young people's needs* at the heart of the curriculum.

It is also not clear how the objection that **controversial issues make specifying objectives problematic** will be overcome. As we have seen, unless the topic in question approximates to 'factual information' the knowledge in question is bound to have a 'normative element', leaving it open to debate and controversial enough to make the specification of objectives problematic. For example where factual information in relation to the effects of drugs is discussed how would one go about setting objectives for a discussion, given that an important principle of youth work is that young people 'make their own decisions' based on information provided for them.

Indeed, if the important youth work principle of self-determination (Banks, 2001; NYA, 1999) which underpins the right of young people to make their own choices is not adhered to, the curriculum would fall foul of the criticism that the educational process would end up being **indoctrination and not education**. The very setting of objectives by the workers must be carefully negotiated if it is not to be guilty of this criticism. As Shropshire's curriculum document states, 'the process is negotiated with young people so that it is acceptable and appropriate' (2001: 4). Similarly, 'It is the right of young people to influence and inform the curriculum' (Hampshire, 1991: 6).

Similarly, it is difficult to see how the problems concerned with the **linear conception of learning** could be countered, as planning by objectives necessarily entails this conception of learning. Finally, the extent to which the objection that product models become **training not education** would depend on the extent to which planning by objectives became the sum total of the youth work. If all the work was delivered through the pre-specification of objectives it would be difficult to see how dynamic, spontaneous and fun elements of the youth work process could be incorporated, and it would end up being a crude form of 'life training' not education in its fullest sense.

It should not be interpreted that in criticising the application of the objectives or product approach to curriculum that an abandonment of an emphasis on outcomes or planning is being advocated. Far from it, as even Kelly, perhaps one of the most ardent critics of the product approach concedes: 'The objectives movement has rightly drawn our attention to the importance of being clear about the purpose of the curriculum' (2004: 75). Clarity about the outcomes and the educational achievements of youth work is enormously beneficial. As a critical and reflective practitioner it is important for one's own practice, as well as for those with an interest in it, whether that be young people, practitioners, managers, politicians or members of the local community, to be clear about the outcomes of youth work. Evaluation is integral and a critical perspective on the effectiveness of our interventions is crucial in the development of good practice.

However, how outcomes are framed within the curriculum has important implications for the process of youth work. The extent to which workers are expected to have pre-specified objectives in relation to outcomes prior to engagement with young people is of particular importance. It may be at times (though perhaps rare) that a strict product approach is both appropriate and necessary. As Stenhouse rightly points out: 'The objectives model of curriculum design and planning is no doubt a useful one, but it has severe limitations. Accordingly, it is wrong that it should be taken for granted, or advanced as universally applicable' (cited in Hooper, 1973: 123). Before turning our attention to alternative approaches to curriculum we must explore one of the domains within which a product approach is more acceptable: skills acquisition.

Skills acquisition as a legitimate application of the product model

There is one aspect of learning in youth work which can be shown to be legitimately articulated through an objectives approach. That is the acquisition of skills. Even Lawrence Stenhouse, an advocate of a process model of curriculum, admitted that 'The objectives model appears more suitable in curricular areas which emphasise information and skills' (1975: 97).

We have dealt with the problem of information comprehensively in the previous section on content and considered the difficulties of incorporating the passive process implicit in the giving and receiving of information into the dynamic situation of youth work. However, it is to skills which we must now look.

The acquisition of skills is a legitimate part of youth work. Whether they are particular skills which have been identified by either the worker or the young person, skills in chairing meetings, for the recently elected chair of a youth forum or interview skills for a young person going for a job – they are a legitimate part of the youth work curriculum.

Also through the activities that are undertaken in youth work, skills are acquired. Whilst these activities are perhaps not the raison d'être, as Spence suggests, 'Activities based youth work has never been the full story of youth work' (2001: 171). None the less, whether it is DJ-ing or photography, cooking or managing a budget, ICT or outdoor education, there are a wide variety of activities which are incorporated into the youth work curriculum, or could be if the young people choose them to be, through which skills are developed. If these skills are to be specifically taught it is widely accepted that they are reducible to specific behavioural objectives, and that a product model is the most suitable. Specific outcomes or objectives can be identified prior to each and every session and a series of sessions can be programmed together to ensure adequate teaching and learning. These skills are in themselves valuable outcomes. It should be remembered however that skills acquisition alone could never account for the whole of youth work and the purposes of youth work must encapsulate the wider issues of personal and social development (Young, 1999: 10). However, where such acquisition is an identified part of the curriculum it is right and proper to approach these within a product framework.

Products as vehicles for learning

It is important to distinguish between activities through which skills are developed for their own sake and therefore as ends in themselves, and activities which are undertaken as a means to an end. It is the latter which is most significant, indeed if youth work only incorporated the former it would cease to be youth work. 'Activities are a framework around which the educational aspects of the work with young people are structured' (Spence, 2001: 171).

Importantly, these 'educational aspects' are not reducible to the specific 'skills' which are acquired through the activity. For example, one could undertake outdoor activities for the acquisition of new skills in themselves, whether map reading, rope work or camp side cooking. But in youth work outdoor activities are more important as a vehicle for learning. For example, through outdoor activities young people could set themselves a challenge of undertaking an abseil to overcome barriers or come to terms with fears, trust one another whilst being held on a rope, or support and encourage each other through a gruelling hike. The activities are important and they define the learning opportunities but the activities and the skills needed to undertake the activity are not the whole picture; the process that develops out of the engagement in the activities is more significant, and provides the opportunities for learning.

These activities are often referred to as the products of youth work; the tangible, visible aspects of the work. As products however they must be distinguished from 'curriculum as product' with its emphasis on 'planning by objectives', which was criticised previously. This is important because many of the outcomes of these activities or products will not, and could not, have been predicted, and therefore pre-specified. They will have emerged out of the process. For example, one could not predict what the outcomes would be for a group undertaking a two day expedition, one could build a plausible educational purpose around facing challenges and group reliance, team work and mutual support, but the 'actual outcomes' or impact will only be apparent after the process has developed during the activity. This is an important point which will be expanded upon later.

The importance of quality products

It is important to note that whilst many youth workers perhaps understandably focus on the process of youth work they do at times neglect the product, as, very often, a quality process requires a quality product. For example, to encourage ownership of a building through a graffiti art project one needs the skills of the graffiti painting. To produce a film of your local environment to tell the young people's story, to encourage critical reflection on their experiences and communicate this to the wider community, one needs to be able to use a camera and edit the film, as well as of course having access to those resources. On this basis Ingram and Harris are right when they maintain that the received curriculum is dependant on 'Resources, both human and physical' (2001: 38).

This is perhaps why it is galling for youth workers who have consistently worked in under-funded youth clubs, who can barely afford a residential once a year to be criticised by the previous Minister for Children and Youth, about the quality of the learning which they provide (Hodge, 2005) and by the current Youth Minister Beverley Hughes, who described the record of statutory services as 'appalling' (cited in *Young People Now, News*, 2006: 2). Anyone who has knowledge of the provision in some of the local authority youth services which top the per capita funding tables (*Young People Now*, 19–25 November 2003; 1–7 Sept 2004) will be well aware of the possibilities that quality resources and quality products well managed within a youth work framework can provide.

The London Borough of Wandsworth provide a case in point. In 2003/4 they allocated £216.94 per head compared to the average of £86.75 (*Young People Now*, 2005) however even 'that is slightly skewed by a few very high spenders' and many are much lower (ibid.). As a result of Wandsworth's considerable commitment to youth provision they have for example, a young person's radio station, run entirely by young people, on air 12 hours a day, seven days a week for four weeks in the summer holidays (Wandsworth Youth Service, 1999; 2003). That is the power of a well resourced and structured curriculum. This was perhaps one the biggest failings of *Transforming Youth Work* (DfES, 2001, 2002) that the laudable £100 per head for every young person between the ages of 13 and 19 in every locality never became a reality (Barrett, 2005).

Having exhaustively dealt with the dominant theory of curriculum: curriculum as 'product', it is necessary to turn our attention to the lesser known, but no less important theory, particularly for youth work, that of curriculum as 'process'.

Curriculum as Process

The previous chapter dealt with some of the problems of implementing a curriculum as product, which is reliant on the setting of pre-specified objectives, whether in terms of intended learning outcomes or behavioural changes. The starting point of this chapter is a further criticism of curriculum as product: That in certain circumstances it may not just be the case that there are some unfortunate consequences for a curriculum based on pre-specified objectives, but that it might actually be illogical and therefore fundamentally flawed to even begin to try to set objectives for certain types of learning.

Despite the dominance of product based curriculum, there is a distinctly different approach, which though conspicuous by its absence in much of the contemporary debate about curriculum, is logically more consistent with the certain forms of educational enquiry, particularly youth work – that is a curriculum conceived of as a process. Evidence of the omission and denial of process based curriculum is widespread. For example, contemporary curriculum text books like *Key Concepts for Understanding Curriculum* by Marsh (1992) or *Engaging the Curriculum in Higher Education* by Barnett and Coate (2005) give it no mention. Despite this, curriculum as process was once an important method of understanding the curriculum. Pope suggests that it may even once have been the dominant ethos, and that Bobbit's objectives approach was itself created to 'challenge established practice'. 'The process model . . . contains some features which appear to have a long pedigree . . . Because they are so well established by tradition, these characteristics of the process model might seem to be second nature to many teachers' (1983: 23).

Curriculum theory as process

The premise of the processes approach is best summarised by Taylor:

> It is established folk lore at many levels in education that the essence of good teaching is a knowledge of one's subject. Given that the teacher knows his subject the folk lore has it, all that is required further are some techniques for presenting it. Nothing could be more a half truth . . . what results is teaching from conclusions, whereas what is needed by the pupils is teaching which leads him towards conclusions. The first concentrates his attention on knowing what, and the second on knowing how.
>
> (1973, 163–4)

The process approach does not therefore start with the end products – what is to be learnt, rather its starting point is how learning is best facilitated.

Stenhouse and curriculum as process

No one has done more in articulating the notion of curriculum as process than Lawrence Stenhouse. He was an influential figure in education during the 1970s and early 1980s before his death in 1982. Ruddock notes that his primary concern was 'the emancipation of the individual through knowledge' (1995: 1). Though Stenhouse himself thought that schools did value achievement they did not value the emancipation of their pupils.

His starting point, according to Elliot, was not the dominant question, 'What are the objectives of the curriculum?' but with a problem-situation that faced teachers, in attempting to make the school curriculum more relevant to the lives of young adolescents. The problem was 'how do teachers handle value issues in classrooms within a pluralistic society' (1995: 55).

Equally importantly was the methods and their philosophical foundations which most concerned Stenhouse. He argued strongly against what Elliott (1995) calls 'technical rationality'. This is an important concept and the focus of much criticism from writers who oppose a product based methodology. For example, Cornbleth (2000) refers to it as the 'technocratic curriculum' and Kelly (2005) refers to it simply as a 'technicist' approach. What these criticisms embody, along with Stenhouse, is a view that the terminology and approach of the production line of analysis as simply 'means to ends', and of an overriding concern with quantifiable outcomes, has erroneously permeated the curriculum as well as the social world:

Technical rationality represents the generalisation of an engineering mentality to the manipulation of cognitive and social as well as material objects. It carries assumptions of machine like functioning, reproducible linear process . . . and measurable output.

(Cornbleth, 1990)

Grundy (1987) locates this criticism in Habermas' technical interest, but it is founded on an age old philosophical distinction made originally by Aristotle (Irwin, 1999) between what he referred to as *Techne* and *Phronesis*. Techne is the kind of reasoning associated with the making of products and phronesis being the kind of reasoning associated with 'doing something well, in the moral sense'. What Stenhouse and those who have followed him are objecting to, is the inappropriate intrusion of the product making mentality into the social realm. As Elliot importantly points out 'encroachment of technical rationality into every area of social life is endangering fundamental human values' (1995: 57). Technical rationality has beset the educational curriculum with its preoccupation with objectives and product approaches; the process approach is fundamentally opposed to this, not least because educational outcomes are aspects of people and the social world which are not translatable into end products of a production line mentality.

Stenhouse therefore set out to formulate a rationale for the school curriculum which was completely independent of objectives. His starting point was 'uncertainty' and controversy in educational environments, which is, he maintained, widespread in issues of knowledge and understanding. In such uncertain environments attempting to be guided by the pre-specification of objectives was not only difficult, and disingenuous to students, but inappropriate. As Stenhouse himself puts it: 'The great problem of the objectives model lies in the area of induction into knowledge' (1975: 81). It is the unpredictable nature of knowledge acquisition which makes the setting of objectives for it logically inconsistent. Objectives are not suitable because they do not '. . . take account of the indeterminacy of knowledge which arises because the structures of knowledge are not mere classification and retrieval systems but constitute a raw material for thinking' (ibid.).

Stenhouse recognised that students must come to their own understanding and the knowledge acquired will reflect this. In a sense all knowledge is a synthesis, not necessarily of opposing positions, but certainly in the light of previous experience (Kolb, 1984). It involves the individual coming to 'their' understanding. Knowledge is not conceived as a separate 'product'. It is therefore not reducible to objectives, because the particular understanding will be specific to that individual and their particular thinking, their circumstances and contexts. Knowledge in this sense is phenomenological, that is, it is an experiential concept, integrally linked to the lived experience of that individual. The thinking could be based on false premises or fallacious reasoning, and this could be pointed out to the student, but implicit in contentious issues or knowledge, which is inherently debatable, is the assumption that there are opposing views which are equally justifiable. Whilst the outcomes are observable and detectable after the event none of this synthesis is specifiable before hand. As Stenhouse puts it: 'Knowledge is primarily concerned with synthesis . . . the objectives approach readily trivialises it' (1975: 83).

Stenhouse then asks himself the important question: 'Can curriculum and pedagogy be organised satisfactorily by a logic other than that of a means-end model? (1975: 84). The method Stenhouse proposed is based on process, as in an uncertain education environment one is, both practically and theoretically, best guided by principles rather than by objectives or pre-specified outcomes.

Put simply his argument runs thus:

- Knowledge is inherently controversial and contains opposing viewpoints.
- Knowledge as an educational end point therefore involves individuals coming to their own understating based on a synthesis of those opposing views, and their own experience.
- The eventual outcomes therefore will be indeterminate at the outset.
- As a result no objectives can be set meaningfully in advance.
- On this basis therefore the curriculum must be based on the *process* by which the students can best be facilitated in acquiring knowledge and understanding of the topic in question.

In specifying the details of the process curriculum Stenhouse borrows from Peters (1959) concept of 'principles of procedure'. That is principles which guide the means by which learning is facilitated. Examples of these (based on Raths, 1971) would include:

- Students are encouraged to make informed choices.
- Students are active in the learning environment.
- Students are encouraged to enquire into current personal and social problems.
- The activities should be meaningful to students.
- The activities should be relevant to the expressed purposes of students.

There remains the problem of content for the process model, but this is no less the case than for other curriculum models. However the problem of content is mitigated by the formulation of content both for, and within the process, generated from the expressed concerns of the pupils. Stenhouse also suggested that 'education be founded on the disciplines of knowledge, because they provide a framework' (1975: 93) and these do to some extent fulfil the criteria for being intrinsically valuable (Kelly, 2004). The framework for the youth work curriculum would be the 'content areas', the overarching concepts, found in the curriculum documents, and from which specific content is derived within the process.

Finally, it is perhaps obvious why Stenhouse's model was not widely accepted by mainstream formal education. As he acknowledges 'the process model is essentially a critical model, not a marking model'. (1975: 95). It is in the realm of assessment that it is most weak. As youth work is not subject to the same assessment demands, for example in terms of testing and exams, this makes the application of Stenhouse's process model to youth work less problematic.

The child (or young person) centred curriculum

The young person centred curriculum is another important feature of a process curriculum.

Rousseau

Ross (2000) rightly cites Rousseau as the original source of the child centred approach to

education. In his classic text *Emile* (1762) describing the education of a fictional child, he sets out his beliefs about naturalistic education. Ross suggests that Rousseau's philosophy is founded on two principles. Firstly, that 'nature is always right' and secondly that 'the child is naturally good'. Ross suggests Rousseau's approach to education follows from these assumptions and summarises his approach as a belief that: 'the child will develop naturally, given a suitable environment; the child's development is best self-directed; the role of the teacher is to enable learning, not to transmit knowledge; and the learning should be organised for individuals and not class sized groups' (2000: 136).

This final point is Rousseau's biggest flaw, and to think that any individual is independent of the social setting into which he is born is being naïve. His inability to incorporate the development of a 'social side' to his philosophy of education is a major weakness. However, the other principles have, to some extent, stood the test of time as foundations of a child centred approach. In formal education, in the UK, this approach is often more associated with primary schools, where until the early 1990s this was still the dominant philosophy underpinning the primary curriculum (Ross, 2000).

Young person centred youth work curricula are thus posited around the four remaining central positions, each of which can be traced back to Rousseau:

- Children will develop naturally, given a suitable environment.
- Children's development is best self-directed.
- Subject/discipline divisions are artificial.
- The role of the teacher is to enable learning, not to transmit knowledge.

(Ross, 2000: 138)

Pring (1978) summarises the case for a child centred curriculum suggesting that two principles underlie the argument in favour. Firstly, as all selection of content, subject matter or educational focus is made on the basis of a value judgement, the curriculum should therefore not just focus on encouraging children to focus on what the individual teacher, policy makers or society as a whole deems to be worthwhile, it should also develop in children interests intrinsically valuable to him or herself. 'The school should (therefore) organise at least part of the curriculum around what it diagnoses to be the potentially satisfying interests of each child' (1978: 24). Secondly, as all knowledge is ultimately derived from a process of enquiry, knowledge should not be presented independently of that enquiry. Furthermore, the skills and abilities which form the basis of that enquiry, the processing of information, the balancing of arguments, and the solving of problems should be incorporated into the curriculum. Importantly it is the pupils' own skills and abilities which constitute a valid focus of the educational enterprise, independently of the end products.

Pring summarises the call for a child centred curriculum suggesting, 'There should be more concentration upon the child's active reconstruction of experience as he pursues some interest than upon the adult's ways of conceiving experience as it is enshrined within particular subjects' (1978: 24–5).

Gestalt: learning as a holistic process

Lawton (1996) suggests that the role of Gestalt psychology 'should not be underestimated' in its influence on the child centred curriculum. Gestalt places an emphasis on the whole being greater than the sum of its parts. It rejects behaviourist approaches which try to dismantle learning into specific associations between stimulus and response. Instead Gestalt placed greater emphasis on the whole person as 'configurer of reality' or as 'meaning maker'. When applied to learning in education, the curriculum is seen not in terms of its dissection into constituent parts, but as an 'holistic process', which maintains the integrity of the whole person.

Dewey: education as experience

Dewey is one of the most influential of the child centred educational philosophers. He is associated with the development of progressive schools and is highly critical of traditional formal educational practices: 'The traditional scheme is, in essence, one of imposition from above and from outside' (1997: 18) and the attitudes it fosters are 'docility, receptivity and obedience'. He contrasts traditional education with the approach of what he calls the 'new education' of progressive schools as:

To imposition from above is opposed expression and cultivation of individuality; to external discipline is opposed free activity; to learning from texts and teachers, learning through experience; to acquisition of isolated skills and techniques by drill, is opposed of them as a means of attaining ends which make a direct vital appeal; to preparation for a more or less remote future is opposed making the most of opportunities of present life; to static aims and materials is opposed acquaintance with a changing world.

(1997: 19)

Dewey's primary concern is learning through experience and he is therefore described as the founding father of experiential education. He is quite specific that the primary vehicle for education should be the experience of the individuals being educated. 'Education in order to accomplish its ends both for the individuals and for society must be based upon experience – which is always life experiences of some individual' (1997: 89).

Dewey's experiential education is based on two fundamental principles of Continuity and Interaction. It is these principles which define the educative quality, or otherwise, of experience: 'continuity and interaction in their union with each other provide the measure of the educative significance and value of experience' (1997: 44). Continuity refers to the ability of the particular experience to build upon previous experiences, develop and extend present experiences and importantly lead to further experiences '. . . the principle of continuity of experience means that every experience both takes up something from those which have gone before and modifies in some way the quality of those which come after' (1997: 35).

The second principle of interaction is founded on 'the fact that all human experience is ultimately social: that it involves contact and communication' (1997: 38). It is a unique combination of people, places, and objects; it is the interaction of these factors with 'the personal needs, desires, purposes and capacities (of individuals) which create the experience which is had' (1997: 44). Importantly the interactions in Dewey's rationale gives equal weight to both the individual whose experience constitutes the education 'the internal conditions' and the environment which the educator manipulates or facilitates to provide the experience; 'the objective conditions'. Dewey '. . . assigns equal weight to both factors' (1997: 38). Dewey argues that formal education pays too much attention to the external conditions and not enough or no attention at all, to the internal conditions. 'Any normal experience is an interplay of these two sets of conditions. Taken together, or in their interaction they form what we call a situation' (1997: 42). It is these experiential situations which provide the grist for Dewey's educational mill.

Curriculum and the development of cognitive 'processes'

The starting point of the cognitive approach is 'how' people learn. It grew out of the developments in cognitive psychology and utilisation of the analogy of 'information processing' as a model for learning. The focus therefore is not so much on teacher input, the information itself, but on the manipulation of that input by the learner, what the pupil does with the information. 'Learning is a cognitive process involving the learner *acquiring* new information, *transforming* his state of existing knowledge and *checking* the adequacy of that state of knowledge against the demands of new situations ... *Knowledge is a process not a product*. The acquisition of knowledge is an active process and depends for its effectiveness on the learner's relating incoming information to previously acquired frames of reference' (Curzon, 1990: 84, author's italics). In this approach it is the processes themselves that are regarded as most valuable and it is the development of these which becomes the primary focus of curriculum. As Burns and Brooks maintain, 'Curricula must be process orientated if learners are to develop processing behaviours.' (1974: 43). Or, as Eisner and Vallance suggest, 'content in history or biology is considered less important than the development of the student's ability to infer, to speculate, to deduce, or to analyse. These abilities, it is argued, will endure long after the particular content or knowledge is forgotten ...' (1974: 19).

Bruner

One of the most influential writers to have applied the principles of cognitive approach to curriculum was Jerome Bruner (1960). His starting point is the means by which learning can best be facilitated, and this must, according to cognitive theory, involve the active manipulation of information. The learner must therefore be active in the learning process. He proposes a method of what he calls 'discovery learning'. Essentially, this involves not the teaching of knowledge as a finite entity but as something which must be arrived at through a process of enquiry. He recommended the setting of problems and encouraging the pupils to solve them, thereby enabling them to come to their own understanding. Importantly however through this process of problem solving they are developing the essential cognitive or intellectual skills (Bruner, 1960). Although Bruner is often criticised as we shall see later, for his exclusive focus on intellectual and cognitive development, it is noteworthy that in certain respects he laid the foundations of Stenhouse's work through his early enquiries into process curriculum with his experimental work on social science curriculum – *Man: A Course of Study* (Bruner, 1966).

Kelly and curriculum as development

Kelly's (2004) concept of curriculum as development builds on the previous three theoretical strands; Stenhouse's procedural principles, Dewey's learning from experience, and the cognitive school's conception of how children best learn.

Aims and principles

The starting point is a specific rejection of the objectives or product model of curriculum. Arguing against the overriding assumption that specific objectives can logically or meaningfully be derived from general educational aims, Kelly argues it is the 'general aims' which provide a more legitimate basis for a curriculum. The objectives approach to curriculum planning is replaced by an adoption of Stenhouse's procedural principles. Kelly argues it is procedural principles which best form the basis of 'enquiry' method of curricula. They approximate to educational aims but importantly they implicitly contain reference to 'how' the process will develop. For example, as Stenhouse suggests, within an overall educational aim of the 'elimination of racial tensions', these procedural principles would follow:

- We should help pupils become aware of their own attitudes.

- We should assist pupils to detect bias and the motives behind this.
- We should help pupils to see that many problems which appear to stem from racial causes may be predominantly social.

(Stenhouse, 1975: 131)

The advantage of this method, as Kelly (2004) notes, is that it copes with the bane of product curricula: the 'unintended learning outcome', because it welcomes the unexpected. Pre-specification it is argued would actually reduce the opportunities and possible range of educational outcomes, as one is preoccupied with the attainment of the set objective. As Stenhouse points out, 'Pre-specification of explicit goals prevents the teacher taking advantage of instructional opportunities unexpectedly occurring in the classroom' (Stenhouse, 1975: 73).

Education as democratic empowerment

Unlike previous models which disingenuously claim to be value neutral, Kelly's concept of curriculum is explicitly value based. Its starting point is a commitment to democracy, by which Kelly (2004, 1995) means the morality which underpins the more formal political democracy. Democracy therefore includes a respect for individual freedoms, equality of treatment and either an opportunity to participate in governance, or to evaluate the decisions and policies of those who do. As a consequence of this commitment to democracy, education must therefore make adequate provision for moral development, that is the knowledge and understanding necessary to take an active part in the democratic process: 'The young must be initiated into democratic morality' (Kelly, 2004: 89).

Curriculum as development

The means by which the moral and political dimensions of democracy can be advanced is through a concept of curriculum as development, that is the process by which individuals are 'developing a real sense of involvement and control of the social context of one's life' (Kelly, 2004: 89). For this to be realised, however, the education must also be concerned with social development, not only the cognitive processes

and functions necessary for conceptualising our place in the social world but also the affective or emotional aspect of development. The exploration of who we are and learning about ourselves, in relation to others, as well as developing an appreciation of difference.

The 'education provided must be focused on ensuring the emancipation and empowerment of every individual' (2004: 89). It is not therefore prescriptive and controlling. It does not have a prescribed view of what should be taught and is not focused exclusively on bodies of knowledge-content which it is thought must be communicated. Neither has it translated the possible outcomes of the process of development into measurable objectives. For its democratic basis provides further justification for the rejection of an objectives/product based approach. Firstly, as the primary focus of this approach to education is the individual's own emotional, social and moral development. If the teacher were to attempt to specify in advance what the objective would be, it would not be development from within but social control from without. Secondly, bestowing the teacher with absolute power and responsibility to plan, deliver and assess an educational enterprise based on objectives established exclusively by them, is anti-democratic and fundamentally runs counter to the principles which underlie curriculum as process.

Problems of curriculum as process

Problems with a cognitive approach

The problem with the cognitive development model is that it sees education solely in terms of intellectual development, independent of wider educational questions of values and wider purposes. It is also specifically formulated independently of content. In its crudest form therefore it would not matter what one focuses on as long as it is a stimulus for the manipulation of data, and therefore develops the necessary skills. For example, questions about how one should live one's life or treat other human beings are relevant only in terms of the development of the specific problem solving skills which may or may not equip one to actually answer the question of how one should actually live. The important issues of an individual's own life appears secondary to the development of specific cognitive skills. It should be noted though that to some extent Bruner has developed and revised his own ideas and for example in *The Culture of Education* (1996) he expands on the role of 'the social' in education and moves beyond mere cognitive development in his framing of the educational process.

This problem of an exclusively cognitive approach can only be overcome if it is integrated into an explicit 'value based' educational framework, which is what Kelly does in his 'process as development' model. However this in itself is not beyond criticism.

Problems with 'process as development'

Development is a normative concept

Process based curricula which focus on 'development', like Kelly (2004), are criticised on the basis that development is itself a normative concept. This criticism is twofold: Firstly, because it is a normative concept it can mean different things to different people. This criticism can be countered by an admission that given this is the case, it is therefore the responsibility of those who are working within process based curricula to make it explicit what they mean by development. Secondly, the normative criticism is used to undermine the process based approach because it is value based. However, this criticism can be countered, because the approach is explicit about its value stance and furthermore it is critical of the attempts to remain value neutral, in that all attempts to choose curricular content or select objectives involves value choices. The process approach it is argued is at an advantage because it does not deny the presence, stated or otherwise of the values behind the educational endeavour. It proudly asserts that it is value driven and makes those values explicit.

Lack of specifying end points to the process

Process based approaches can be criticised for a lack of specifying end points to the educational process. This is often made by those who would advocate a 'product approach' to planning a curriculum by objectives. This criticism would appear to have some validity and needs to be

addressed. Dewey's approach, for example is to a large extent opposed to end points.

According to Dewey the criteria with which one can judge the educational quality of experience is via the continuity principle and quality is dictated by the extent to which the particular experience is likely to lead to new experiences.

Within this however there is an implicit moral assumption, which underlies Dewey's philosophy, contained within the principle of continuity. It is alluded to in his discussion of growth as an example of the continuity principle. Growth cannot take any course '. . . growth is not enough; we must specify the direction in which growth takes place, the end to which it tends' (1997: 35). He uses the example of the burglar who improves his ability to burgle, which might on the one hand imply that growth has taken place. However, Dewey argues that in fact the burglar, in choosing to extend his experience down one particular avenue, has in fact closed off more than he has opened in terms of the principle of continuity and the scope for future development and growth. The continuity principle is set implicitly in a belief in holistic growth, which is best described as an Aristotelian holistic framework of what constitutes the 'good life' (Irwin, 1999). Lifelong learning and continuity of experience is fundamental to Dewey's particular concept of what constitutes the good life. However, this too is problematic as experience both constitutes and is a justification for the good life, which is tautological or circular.

This is perhaps where Dewey's theory falters, for he is very reluctant to specify educational ends beyond 'experience'. His argument, based on the principle of continuity, that growth is desirable if it is the kind of growth that would lead to more experience is circular: in that experience is justified by growth and vice versa; as well as being a reduction ad absurdum, the educational enterprise is necessarily never ending, which is not necessarily the case. One could say that, as a whole, human beings are always learning and therefore it is never ending, but to explain every focus of an educational enterprise on these terms appears illegitimate. For example, someone may want to understand the origins of the Second World War. This educational endeavour may be enhanced through the 'experience' of visiting historical sites and seeing archive footage, and the experience of developing knowledge would no doubt lead to further enquiries and open new avenues of experience etc. But is there not a point at which they are satisfied with their conclusions to the original question? To argue that there are no end points other than those that lead to new experiences appears untenable.

So the question remains what are the particular end points of the educational process?

To some extent it is just the nature of educational enquiry that given both the controversial nature of knowledge, the child centred curriculum as well as the democratic principles upon which the educational enquiry is founded; it is just not possible for the educator to specify the end products, in any great detail, prior to commencing the process. The problems of pre-specification have already been documented and in relation to knowledge based education, the development of understanding, as well as personal, social and moral development it appears to be the case that it is neither possible not desirable to specify end products in any logical or meaningful manner prior to the educational encounter. The problem is the degree to which it makes sense to specify prior to the

event. Process based curricula are not logically opposed to end points or outcomes. It is only logically opposed to the pre-specification of those outcomes.

An important way of overcoming the criticism of a lack of specification is through the specifying of content areas, which necessarily imply a focus. The process approach to curriculum is not opposed to the specifying of content, and in the specification of content there is an implication of possible end points even if there is not detailed specification of them. As Stenhouse suggests:

> *It is quite possible to evolve principles for the selection of content in the curriculum in terms of criteria which are not dependant on the existence of a specification of objectives and which are sufficiently specific to give real guidance . . .*
>
> (1975: 86)

An authentic curriculum incorporates therefore the aims, principles of procedure and content it neither relies on, nor requires, objectives; but clarity of its end products can only be attained during and after the process.

Curriculum as Process in Youth Work Practice

Process in curriculum documents

The process of youth work, that is 'how' the work is undertaken, facilitated and delivered, was clearly highlighted in the review of curriculum undertaken by Ofsted in 1993. They focused on methods of delivery, stating that, 'Often the method is experiential – learning by doing . . .' (Ofsted, 1993: 5) and they go on to describe in more detail some of the broad 'curriculum areas', including sport, arts and outdoor education. Importantly, this document clearly acknowledges the role of process in the youth work curriculum. Many of the curriculum documents produced in the field also incorporate a focus on process, including Cumbria (undated) Gloucestershire (circa 1992) and West Sussex (2000). As do Hampshire who focus on the 'reflective' aspects of youth work, when stating that, 'Young people will be offered the opportunity to explore their own beliefs, attitudes and values' (1991: 7). Shropshire highlight that: 'The process is negotiated with young people so that it is acceptable and appropriate to their needs' (2001: 4). Whilst Merton emphasise the unpredictable nature of the learning environment and implicitly highlight the skills needed to maximise the learning from unpredictable everyday events: 'Learning comes from the skilled use of spontaneous events and relationships which occur. An incident during a game, a question or comment at the coffee bar, for instance, can be the starting point of a meaningful conversation or response which can help the young person think and, as appropriate, change' (1997: 3).

Perhaps the most creative incorporation of process comes from Devon Youth Service (2002). Devon has produced its own unique concept of the youth work curriculum, and coming from the South West this appropriately is 'the youth work curriculum wave'. 'The wave is organic like the "organic process" of youth work. It suggests that there has to be a vehicle of some sort . . . where relationships are built with youth workers . . . in our (Devon's) model the vehicle happens to be the surf board' (2002: 8). Progression, development and change are an important aspect

of the process and this is represented by the movement of the surfer on the board. 'The progress the young person makes is seen along the face of the wave' (ibid.). Interesting analogies emerge from 'the process as a wave' like for example 'the surf is too big – the issue too heavy or youth worker too authoritarian', 'too flat – uninspiring, not enough going on', 'missed the wave – there are always more learning opportunities as well as waves'. 'The waves are too crowded – the youth workers just end up policing' etc. (Devon, 2002; 2006).

It is of concern that some curriculum documents make no reference to process. It could be that the process is implicit and therefore unspoken within the framing of youth work practice in their curriculum. For example, Milton Keynes (2003) highlight that young people will be involved in the 'design and delivery of the service' as well as being involved in 'decision making', which are clearly aspects of a process approach. Similarly Wiltshire (2005) incorporate 'experiential learning' which 'is about enabling young people to learn by reflecting on their own experiences whilst also becoming involved in designing new ones'.

However, it is not completely clear to what extent curriculum which do not provide an explicit commitment to, and incorporation of, the process of youth work are veering towards a product model. The extent to which youth work is retaining a commitment to process is a question both for the framing of youth work through curriculum as well as the application of the curriculum to practice. Are workers creating, dynamic, exciting and challenging experiences, over time, with young people? Have the young people through engagement in activities, learnt to trust and engage in conversation and from which understanding and learning can emerge, as well as through which new skills can be acquired? Or are youth workers more likely now, with the arrival of curriculum, to be conceiving of their work on a pre-programmed basis, with session specific input, to achieve pre-specified outcomes, related directly to organised input, thereby ignoring the long term organic process?

It has been argued, (Ofsted, 1993; Ord, 2004a) that the 'process is complex'. Devon (2002; 2006) also acknowledges this:

> *The process through which it (youth work) is delivered and young people learn is the tricky bit, because it is an organic process ... anything that is organic is growing and developing and is also a mixture of ingredients. It is precisely because of this complexity that people could be led to switch off from trying to understand, let alone trying to deliver.*
>
> (2002: 7)

Perhaps it is this complexity, or at least the lack of simplicity, in the process that has led to some youth services making only implicit reference to it. However, one should be wary of any less than an explicit and full articulation of process. For it is only through an authentic youth work process that many of the genuine benefits that youth work provides can be achieved. It is one of the principle aims of this book to assist in the task of articulating the process more fully.

The process of youth work is perhaps the best understood and least articulated aspect of the rationale of youth work. 'Historically youth work has failed to fully clarify the meaning of process and consequently has been accused of being "woolly"' (Ord, 2004a: 53). Intuitively youth workers negotiate and navigate the maze of interactions and interventions that the work with both individuals and groups demands, maintaining a commitment to and knowledge of the process that is being worked through. But for something that is so integral to youth work it is alarmingly absent from detailed explanation. Not surprisingly then the process of youth work is not particularly well understood by non-youth workers, whether they be allied professionals like teachers and social workers or local and national politicians. The work of Dewey, Bruner, Kelly and in particular Stenhouse can provide an important theoretical basis for a process based youth work curriculum, and thereby make more explicit the intuitive interventions of youth workers.

Application of the theory of curriculum as process

Young person centred curriculum

Dewey will be referred to in Chapter 3.5 when we look at experiential learning in more detail. It is perhaps a bit more obvious how the child centred

or in youth work's case the 'young person centred' curriculum is directly relevant. One of youth work's defining features is its focus on and commitment to young people. For example, Leicester acknowledges the 'young person-centred approach, which is central to the youth work process whatever the context' (2003: 10). This has historically also been the case, as the Albemarle Report suggests we '... try to see the world as young people see it' (1960: 139). In addition latterly the young person centred perspective has been incorporated into the Davies manifesto:

- Young people are received and perceived as young people rather than ... through adult imposed labels.
- Practice starts where young people are starting.
  (Davies, 2005: 11)

Leicester Youth Service's curriculum document suggests the following qualities describe a *'young person centred approach'* (their emphasis), which is central to the youth work process whatever the context:

- Active listening.
- Recognising and respecting the importance of young people's experience and how it shapes their lives; not being judgemental.
- Acknowledging their capacity to think and act for themselves and their peers in a responsible way.
- Valuing young people even when at times, their behaviour is unacceptable.
- Allowing young people to set the pace.
- Being interested in their lives and wanting to spend time with them.
- Enjoying their company and having fun together.
  (2003: 10)

Curriculum as Development in Practice

The cognitive processes approach to curriculum does not have too many parallels with youth work practice. It did, however, have an important influence on Stenhouse and others in the development of curriculum as process, and the development of cognitive abilities has been incorporated into the more relevant 'curriculum as development'. It is this and in particularly the ideas of Kelly (1995, 2005) which are much more applicable to youth work. Indeed, there are striking parallels between the articulations of the key purposes of youth work by Young (1999, 2005) and the work of Kelly. For Young, development is central to youth work:

> *Concern about the development of young peoples' values and the 'sort of people' they are to become is, and always has been, a fundamental feature of youth work thinking and practice.*
>
> (Young, 1999: 10)

She goes on to suggest that despite youth work's disparate history, and the variations in practice from voluntary sector to statutory, as well as across the variety of texts and reports that are written about youth work, there is a 'remarkable degree of consistency in the youth service's concern for the personal and social development of young people' (ibid). There is also the common thread of 'emancipatory democracy' within the key purposes of youth work articulated by Young which are also consistent with Kelly. She suggests:

> *Youth work is educational and therefore, following Dewey, it is not an activity for inculcating rigid patterns of socially accepted behaviour. It is not a static yardstick but a set of processes which must be reassessed to meet the needs of the different individuals, situations and circumstances. Also, education is its own end – a liberating experience which encourages reflective behaviour and promotes growth and health; developing the individual and supporting their participation in society (Dewey, 1966). As such, youth work's intention is to liberate, as opposed to domesticate, young people*
>
> (Young, 1999: 79)

Many of the curriculum documents similarly incorporate an acknowledgement of, and a commitment to, development. Milton Keynes suggests: 'Youth work provides a rich diversity of personal and social development opportunities and choices to young people' (2003: 3). Likewise, Nottinghamshire maintain: 'Youth work is a powerful process which adds to the social and personal development of young people' (2006:2).

Gloucestershire similarly concur that: 'The youth work curriculum is a conscious process where by youth workers provide opportunities for young people to explore life in its various aspects . . . which complements the natural journey taken by young people as they make their transition to adulthood. The skilled worker consciously intervenes to promote young people's development . . . young people further the understanding of themselves, others and the world around them' (2004: 8).

Whilst the commitment to young people's development is a key corner stone of practice, and an identification of it provides one of the broad aims and goals of youth work, more needs to be done to elucidate the basis of the process curriculum of youth work. To this end we need to look to the lesser known work of Stenhouse as he can offer an important theoretical framework which offers educational validity to a youth work curriculum.

Stenhouse and 'procedure principles' for youth work

It is often said that youth work is a value driven profession (Jeffs and Smith, 2005; Young, 1999). What are most often being referred to in this assertion are the value principles underlying practice. The NYA have gone some way to producing viable principles for youth work which articulate these values in their *Ethical Conduct in Youth Work: A Statement of Values and Principles from the National Youth Agency* (1999) identified below:

1. *Treat young people with respect,* valuing each individual and avoiding negative discrimination.
2. *Respect and promote young people's rights to make their own decisions and choices,* unless the welfare or legitimate interests of themselves or others are seriously threatened.
3. *Promote and ensure the welfare and safety of young people,* while permitting them to learn through undertaking challenging educational activities.
4. *Contribute towards the promotion of social justice* for young people and in society generally through encouraging respect for difference and diversity and in challenging oppression.

These principles provide an important foundation for good practice and provide bench marks, as well as clearly defining the value base of the profession. 'They fulfil the role of 'underpinning the work with the aim of guiding the conduct of youth workers' (1999: 3). They are broad enough to cover the full range of youth work practice as you would expect from ethical principles, however, they are as a result often too broad to adequately guide each and every setting. This is partly because they are just 'general ethical guidance for practice' upon which judgements must invariably be made. 'It is not a rule book prescribing exactly what youth workers should do in every situation' (ibid.), nor would this be desirable or possible. In addition, it is not clear how they guide practice in anything other than a very general way, because as Banks (1999) points out the ethical principles can and do conflict in practice.

What is required is something that is specific enough to relate more directly to practice as well as offer genuine guidance but does not tie the practitioner to a prediction about end products. It is Stenhouse's procedural principles which provide the solution. Stenhouse's great achievement was to have produced a rationale for education, a pedagogy, which whilst giving sufficient detail to both guide the educator, and provide justification to the onlooker (other professional or politician etc), does not rely on specifying the expected outcomes of a session in any detail, beyond the statement of broad educational aims. These 'principles of procedure' are the guide for the process of youth work. They are to be distinguished from value principles which though important as a framework within which practice develops, are not detailed nor specific enough in many instances to provide genuine guidance on practice, nor do they provide sufficient detail for non-youth workers to understand the process of youth work. Principles of procedure although often derived from value principles relate more specifically to 'how' the educational process is delivered. Procedural principles fill the gap between values and practice.

Procedural principles provide more detailed guidance. Many of these principles remain implicit, and they are to some extent determined by the value principles; they will at least not be inconsistent with them. The NYA go some way to articulate this in their reference to 'practice principles'. They offer between two and five practice principles for each of the four ethical principles. For example under the first principle to 'Treat young people with respect' they suggest '. . . acting in a way which does not exploit or negatively discriminate against young people on irrelevant ground, such as race, religion, ability and sexual orientation' (1999: 5). Under the ethical principle of 'promoting and ensuring the welfare and safety of young people' they offer the following practice principle: 'taking responsibility for assessing risk and managing the safety of work and activities involving young people' (1999: 5). The practice principles to some extent 'put more meat on the bones' and as such help to translate the ethical principles into practice, and

therefore apply them to the process of youth work but they fall short of procedural principles.

Davies: 'manifesto' for youth work

A better example of procedural principles would be the principles contained within Davies' *Youth Work: Manifesto for Our Times* (2005). To my knowledge they were not written with the purpose of providing specific guidance for practice; rather to define and articulate youth work practice to those, often in positions of power, who did not necessarily know much about it. As a result some of the principles are more like reference points which accurately define practice but do not in themselves guide one during the process. For example: 'Have young people chosen to become involved; is their engagement voluntary? (2005: 11) However, others do offer genuine on going guidance: For example 'Is the practice concerned with *how young people feel* and with what they know and can do?' (ibid.).

This not only provides a yard stick with which to distinguish youth work from other practices, it also provides a continuous reminder of a focus for practice as it is unfolding. How young people feel is not just something one does before starting a session, making a judgement and then working from that basis. It is possible that a worker might reflect upon certain individual's feelings, given an incident the previous week; perhaps knowing that someone had split up with their boyfriend, or who was upset by their parent's divorce. It would be right and proper in those instances to make time to check out how these young people are. The feelings may also be collective, perhaps a group were annoyed at the cancellation of a residential, or are stressed out by exams; this too would be an appropriate 'port of call'. But an important part of the youth work process is the continuous and on going monitoring of feelings as part of the process, intervening as necessary, perhaps challenging, supporting, guiding as appropriate.

Another of Davies' principles which offer guidance for practice and therefore equate to procedural principles is:

> *Is the practice seeking to go beyond where young people start, in particular by encouraging them to be outward looking, critical and creative in their responses to their environment.*
>
> (2005: 11)

This again provides both a bench mark for youth work practice but also a principle of procedure with which to continuously monitor and apply to each and every session. To what extent are the youth workers 'moving people on', not literally in the sense that the police might move a group away from a street corner, but metaphorically in terms of their learning and development. What can they do now that they were not able to do before; how do they see the world as a result of conversations they have had through their involvement in the project? The question of, 'Are young people being encouraged to "go beyond"' is one which continually interrogates practice and informs the process. Importantly it refers to what you can do, or are doing, 'now' in the process of engagement. If the answer to the question, 'How are young people seeking to, or being encouraged to, go beyond where they start' in any given project was – 'they are not' – the quality of practice would be very poor.

Whilst these insights are in themselves very valuable they do not provide all the answers because the youth work process is multi-layered and multi-faceted. It is holistic, that is, it incorporates a number of different and diverse elements at one and the same time. Perhaps first and foremost is the fact that youth work is work with individuals and groups, at the same time. Youth workers must be aware of the individual issues, interests and needs as well as their progression and development. However, they are also concerned with the development of the group, the relationships within the peer group, as well as any sub groups.

Given the dominance of the product theory of curriculum it is perhaps not surprising that procedural principles do not feature heavily in the youth work curriculum produced in the field. This is not, however, because they are not utilised in practice. They do in fact make up much of the implicit curriculum which youth workers intuitively and through their 'unconscious competence' employ regularly. Many documents will also allude to and incorporate the broad procedural principles similar to those originally offered by Raths (1971) and which were developed by Stenhouse, such as 'students are encouraged to make informed choices' and 'students are active in the learning environment'. But any detailed incorporation of procedural principles which are either derived from values or from the content areas defined within the curriculum is limited. However, there is one

remarkable document which incorporates a pedagogy of process akin to that recommended by Stenhouse: Isle of Wight (2000). Although this is not explicit, which perhaps would be truly remarkable, they do articulate their curriculum implicitly in relation to procedural principles.

Interestingly what Isle of Wight have done is to implement a process approach to curriculum which is implicitly along the lines Stenhouse suggested. They offer specific guidance as 'procedural principles', that is, the content areas are not translated into practice through desirable outcomes or attainable objectives as in a product approach but through guidelines for intervention. There are specific curriculum guidelines for each of the topics.

Each curriculum topic starts with the statement 'Good youth work practice will result from asking' (2004: 14) and what follows are a number of key questions. The questions inform and interrogate practice on an 'on-going' basis. For example, in relation to 'Leaving Home/ Homelessness' the questions include:

- Am I working from the young person's starting point?
- How can I best help the young people to explore all the issues around leaving home?
- Am I enabling young people to make informed choices?

(2000: 24)

In relation to sexism: 'Good practice will result from asking':

- How sexist am I? Do I collude with sexism?
- What do I do to challenge sexist attitudes, assumptions, language and behaviour of colleagues and young people?
- Does the environment reflect sexism? Look at the activities. Do they involve both young women and men? What are the notices, displays and posters like?

(2000: 10)

In many respects Isle of Wight have shown the way forward for the youth work curriculum and begun the process of applying procedural principles to a youth work curriculum. There is perhaps much to be improved within their initial undertaking but it is to be merited highly for its innovation. It is the task of others to follow their lead and make explicit the implicit principles that underpin practice.

Section Three
Essential Elements

Participation and Power

Participation

'Participation is a fundamental principle of youth work' (Leicestershire, 2000: 7). Few, if any, of the curriculum documents produced in the field have not incorporated a specific reference or commitment to participation. Historically, Young (2005) notes participation has been a consistent feature of practice, for example all the major post war government reports of Albemarle, Fairbairn-Milson and Thompson contain a commitment to participation.

However, as Smith points out, 'Participation has a long and untidy history within youth work. It is an idea much talked about and much misunderstood' (1983: 17). It is important therefore to be clear about what is meant by participation in the youth work sense. It is much more than merely 'joining in', the ordinary use of the word, though this association often leads to confusion within the youth work. It is one of the four key features of the nationally agreed Statement of Purpose, which offers some clarity: 'Youth work offers opportunities which are: Participative – through a voluntary relationship with young people in which young people are the partners in the learning process and the decision-making structures which affect their lives and their environment' (NYB, 1991).

To fully understand participation in the youth work sense one must acknowledge its four underlying factors:

- Responsibility.
- Decision making.
- Engagement.
- Action.

A prerequisite for one's participation is the need to take responsibility for one's involvement and to be party, where possible, to all the relevant decisions which are taken in relation to the object of participation. These two factors will determine the extent to which one is engaged in the process of participation. Finally there must be some action which results from the participation process – one must actually 'do' something.

The following analogy of 'voting in an election' will illustrate these factors. Firstly, one could turn up at the polling station and arbitrarily put a cross on the ballot paper, or one could vote for the party their family and friends have always done but without paying much attention to the detailed policies. Thirdly, you could have studied the literature from the respective candidates, considered the issues and made an informed choice. Finally, one could encourage others to discuss the election, debate the issues, perhaps even canvass for the particular candidate you intend to vote for. What this analogy shows is that participation is a combination of the above factors. The degree of responsibility one takes for one's actions, the decisions one takes in relation to those actions, how engaged in the process one is and importantly the action one takes as a result of the engagement. Interestingly in the above analogy an informed abstention, thereby 'not joining in' the election, could be more participative than joining in with little engagement or informed decision making!

Participation is perhaps the defining 'procedural principle' of youth work: 'It is an underlying principle upon which the curriculum is based' (Baker, 1996: 51). Responsibility for decisions and the actions young people take should wherever possible be delegated to the young people themselves. This delegation must be done appropriately and sensitively, and judgements need to be made about the extent to which young people are ready to take such decisions. How participative youth worker's practice is, should be a question which continuously interrogates their practice. As Ofsted (2002b) put it, the extent to which youth workers are 'doing things with', as opposed to 'doing things for' young people is a key indicator of the quality of their practice. Everything that is done in and around the youth project or club should where possible be delegated to young people from the simplest of tasks, like the phone call to book a trip or where to go on a residential, to tasks which it is all too easy to think are beyond their reach, like budgeting and responsibility for decisions about the running of the project.

Effective participation must include informal but systematic implementation of participative 'procedural' principles, whereby every aspect of one's youth work is informed by a commitment to communicate, involve and delegate decisions to young people. However, participative practice must also contain the necessary formal structures to maximise involvement and enable young people to be sufficiently involved in all aspects of the club or project. West 13, a youth club in Ealing, West London, shows how effective a commitment to, and implementation of, a combination of informal methods of participative practice and the more formal implementation of a 'running committee' can be. They set up an effective young people's advisory committee and they implemented the 'effective take over (of the adult's advisory committee) with young people acting as secretary and treasurer of the committee' (Baker, 1996: 36).

The origins of participation can in some part be traced to Dewey:

There is, I think, no point in the philosophy of progressive education which is sounder than its emphasis upon the importance of the participation of the learner in the formation of the purposes which direct his (sic) activities in the learning process, just as there is no greater defect in traditional education greater than its failure to secure the active co-operation of the pupil in construction of the purposes involved in his studying.

(Dewey, 1997: 67)

Participation is much more than securing the co-operation of young people however, which this quote, although not necessarily Dewey himself, implies. 'Participation is ultimately geared towards self-direction and ownership by the participants. It is not merely concerned with securing the agreement of the educator's plans and intentions' (Shenton, 2004).

The profile of young people's participation has moved up the political agenda in recent years, in part due to the UK's adoption of the United Nations Convention of the Rights of the Child in 1991 and in particular Article 12 which states: 'parties shall assure to the child who is capable of forming his or her own views the right to express those views feely in all matters affecting the child' (United Nations, 1989). In addition, and perhaps more importantly in the UK, is the Children Act (1989) which together with its subsequent amendments have produced a 'recognition of the right for the children and young people to

participate in decision making' (Save the Children and Dynamix, 2002: 5). Whilst clearly these changes are significant milestones in terms of advancing at least structurally the cause of participation, 'to this day consultations with children and young people show that they still feel that adults do not listen to them or respect them. They have low status, little power and almost no control over their lives within family, school, public services or in relation to politicians and policy makers' (ibid.). In some respects therefore the language of one of the fundamental principles of youth work has been appropriated. Although it could be argued that youth workers have been and still are in a better position to work participatively with young people because they create a 'culture of participation' and participative practice is 'built in' to their work, whilst in some other sectors it is at best 'bolted on' and rarely approximates to the genuine article. This is in part because within youth work there is recognition that participation is integrally linked to power.

Power and empowerment

Participation is ultimately about power, if it is to be genuine participation. If it is not, it merely becomes a method of attaining someone's commitment or even a sinister and coercive method of producing conformity. This criticism could be levelled at some of the participative practices associated with the connexions service (DfES, 2002a, 2002b). Much of the emphasis is on 'active involvement' whether that be in a consultation on local services or the election of the new manager or even the chief executive. The question of what, or how much, power the young people have in any of the decision making processes they are asked to be 'actively involved' in amounts to little, if any real, power.

This lack of power is evident in some of the 'newer' incorporations of participation which conceive of participants as 'consumers' rather than as 'genuine participants'. The involvement of the young person is seen as necessary in order for the deliverer of the service to be able to receive feedback on the service and make alterations accordingly. It is not a model founded on equality, mutuality, joint responsibility and empowerment. One should for example be wary of the model of 'participant as consumer' infiltrating the potentially genuine youth forum initiatives.

Interestingly, with the rise of 'active involvement' within recent formulations of participation, empowerment has significantly begun to disappear from descriptions of practice. Active involvement has to a large extent superseded empowerment. For example, in the recent standards on young people's participation published through the NYA's *Hear by Right* (Wade and Badham, 2004) there is little if any mention of power or empowerment, only of the 'active involvement' of young people:

As Shenton correctly acknowledges:

> *When looking at participative practice, there can be confusion over terms such as involvement and consultation with young people. It is important to point out that they are not the same, and are not the same as participation.*
> (2004: 15)

As Shenton (2004), and Hart (1992) before her point out, without any real power to influence or instigate change, participative practice too easily becomes tokenistic, and not participation.

Participation and empowerment are integrally linked, because power is fundamental to participation. In fact empowerment is best seen as 'the end result of participative practices where each participant gains control and/or influence over issues of concern to them . . . empowerment cannot be achieved without having participation as a precursor; and that the level of participation will determine the level, if at all, of eventual empowerment' (Barry, 1996: 3).

Empowerment is central to many curriculum documents. For example, Kingston Youth Service has as its main aim 'To empower and optimise the potential of young people' (2002: 4). Similarly, Davies' manifesto also recognises the crucial role of power in defining youth work: 'Practice proactively seeks to tip balances of power in young people's favour' (2005: 11). Empowerment is one of the four key elements of the Statement of Purpose (1991): 'Youth work offers opportunities which are: Empowering – supporting young people to understand and act on the personal, social and political issues which affect their lives, the lives of others and of the communities of which they are part' (NYB, 1991).

Models of participation and empowerment

Participation in practice and its relationship to empowerment has been developed through a number of related models. The first model was created by Arnstein (1969) who utilised a ladder to denote progression. This was elaborated by Hart as 'The Ladder of Participation' (1992). The theme of ladders or steps as a model of participative practice was continued and applied within curriculum models developed in the early 1990s, most notable of which was that developed by Gloucestershire Youth Service (1994) and latterly incorporated into other curricula, for example, Wiltshire (2005). Gloucestershire developed an eight stage step model which moves from levels 1 and 2 at the beginnings of participation, concerned respectively with 'accessing information and opportunity', and with 'making contact and developing relationships' through to level 6 where young people share control and responsibility for action and level 7 where young people 'take control and responsibility'. The Gloucestershire model was then developed a little further by Huskins (1996) into the Curriculum Development Model, where he added 'levels of activity' to each of the stages and linked to the development of youth achievement awards (see 3.1.1). It should be noted that although this model has now become known as the 'Huskins model', in reality it was a model developed by Gloucestershire Youth Service and could perhaps more accurately be referred to as the 'Gloucester model'. Either way it does give a good diagrammatic account of participative progression. This, or related, models are utilised by other services and incorporated into their curriculum documents e.g. Bournemouth (2005), Hartlepool (2005), Bristol (2002) and Cheshire (2005).

One should not think that the model is a prescription for practice. For example, it is not necessarily the case that all young people should or could progress to the top. What they want and need out of the project may well not necessitate progressing to the upper stages. Interestingly as well, it should be noted that in different social settings young people could operate at different levels of the ladder. In their own peer group, a young person may well be a leader taking responsibility for key decisions, but in a more formal setting like school, be considered as not capable or interested in participating at all. It is all too easy to see the ladder as an irrevocable ascent, whereas one could move down the scale as well as up, for example where personal circumstances could necessitate less of an involvement, or one could feel like one's input

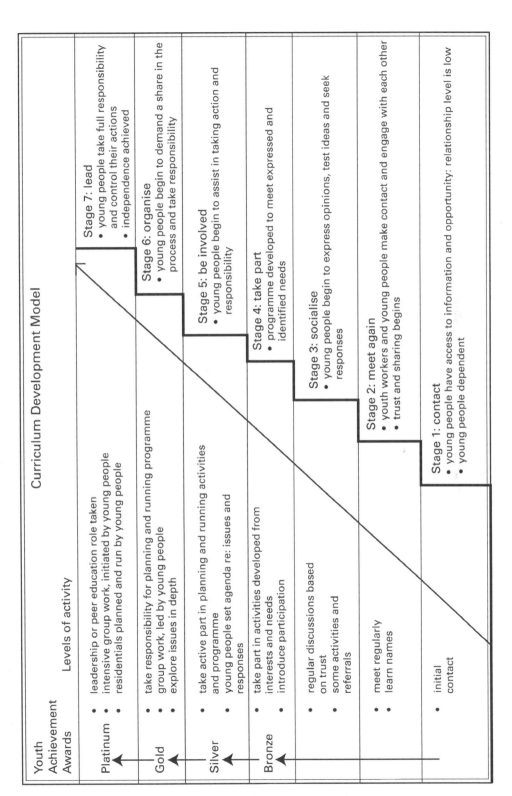

Figure 3.1..1   A progressive model of youth worker involvement with young people (after Gloucester Youth and Community Service) (Huskins, 1996: 13)

has been acknowledged or an issue which prompted one's involvement addressed and the involvement or participation decreases.

Dilemmas in practice

However, with the question of participation, and the delegation of power, comes the difficult question of the young people's 'problematic choices'. There must be potential for young people to choose, and this choice must be genuine and authentic but therein lies the dilemma, as these choices do not take place in a moral vacuum. What if young people choose to access pages on the internet which are sexually explicit or gratuitously violent, or if they choose to exclude other members of the community from their club? Leicestershire recognise this when they describe the '. . . potential conflict since young people or communities are not apt to make "the right decisions"' (2000: 7). Youth workers clearly have responsibilities in these instances and part of their educational role would be to encourage young people to appreciate their own responsibilities to others, and to enter into a dialogue around what might be considered 'problematic choices'. This limitation on participation and empowerment which the workers must, in their welfare and educational role, administer, is what Jeffs and Banks 'have called 'control in practice' and is essential for all good educational practice' (1999: 105). This is the moral framework of the interplay of rights and responsibilities which is played out in participative practice. The tension between young people's choices and actions, and the framework of 'acceptability' is worked through in an on-going dialogue between youth workers and young people, and importantly workers will be required to make judgements.

Equality of opportunity and anti-oppressive practice

Empowerment can be a useful term to describe the certain aspects of effective youth work practice which 'moves young people on in gaining control and influence over their lives'. Perhaps describing the growth and development a young person experiences completing a successful challenge or benefiting from a period of support, they are empowered: to make the

most of their talents and abilities. However, power and empowerment cannot be solely understood, nor can youth work itself be conceived of, as operating solely in terms of the individual. The Statement of Purpose (NYB, 1991) makes this clear, referring as it does to the 'social and political issues' which affect both individuals and communities. The key social divisions and how power operates in relation to them is an important aspect of the youth work curriculum. How practice articulates itself and responds to the oppression that operates in society, which results from inequalities of power, is integral to it. Thompson (2001) rightly alerts us to the cultural and structural contexts within which power operates. The youth work curriculum must acknowledge this and attempt to develop its practice, which as Tomlinson and Trew (2002) suggest 'equalises opportunities and minimises oppression'.

The Statement of Purpose incorporates this commitment and suggests 'Youth work offers opportunities which are:

> *Designed to promote equality of opportunity through the challenging of oppressions such as racism and sexism and all those which spring from differences of culture, race, language, sexual identity, gender, disability, age, religion and class; and through the celebration of the diversity and strengths which arise from those differences.*
>
> (NYB, 1991)

Many, if not all youth work curricula, incorporate a commitment to either equality (Norfolk, 2005) or equality of opportunity (Kingston, 2005; Bradford, 2006) as one of their core values. Work in relation to equality of opportunity takes many forms in the youth work curriculum. It could take the form of specific anti-racist projects such as 'peacemaker' – a voluntary sector project which trains anti-racist peer mentors in Oldham (Redfearn, 2003: 14), or through specific targeted detached work (ibid.). Another important aspect of work in relation to equality of opportunity is in the development of support to vulnerable groups. For example, 'GLYS', the Gay and Lesbian Youth Support group in Halton which appears as a case study of best practice in Merseyside (2004). Their '. . . main objectives are to provide a safe and confidential environment for young people to meet and discuss issues that are important. Meanwhile, staff aim to identify the groups' needs and educate appropriately' (2005: 48). They claim that 'Young people benefit greatly from this provision, they feel less isolated by the community they live in and develop new skills through informal learning' (ibid.). In addition, groups who are either vulnerable or likely to suffer from discrimination are also identified as: 'young people with the greatest need' and identified as 'priority groups' e.g. in some curriculum documents such as Buckinghamshire (2004: 3).

Equality of opportunity is however equally important as a procedural principle which informs and interrogates practice on an 'on-going' basis, whether that be targeted work on anti-racism or disability integration, or through generic or project work which does not ostensibly have an equal opportunities focus. Thompson (2001) argues that this aspect of practice is better described as 'anti-discriminatory practice', as this distinguishes it from the restrictive notions of equal opportunities which are exclusively concerned with 'fairness'. Anti-discriminatory practice more broadly acknowledges the embedded discrimination extant in society. Youth workers must therefore critically reflect on their practice in relation to issues of equality of opportunity, discrimination or oppression, ensuring they are alert to their own and others prejudice and challenge this where appropriate. As Thompson suggests: 'Even if we are full of good intentions in relation to anti-discriminatory practice, unless we are actively seeking to eliminate racist thoughts (for example) and actions from our day-to-day dealing, they will filter through from the culture and structure into which we were socialised and which constantly seek to influence us . . .' (2001: 25).

Challenge needs to be done with sensitivity, as prejudice inappropriately challenged can all too easy become entrenched. One must be wary of working from a premise that means one is merely attempting to ensure young people hold the 'correct' attitudes and beliefs. As Williamson suggests: 'The rhetoric of valuing "expression" and respecting 'difference' has, over the years, become heavily constrained by a reality that only certain viewpoints, conveyed in certain ways were "acceptable"' (2003: 11). Young people need to be given space for 'admission of irrational prejudice' or be allowed to work through 'discriminatory views they needed to reveal' (ibid.).

Citizenship

For some authorities, citizenship is an equally important element which informs and defines their curriculum. It is sometimes seen as a development of the participation, empowerment and equality of opportunity agendas, and one of Hounslow's curriculum themes (2005) is described as 'Citizenship and Participation'. However, subsuming all these debates under one term, which is in itself contested, can be problematic as it confuses a number of the subtleties and complexities of each of the separate concepts.

More recent notions of citizenship in the curriculum have had a distinct emphasis on community involvement and this is linked with the *Every Child Matters* outcome – 'Making a Positive Contribution' (DfES, 2003). For example, Merseyside, who link citizenship with 'young people's rights', argue 'Citizenship is therefore concerned with promoting active participation both in local communities and with wider issues. It encourages young people to have a voice and influence the world around them' (2004: 20). However, with its emphasis on the interplay of rights and responsibilities it can provide a framework for working on issues of community engagement as well as the development of social skills and social relations.

Citizenship appears in a number of curriculum document's designated 'areas', including Redcar and Cleveland (2006) and Hull (2003). It is highlighted as one of ten 'specific issues' in Milton Keynes where it is explicitly linked with volunteering, suggesting, 'youth workers will provide opportunities, training and preparation to enable young people to see the benefits of active citizenship as a part of developing their self-esteem, adding to their future study and employment prospects, and gaining a 'feel good' factor from contributing to society and helping others' (2005: 13).

The notion of citizenship, however, raises as many questions as it provides answers. The concept itself is a contested one. Fundamentally a disagreement exists about the relative merits of rights and responsibilities in the establishment of an individual's citizenship. Hall et al. (2000) and Hall and Williamson (1999) argue that a shift has occurred in the conception of citizenship whereby members of a society no longer automatically have citizenship by right bestowed upon them, instead they earn their citizenship through the exercising of their responsibilities. This shift in the notion of citizenship now informs policy and can be seen in operation for example within the new right welfare reforms which removed people's 'rights' to benefits. This has, it can be argued, not lessened under New Labour which has directly, with its 'New Deal' for the long-term unemployed, linked the 'rights' to welfare benefits to one's responsibility to society. Thus an under 24-year-old, who has been unemployed for more than six months, cannot receive their benefit for merely seeking work, they must be seen to be making a contribution to society, through, for example, volunteering on an environmental task force (Exell, 2001; Mizen, 2004).

Subsumed and sometimes lost within the citizenship debate is the critical dialogue about what kind of a society we wish to live in. All too often citizenship is thought of merely as a legal concept defining rights and responsibilities and unifying a social group. In this sense citizenship is reduced to a consideration of how each individual makes a contribution towards the maintenance of the status quo and making improvements within existing social relations. Hall and Williamson suggest that citizenship as a 'lived' concept, that is the reality of people's lives or 'the character of shared life as we experience it' (1999: 4) or citizenship as a 'normative' concept, as an ideal or something to aspire to beyond the existing legal parameters, do offer alternative means of conceptualising citizenship which should not be lost from the debate. This important aspect of the curriculum and its relationship to wider society will be addressed more fully in the final chapter on Curriculum and Culture. We must now consider other essential elements of curriculum.

Relationships and Group Work

Relationships

'Relationships are, and always have been, at the heart of youth work' (Young, 1999: 63). They are the foundation of the youth work process. The relationship between the young person and the youth worker is the guiding thread of the process, without them no process can develop.

In any given youth work setting, whether it be a residential weekend, a street corner, a youth club or a specific project, what occurs as a result of the interplay of the relationships, and the resulting dynamics between youth workers and young people, and between the young people themselves, will provide the 'grist for the mill' of the personal and social education. Youth workers are therefore undertaking a distinctly different role to other social professionals in that they are 'real' people, and have authentic relationships. They have genuine relationships which although they are professional relationships which have clear boundaries, there is a reality to them that is missing from the relationships of teachers and social workers.

This point could be contended. 'Are teachers, and other professionals, not real people, concerned with the welfare and development of young people?' Indeed the emphasis on the difference in the nature of youth workers' relationships and other professionals' relationships can, on the face of it, appear to be overstated. The difference is subtle but significant and therefore justifiable, that is, for youth workers, unlike other professionals, the starting point is the relationship with the young person, and importantly everything else follows from this. No specific agenda is set prior to the youth worker getting to know that young person. All other professionals, at least to some extent, have a prior agenda. Education welfare officers' priority is to return young people to school; social workers may have a number of priorities depending on the nature of the 'referral'. With drug and alcohol issues, family problems etc., youth justice workers quite clearly have criminal offences as their primary focus.

Four of Davies' nine defining principles of youth work articulate this point:

- Is practice starting where young people are starting?
- Are young people perceived and received as young people rather than, as a requirement, through the filter of a range of adult imposed labels?
- Is a key focus of the practice on the young person as an individual?
- Is practice concerned with how young people feel?

The 'relationships as the starting point' are the vehicle through which the priorities are articulated and this importantly is as the young people see them. In addition therefore, it is not just the starting point which is significantly different, but implicitly the end point as well. In the formation of the youth work relationship there is no ostensible end point, which the worker implicitly or explicitly is intent on. The worker is in the process of getting to know the young person. This is a defining difference between youth work and other professionals. This does not mean therefore that other professionals do not work in successful ways with young people, but the 'starting point as the development of a relationship' is unique to youth work and so therefore is the curriculum that follows from it.

The 'relationship as starting point' can be seen to be derived from the child centred, or rather, young person centred curriculum which youth work adheres to. The only group of professionals which approximates to this starting point are perhaps counsellors, but of course counsellors have exclusive one to one relationships. There are other similarities in their approaches however. For example the 'unconditional positive regard' – the attitude of unconditional acceptance which Rogers (1967; 1994) describes as a necessary condition of the helping relationship can be seen to be akin to the empathy, acceptance and optimistic approach that belies the youth work relationship. Other important factors which belie both approaches would include a consistency of approach, a commitment to seeing the young person's point of view, honesty and integrity.

Though there are similarities between the depth of relationship that both counselling and youth work develop, a significant difference within the youth work relationship is that it is mutual. There is an equality and openness of exchange, and expectation of response from youth worker to young person which is absent from counselling. If a client asks a counsellor a personal question like 'Are you bisexual?' an appropriate response would more likely be to ask a question in response – 'Why are you asking? Why is it important to you? Are you bisexual, and you think that if I am, I will accept you more?' The counsellor's job is to avoid themselves becoming the object of attention and to always make the client the focus. On the contrary the youth worker is 'present'. The mutuality in youth work is partly what defines it as a profession. Perhaps youth workers don't have to answer every question ever put to them, but they would be very unsuccessful if they made it their point to answer very few! The boundaries between personal and professional life in youth work are narrower than other professions, both the quantity of information one is expected to disclose and the quality of information – the type of information one is expected to disclose is greater. Who you are as a person, as well as a professional, is of vital importance in youth work.

Heather Smith builds on the counselling insights into the dynamics of relationships. She re-emphasises Rogers' stress on the need for the facilitator to be 'real' and for the person who is learning, or being facilitated, to experience this realness as authentic. Smith encourages youth workers to 'take personal responsibility to seek out the gift of authenticity' (2002: 31). Whilst there is much to be valued in this approach, one word of caution should be heeded, in relation to the realness that youth workers are seeking. They are not real in the sense that they are completely themselves, because they are not there to meet their own needs but those with whom they are working. This is why they are founded as professional relationships. It is the check which they hold their own needs in, that defines the relationship as professional and not personal.

Despite the overwhelming importance of relationships in youth work it should not be forgotten that they are a means to an end and not an end in themselves. Too often youth workers are content with building successful relationships and forgetting to 'go beyond' (Davies, 2005).

Nottingham City's *Curriculum Framework* articulates this point very well:

> *Relationship building with young people lies at the heart of all youth work. The relationships developed by youth workers with young people are the means by which we assist young people to learn and develop . . . It is vital that everyone working in the youth service understands this process of connecting and communicating with young people, so as to help them identify what is important in their lives and take steps towards achieving their goals and aspirations.*
>
> (circa, 2003: 3)

Group work

The relationships in the process of youth work are, however, inherently complex. This was recognised by Ofsted's original guidance on curriculum in 1993: 'The youth work curriculum is complex because its dimensions include not only the activities that young people take part in but also the relationships they develop through the process' (Ofsted, 1993: 16).

The youth work relationships are complex in part because they are multi-dimensional. Youth work is not case work, or exclusive one to one work. Youth workers rarely have exclusive relationships, like social workers or counsellors. So the process involves the totality of the relationships the youth worker and co-workers, have with a given group of young people, both as the sum total of the individual relationships, as well as the relationship with the group as a whole (as a social group is often more than the sum of its parts). In addition, the relationships between young people are of equal importance. What occurs between the young people is as important as what goes on between the young people and the youth worker. The dynamics that emerge as a result of the establishment, maintenance and development of these relationships will determine many of the important aspects of the process. Group work is founded on what Collander-Brown refers to as this 'complex melee of factors . . . interacting simultaneously' (2005: 34).

Group work as development

Group work is, however, more than the establishment and maintenance of these relationships; for the relationships are not an end in themselves, they are a means to an end. It is through reflection on and analysis of the relationships in youth work that development can take place. As Button explains, 'Group work is about helping people in their growth and development, in their social skills, in their personal resources, and in the kind of relationships they establish with other people' (1974: 1). It is through the relationships that develop in groups that this growth can take place.

For Button, group work is particularly pertinent for adolescents as they are in a 'period of transition'. This includes a freedom from childhood constraints of the family and of society: 'For a few years he (sic) is foot loose, neither a child nor an adult' (1974: 15). As a result, there are specific developmental needs which, though not exclusive to adolescents, are of extra importance due to the exaggerated period of change. These developmental changes include a development of a number of new roles, including 'sexual and gender roles', and 'peer and group roles'. Group work allows for an exploration of these roles.

Needs in group work

Group work also allows for an exploration of young people's needs. Button cites three particularly important needs which are addressed through developmental group work:

- The need for significance.
- The need for security.
- The need for adventure and new experience.

This is not an exhaustive list, and can be augmented, for example by the needs suggested by Kellmer Pringle (1980) such as the need for 'love and security'; 'new experiences'; 'for praise and recognition' and the need for 'responsibility'. Of course, these needs are not necessarily the sole preserve of young people. None the less they do form the basis of much group work practice. Through involvement in the group 'our need to be somebody, to matter' (our need for significance) can be acknowledged, explored and addressed. Our need for security can similarly be met through identification with the group. Security is, however, also the foundation of the developmental process in that young people will be deterred from exploring or sharing aspects of themselves in any depth if there is not a foundation of safety and security in the group. Button acknowledges that it can appear

incongruous that alongside the need for security and a concomitant desire for stability, order, consistency and reliability also comes the need for adventure and new experiences. But he rightly acknowledges that too much stability can lead to boredom and the cycle of development needs to alternate between periods of novelty and familiarity. This new experience is not interpreted necessarily in terms of activities, though these can provide important sources of experience, and new experience can be in the form of dialogue and through the development of relationships.

Group work and social skills?

Group work is not, however, necessarily solely concerned with meeting needs. It is also concerned with enabling young people to meet their own needs, for example through the development of social skills. Button describes the example of a young person's inability to form and sustain friendships through a lack of social skills, and it is therefore through the development of social skills that the young person can in turn meet that need themselves. Importantly the learning of social skills is an active process: 'social skills can only be learnt in contact with other people, it is the purpose of group work to provide the individual with the opportunities to relate to others in a supportive atmosphere, to try new approaches and to experiment in new roles' (1974: 1).

This lack of social skills development is cited by Button as one of the primary reasons behind an individuals' lack of fulfilment: 'In most situations, people who are living rather less fully than they would like (is) because of the limitation within their own personalities and a lack of social skills' (1974: 23). This is often criticised as leading to a deficit model of young people. However, it is not being suggested that all young people are to be conceived of in this light, nor indeed that an equal number of adults are equally 'in deficit'. Neither is it being suggested that youth work itself should operate entirely from a deficit model. However, the development of social skills is an important part of the youth work curriculum. How often have youth workers been hampered in their attempts to work participatively by the inability of young people to undertake simple tasks like making phone calls to book trips, or appreciate and value the needs of others. And importantly these can be developed through group work.

One should be wary of exaggerating the role of 'skills development', whether social or not, in group work. It is not merely a matter of semantics to object to the totality of group work being described as 'social skills development'. Some of the developmental benefits of group work, like, for example, the ability to talk to strangers in public or on the phone, are specific skills. But some of the benefits of group work are not, like the development of confidence and self-esteem. Confidence and self-esteem are an aspect of ourselves (Ord, 2004b). To insist that confidence is a skill would be committing a 'category mistake' (Ryle, 1949). This distinction is one that does have importance, not least for appreciating the importance of the process of group work. As we saw in our analysis of the difference between a product and process approach to curriculum, one can teach skills (whether social or not) through a product approach but one can't 'teach' knowledge or understanding (whether that be self-knowledge or self-esteem) through a product approach, and it can only be facilitated through the development of a process.

Much group work therefore is not concerned with the development of social skills as such but with individual personal and social development, whether this be one's attitudes, dispositions, one's self- esteem or confidence. Indeed as Button suggests, much of the focus of this development is on, 'The way in which a person feels about himself (sic) (which) is usually called his self-concept' (1974: 117).

Group work as a process

For group work to be effective in a youth work environment, it must retain a commitment to process. Teachers and many other professionals work with groups; this does not make them 'group workers'. A necessary condition of group work is an appreciation, and utilisation of, group dynamics. These dynamics are described by Houston (1993) as forces. 'Group dynamics make up the group process which can be defined as everything that happens in the group apart from the overt task', Adams (2001: 83). They are caused by the behaviour, feelings, attitudes and thoughts of the participants and must be acknowledged by the facilitator and 'worked with'.

The group work process, although having broad educational purposes of 'encouraging self-reliance and self-discovery', (Button, 1974: 5)

works with what emerges from the group. The group has a fluidity of direction and development which precludes the fulfilment of pre-specified ends or objectives. In a similar vein to the methodology proposed by Stenhouse, describing the discovery methods of teachers, the group work approach is an exploratory approach. 'For example, the worker will be leading his group into an examination of their feelings towards authority, and into an exploration of friendships, of loneliness, and of a wide range of other relationships . . .' (ibid.). As a result the group worker does not necessarily know what the outcomes will be until the process is underway. In fact it is arguable whether or not anyone could ever know the full impact of a developmental group work process until a long time after, as who can really say what a young person will do with newly found self-belief.

Youth groups and youth culture

No small part of the success of the group work processes in youth work is because they embrace rather than oppose youth culture. Youth workers, unlike most adults, do not see youth culture as 'problematic' or as a cause for concern. Garrett rightly points out youth culture is, for most young people, 'a means to create and establish an identity in a society where they can find it difficult to locate a sense of self' (2004: 145) and he suggests the threat they pose is an 'adult perception' and it is at worst only a 'symbolic threat'. If it is the case that youth sub cultures 'enable young people to find their own individual identity, yet still have the support of group solidarity' (2004: 151), it is easy to see why youth culture is of over-whelming importance to young people, and why, if any group work with young people is to be successful, it must work within those cultures and give room for their expression. If it works against those cultures or fails to fully acknowledge them the educational process will implicitly be rejecting an important part of the young people themselves and what they identify with.

Wider social significance of group work

Group work is often criticised for its focus on 'individuals' to the exclusion of the wider community and society. However, group work is not just concerned with individual growth, it is also concerned with fostering changes in the community and the wider society in its conception of young people as inspirers of change.

Button makes this point explicitly:

> *It is as a result of this freedom from restraints and commitment that the adolescent and young adult has a special function to perform in questioning the manner of life and mores of his community ... Adolescents may reject the accepted premises as a basis for their thinking and discussion ... However uncomfortable or inconvenient, the contribution that can be made by its young people is indispensable to a changing society.*
>
> (1974: 15)

Button also makes an implicit but never the less important link back to 'participation', by insisting that 'they will not be able to make this contribution unless they are held in a dialogue with the adult community' (ibid.). Importantly, the young people's involvement should enable them to have power and to make changes, it should not be in order 'to neutralise' their influence.

Choice and Voluntary Participation

Choice runs through many of the essential elements of the curriculum. One of the important ways in which power is exercised is through choice. One of the reasons the relationships and the group work process flourish is that young people have the choice to engage at the outset and all stages of the process are negotiated.

Historically this has been an important theme as can be seen in the Albemarle Report: 'Young people must have the liberty to question cherished ideas, attitudes and standards, and if necessary to reject them' (1960: point 142). The notion of 'informed choice' is an important principle which underpins youth work. It is formulated as the second of the four ethical principles by the NYA: 'Respect and promote young people's rights to make their own decisions' (1999: 5).

This is an important aspect of the youth work curriculum and for some it is sufficient to have it implicit in the participative process. Others have felt it necessary to incorporate it as separate and explicit. Kingston Youth Service, for example, has incorporated it as one of their core values: 'The promotion of the young people's capacity to make informed decisions is central to the process of youth work' (2002: 5). For Hampshire, 'It is the purpose of the curriculum to enable young people to make informed choices and decisions on matters of concern to them. It should also provide them with the skills and experiences to make such informed choices and decisions . . .' (1991: 6).

Another important aspect of choice is in relation to access and attendance, and for many this is the defining principle of youth work: 'Voluntary participation'.

Voluntary participation

In many ways the voluntary participation in youth work is unique as there are few other educational or even welfare services which young people are in receipt of which they access of their own volition. The dynamic of voluntary participation does establish an important foundation to the work. The power relations are clearly defined by it and the relationship of mutuality can also be seen to stem from it. Youth work practice has developed out of this tradition, it appears as a key feature of the major government reports of Albemarle, Fairbairn-Milson and Thompson; and historically youth work has consistently operated under this rationale (Jeffs and Smith, 1998).

That young people have the 'ultimate choice' to attend or not is believed by many therefore to be a defining characteristic of youth work. Derbyshire Youth Service for example, maintains that: 'The youth service considers its relationship with young people to be a unique one. It is a voluntary relationship' (undated: 7). Davies concurs arguing that: 'the principle of young people's voluntary participation is a – perhaps *the* – defining feature of youth work' (2005: 12) and it is stated as the first of his manifesto principles: 'Have young people chosen to be involved, is their engagement voluntary?' (ibid.). He goes on to suggest that not only has practice historically developed out of this state of affairs, but there are significant reasons for the importance of voluntary participation. As a result of voluntary participation:

1. 'young people retain a 'degree of power intrinsic to practice . . . this is not just a concession made to the young by benevolent adults who see benefits for themselves in letting the young have their say . . . the power structured into their relationships with the adults (defines) a role and a status' (2005: 12).
2. 'practitioners have no choice but to negotiate with young people' (2005: 13). Importantly this is not just a 'tactical manoeuvre' to ensure compliance as this would be unlikely to ensure long term commitment but must involve 'real give and take'.
3. 'the content of the youth work providers' 'offer' to young people (must be) valuable . . . in the here and now' (ibid.). This content must be relevant in the 'here and now' and is unlikely to involve any degree of delayed gratification.

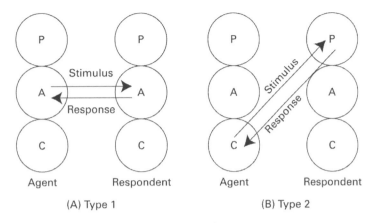

Figure 3.3.1 Complementary transactions (Berne, 1964: 29)

4. 'the way adult and young people each see each other and interact . . . *requires* a greater parity and treatment than most other adult providers and young person exchanges *impose*.'

These are important aspects of practice which are precipitated by voluntary participation. However, it is points one and four which in particular when combined help to define the important relational dynamic between the young person and youth worker which is rarely present in other professional settings. It is perhaps best illustrated with reference to the theory of transactional analysis (Berne, 1964). The theory is based on the assumption that there are three basic emotional positions or to use the technical term 'ego states': parent, adult, and child. Engagement in communication, or 'transactions', are always from one or other of these three positions. It is the transactions cumulatively which form the basis upon which a relationship is developed.

Transactions can either be 'complementary' or 'crossed'. Complementary communication is successful, uncomplicated, and mutually beneficial, and is ongoing. This is illustrated by Figure 3.3.1.

Crossed communication is antagonistic, frustrating and not mutually beneficial. Importantly, 'communication is broken off when a crossed transaction occurs' (Berne, 1964: 8) as illustrated by the diagram below.

Young people are in a developmental stage in which they are separating emotionally and psychologically from their parents (Biddulph, 1984) and do not want to be engaged with as if they are a child. Youth work ensures 'complementary communication', which allows for the development of a relationship, because youth workers consistently and reliably engage with the young person in an adult to adult way. Other professionals do not ensure an 'adult to adult' relationship because they too often either

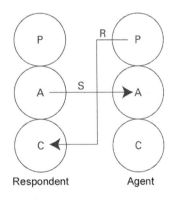

Figure 3.3.2 Crossed transactions (Berne, 1964: 29)

treat young people as if they were a child or operate in such a way that a young person will perceive them as an authority figure which inevitably results in the young person feeling as if they are being treated like a child. As the young person wishes to be communicated with as if they were an adult and communicate as an adult, this inevitably leads to 'crossed communication' and the breakdown of a relationship.

Sometimes this crossed communication is precipitated consciously, when for example a teacher demands respect from pupils but does not necessarily give the same respect to pupils in return, or inadvertently because of the inherent power associated with their position and the lack of genuine power delegated to the young person, for example, when an education welfare officer is attempting to understand why a young person is not attending school, but is inevitably perceived as an authority figure, decrying their truanting.

This simple yet profound analysis may well encapsulate much of youth work's success, that is, it enables dialogue with the young adult because it avoids the natural tendency of the young adult to perceive the other adult who is in a position of authority (by virtue of their professional status) as 'parental'. Perhaps this is best summed up in the words of a young person '(youth worker) 'X' is accessible and reliable and treats me like an adult. She lets me do it/helps me do it (social workers always did it for me) makes me feel good in myself because I've done things' (Merton et al., 2004: 4).

Whilst it is certainly the case that voluntary participation does enable the four important aspects of practice, suggested by Davies above to develop, as well as help define the adult–adult relationship required for 'complementary communication' in accordance with transactional analysis, the points are not all exclusively derived from the voluntary principle. The first point is perhaps the only one that does exclusively follow from voluntary participation and can instil that degree of power to the dynamics of practice, and this should not be underestimated. However, although the other three points do clearly follow from voluntary participation, they also follow from the values of youth work, for example from the NYA ethical principle to 'treat young people with respect' and 'to allow for self-determination' (NYA, 1999); they also have an important role in bringing about the particular aspects of practice, as does the young person centred curriculum.

A necessary condition of youth work?

Undoubtedly, voluntary participation is a powerful defining force of youth work practice and underpins much of its curriculum. However, one should not make the mistake that Jeffs and Smith (1998/99) make and assume therefore that if it is not present it is not youth work. They link voluntary participation with two other criteria:

> *The work undertaken has an educational purpose* (and) *the focus of the work is directed towards young people* (maintaining that) *for over 150 years, (these) three elements have fused to delineate youth work and distinguish it from other welfare activities. It has been distinctive only when all these ingredients are present. Remove one and it becomes obvious that what is being observed may possess a resemblance to, but is unquestionably not, youth work.*
>
> (1998/99: 48)

It is somewhat of a fudge to suggest that criteria can in fact 'fuse'; what is meant by this? How does the whole of the three criteria make up more than the sum of its parts? Are they three separate criteria or is it in fact an elaborate threefold definition of youth work that is being proposed? On either count it is problematic, because of its over-emphasis on voluntary participation. For the criteria to be credible, they must stand up on their own merits. Although voluntary participation is an important part of youth work practice is not a necessary, nor a sufficient, condition of youth work.

A sufficient condition is a condition in which the presence of that criteria or factor alone is enough to produce or define the concept. Voluntary participation is clearly not a sufficient condition for youth work, as young people participate voluntarily in a number of disparate 'leisure activities' which are clearly not youth work.

It is more likely that Jeffs and Smith are implying that voluntary participation is a necessary condition of youth work, that is, although in itself it is not 'enough' or 'sufficient' to define youth work, by the same token nothing can be legitimately described as youth work unless it contains that element; it is 'necessary' or 'essential'. For youth work to take place, therefore, the young people must have voluntarily engaged in the process, activity or session and furthermore been able to, at any point, leave of their own free will, with no repercussions.

I think that although this is seductive, it is in fact untenable, and some very powerful youth work interventions may well take place in settings where young people do not participate voluntarily. For example, if a youth worker who has worked with a young person in a traditional youth club setting and built a relationship through voluntary participation (and so according to the definition can legitimately be described as youth work), then undertakes work with the same young person in a formal setting, perhaps advocating on behalf of that person in a meeting concerning their non-attendance, or is brought in to help encourage the young person to re-engage with their schooling after a bereavement, through one-to-one work, thereby undertaking 'work' with that young person in a setting in which the young person is not choosing to attend. By Jeffs and Smith's definition the worker in these cases would no longer be doing youth work. This is clearly illogical. This work does not cease to be youth work just because it is in a setting in which the young person has not chosen to be. Jeffs and Smith may wish to counter with the observation that 'the relationship had originally been founded on voluntary participation and so that is why those instances can be described as youth work', however, if one concedes that, it is equally plausible to imagine the very same scenario taking place which has not previously been founded on voluntary participation, whereby the worker builds a sufficiently good relationship with the young person within the school environment and either advocates on their behalf on the issue of non-attendance or engages in one-to-one sessions around issues of bereavement and non-attendance, and so the same quality of work is produced without the precursor of voluntary participation. It would be implausible to suggest that one scenario is youth work and the other is not.

Voluntary participation may be a very important dynamic which youth work abandons at its peril, but by the same token neither is it the 'holy grail' by which interventions and approaches are permitted into the realm of youth work.

What the above example alludes to is that it is not voluntary participation in itself which is important; it is what it 'enables'. It is, after all, a means to an end and not an end in itself. Voluntary participation allows the formation of an authentic youth work relationship, one based on honesty, respect, mutuality and a concern for the well being of the young person, as well as importantly a degree of power at the disposal of the young person. It is easy to see why voluntary participation makes youth work relationships flourish. Without it, it may be much harder to form such a relationship, particularly with certain young people at the 'margins'. But it is not a necessary condition of a youth work relationship, as a youth work relationship can form without it.

Part of the problem here is a false distinction operating between voluntary participation on the one hand and compulsion on the other. It is assumed that if a young person has not chosen to do 'X' and they have no right to leave 'X', they are under some kind of compulsion which if removed they automatically would leave. The reality is a little different and life a bit more complicated. There are many things in life for young people, as well as adults, which on the one hand we cannot walk away from, but do not feel 'compulsion' to do. Compulsion is an emotive word which would 'set anyone's back up'. We can all think of situations where we did not particularly want to be or of things we felt obliged to do, which in fact turned out to be enjoyable or we got a lot out of. For example, a party we felt obliged to attend but turned out to be enjoyable, or a walk in the countryside which although we thought we were too tired for, turned out to be refreshing. The fact is just because we do not explicitly choose to be somewhere does not mean that it cannot be beneficial. It is the quality of the experience that is important.

One could imagine a plausible, if unlikely, scenario of a parent insisting on their son or daughter attending a local youth club and then going on to enjoy it. The reluctance to be there would certainly be an initial barrier, but with a quality of engagement on the part of the incumbent youth workers, the young person may actually be glad they were forced to attend. Similarly, one could imagine a youth work project like the e2e (entry to employment) (Redfearn, 2005) which forms part of the government's integration into employment for NEET young people (those not in education, employment or training) fitting this bill. What is more important is the curriculum which underpins the practice of these projects which do not operate voluntary participation as much as the simple fact that the participants do not choose to be involved. Indeed the curriculum could well be more stimulating and exciting, participative and challenging in a project which is targeted, and young people do not choose to attend than within one which you can.

Enabling engagement or choosing to attend

One of the reasons voluntary participation is held up as a defining characteristic of youth work is that it can be used to distinguish it from other welfare and educational services. But this alone should not be used to elevate it beyond its actual importance. Voluntary participation is an important principle upon which much quality youth work is founded. However, one needs a critical understanding of the concept and it cannot legitimately be presented as either a necessary or sufficient condition of youth work. Ultimately it is the quality of the relationship which forms out of the engagement, the degree of choice at the disposal of the participants, and the participative practices of the workers, not simply whether the project was based on the participants being able to choose to attend that defines the potential of the youth work curriculum. Ultimately it is the ability to 'enable young people to engage' which is important. Choosing to attend is *one* of the factors which would assist this engagement but it is not the only one and in itself it is no guarantee.

Targeted youth work may have the initial barrier of compulsory attendance to overcome, but targeted work may also put youth workers in touch with young people with whom they would not have had the opportunity to meet. For those 'targeted' projects that are not founded on voluntary attendance, the guiding principle should perhaps be 'Is this the kind of thing the young people *would have participated in voluntarily, if they had been given the opportunity*?'

What is required is a balance of provision between targeted and universal provision. Worryingly, Merton et al. have noted a shift in practice, whereby 'targeted work with at-risk young people has attracted greater proportions of youth service resources' (2004: (k)). This is believed to be in part because they can better demonstrate their outcomes. They rightly advocate 'sustaining a balance' of youth provision as 'Open access work through clubs and centres continues to fulfil important functions in providing a range of opportunities

for young people's personal and social development' (ibid.).

Emerging essential elements

Before leaving the essential elements of the youth work curriculum it is worth considering briefly two emerging elements: global youth work and spirituality, which are gaining prominence in recent curriculum documents and have recently been given a higher profile by the NYA.

Global youth work

Global youth work is an increasingly important aspect of youth work. According to a recent NYA survey '85 per cent of youth workers think that young people should learn about global issues' (Boagey, 2006: 21). As he points out, 'Youth work might once have approached global issues as a separate activity, but now the world is changing and there is a growing imperative for these issues to be placed at the heart of it, to be woven into the fabric of youth work' (2006: 21). Hopkinson concurs that, 'Youth work has a long tradition of supporting young people's understanding of the world around them and encouraging them to reflect on global issues. Often, though, these have been seen as an optional extra, a bolt on to perhaps the more traditional curriculum areas' (2006: 20).

Global youth work and global issues have been incorporated into some of the curriculum documents produced in the field. For example, in Tower Hamlets (2004) 'Global and Environmental Awareness' is the third element of a programme area entitled political development (which includes 'empowerment and participation' and 'political education and citizenship' as the other two). Their policy statement reads: 'Young people should be encouraged to consider the impact of human activity on the natural environment, both locally and globally. All work with young people will be undertaken with due regard to the impact on the environment' (2004: 18).

For Nottingham, 'Environment' is one of their eight 'key themes' and they have produced a separate guidance booklet on this theme entitled *Environment: A Guide to Learning Outcomes* (Circa, 2003). It is framed within a commitment to Agenda 21, the agreement at the Rio Earth Summit in 1992, which incorporates a commitment 'to meet the needs of all the worlds people whilst ensuring long-term protection of the planet' (Circa, 2003: 2). The types of work the guidance focuses on range from recycling, to fair-trade, animal rights, global warming, conservation projects and environmental improvement projects.

Promotion of global capitalism or global critique?

Global youth work can appear to be consistent with a key government priority. Charles Clarke, the then Education Secretary was quite explicit about the government's commitment to global issues. In *Putting the World into World Class Education, An International Strategy for Education, Skills and Children's Services.* (DfES, 2005b) he states: 'One cannot really educate young people in this country without the international dimension being a very significant and real part of their learning'.

However, there is a contradiction at the heart of global youth work which potentially puts it at odds with policy, not aligning itself to it, that is the extent to which it advocates global capitalism or is a critic of it. The government's position is quite clear, global issues are important primarily because our markets are global: 'Our vision for the people of the UK is that they should have the knowledge, skills and understanding they need to fulfil themselves, to live and contribute effectively to a global society and to work in a competitive global economy' (Clarke in DfES, 2005b).

However, whether described as global youth work, environmental youth work, or education for sustainable development, it must engage in a critical dialogue with the capitalist system which is not only bringing about the imminent destruction of the planet but shows no great desire to cease that destruction. For many young people this will be an area they will be passionate about and youth work can help to mobilise these passions, for example through campaign groups or peer education (Lodge et al., 2006). As global issues ask fundamental questions about how society functions and is structured it is as likely to bring youth work into conflict with government both locally and nationally as it is to support current policy.

The NYA's latest publication in support of global youth work, *Blackberries from Mexico*

(Boagey et al., 2006) has some useful information to guide and encourage practitioners to undertake global youth work which includes links to websites and resource packs. However, it does not explicitly confront the inherent conflict between policy and practice. It cites government policy and stresses how youth work can educate young people about the 'increasingly interconnected world', for example by starting with basic ideas about where our food comes from. It also demonstrates how work on global issues links into the ECM five outcomes.

The problem is it tends to gloss over the complexities and inherently conflictual nature of global issues. It is certainly evidence of a global society that our supermarkets are crammed with food from every corner of the globe. But it is also evidence of global inequality that farmers are paid a pittance for their produce and is also evidence of an environmental disaster that the air traffic which transports the cargo is a major contributor to global warming. Global youth work is inherently political and necessarily critical of the status quo and this must be made explicit in youth work which purports to be such. Plymouth Youth Service's curriculum framework (2006) does emphasise this within their curriculum area of *Me in a Global Society*. They suggest that one of the possible outcomes would be for, 'Young people to develop an understanding of inequality and discrimination globally and young people take responsibility for their community and their world and begin to take action to make it a more equitable place' (2006: 11).

This important of the relationship between the purposes of youth work and the maintenance or otherwise of the status quo will be addressed more fully in Chapter 5.2 on 'Curriculum and Culture'.

Spirituality

Spirituality is another emerging theme. Historically it has been what has most obviously distinguished youth work from youth ministry, the latter having an explicit commitment to religious and spiritual aspects with the former often shying away from them, tending to stress the political rather than the spiritual. Some curricula do incorporate a commitment to the spiritual aspect of young people's lives. Indeed West Sussex, one of the first authorities to produce a document undertaking their consultation on curriculum in 1988 (West Sussex, 1989) incorporated a commitment to 'Spiritual Development' which they suggest concerns 'a personal journey . . . of development and growth' (1989: 26) and involves explorations of 'meaning (and) . . . helps people face difficult and often unanswerable questions' (ibid.). Throughout their five versions of curriculum, culminating in West Sussex (2005) they have retained a commitment to this aspect of practice. Milton Keynes similarly state that, 'The service aims to enable young people to develop an awareness of self and assist them to explore and develop their spiritual side' (2005: 12).

Young (1999, 2006) suggests that youth work is fundamentally concerned with development of the mind, body and spirit as well as exploring aspects of meaning in young people's lives. However, she falls short of explicitly framing this in the terms of the 'spiritual'. Nemko (2006) who advocates the introduction of spiritual development into work with young people, distinguishes it from religion and faith, suggesting spirituality is 'about being aware of our own insignificance in the large scheme of things' (2006: 98) whether or not that is then framed in a religion or faith. Spirituality for Nemko is located in the self and the 'search for purpose' but also intrinsically related to action: 'Spirituality is about engaging in the world in every sense. In the experience of nature and creativity, in our relationships and in every intention and action that leads to a more meaningful experience and positive result. So we can say that human rights, ecology and ethical

globalisation are all universal spiritual issues' (2006: 106). She argues that by exploring the innate spirituality in all of us we can find inner connectedness between people which both breaks down and bypasses the prejudice and stereotypes associated with religion and faith groups.

NYA consultation paper on *Spirituality and Spiritual Development* (NYA, 2005a) claims 'there is an implicit understanding that youth work is holistic' and that this involves the development of the 'spirit' as well as the mind and body. They refer to the guidance on spirituality from the element of the National Occupational Standard Element B.2.2 to:

> *Assist young people in the exploration and development of their spiritual self . . . which is about: exploring the difference between spirituality, religion and faith, encouraging young people to see themselves in a wide setting of relationships with others and of the environment around them. It is about enabling young people to have a sense of, and value their life journey.*
>
> (2005: 41)

They go on to suggest that given that 'funding streams' tend to run counter to this holistic approach the framing of the spiritual aspect of work is as important as ever, as it is one way of ensuring that the holistic approach continues (NYA, 2005a: 16). Whether one adopts the spiritual aspect of the curriculum for pragmatic reasons or not, denying young people a sense of wonder or awe, an opportunity to connect with their innermost feelings, as well as to make connections with those of others, or even address the 'big questions' is denying them an important aspect of the youth work curriculum.

On Methods

Within the methods of youth work a distinction is apparent between what is described as broad methods or *modes of delivery*, and *specific methods* or programmable activities which are the vehicles through which learning is facilitated.

Modes of delivery

There are four primary 'broad methods' or 'modes of delivering' for youth work: centre based, detached, outreach and mobile provision. Each of these methods of delivery or modes of practice are organised differently.

Centre based

Centre based provision is perhaps the most immediately recognisable of the youth work methods, and equates to the traditional youth club. It is what many lay people equate youth work with. This is often referred to as 'generic youth work', and generally operates through voluntary participation. The actual type of centre though can have an important bearing on the potential of the work, whether it is a youth centre, community centre or youth and community centre; or even a church hall or part of a school. Anything other than a designated space for young people, preferably in their own youth centre can provide a conflict of priorities and limit the scope for participative practice which develops ownership of the provision. Centre based work has the added advantage of being able to provide a number of activities within the same space; anything from sports, arts, music or multi-media facilities, depending on resources.

Detached work

Detached work takes place where the young people choose to meet, whether that be on the street, in a park or at a bus shelter. It is 'on their territory' so to speak. For some, this is the purist form of youth work – free from the clutter of rules, regulations, boundaries, ground rules and the policing of the building: it is just the youth worker and the young people and the dialogue that develops between them. For others, it is restrictive without the resources of the centre and they see the scope of the street corner as limiting. It is suitable for some young people, it is argued – perhaps those who were historically deemed 'unclubbable' (Albemarle Report, 1960: 143; Smith, 1988) and who are unable to accept the responsibilities of club membership and the rules and regulations that go with it. In contemporary terminology they may be NEET (not in education, employment or training) and 'at risk of social exclusion' or even on an Anti Social Behaviour Order, and detached work may be the only and best solution. However, regardless of its unique position in being able to make contact with those hardest to reach, detached work is an important method of delivering youth work and should not just be associated with reaching difficult or troublesome young people or in a 'fire fighting' mentality, dealing with complaints about young people on street corners.

Outreach

Outreach is work undertaken in a setting away from a given centre or service, on the streets or in a local park but with a specific purpose which relates to work being undertaken at that centre or service. It could therefore be to advertise the provision at a particular centre and recruit new members for it, or it could be to advertise a service which is being offered at a particular locality e.g. a new sexual health drop-in. It can be seen as related to detached work but having a 'specific remit' means it differs significantly.

Mobile provision

A relatively recent innovation, particularly in the realm of rural youth work, has been the development of mobile provision. Whether this takes the form of a bus, caravan, or a converted minibus, mobile provision enables youth workers to overcome the dilemma of rural youth work, of either having youth centres with lots of resources which young people cannot travel to, or having detached workers who can travel to remote locations but who have limited resources. The vehicles are often kitted out with a variety of computers, music equipment, etc. and could be described as a portable youth centre (Fabes et al., 2003).

Other delivery modes?

'Youth work is organised and delivered in a number of ways' (St Helens, 2001: 7). These ways are sufficiently substantive as to be legitimately defined as modes of delivery as they describe how the work is organised but which are problematic in that they can be utilised as specific methods within other modes of delivery such as centre based or detached work or, for example, a residential as part of the provision of a youth centre, or a trip for a group from detached work. Likewise a youth forum could be a 'stand alone' forum or one created specifically as a vehicle to aid the participation in a local youth centre. Some provision therefore could be described as both a mode of delivery and a specific method, for example a motor project.

As a result the distinction can appear not to be clear cut, as there is overlap. However, it is important to maintain a distinction between methods as 'ways of organising' youth work, i.e. modes of delivery; and methods as vehicles for stimulating learning, i.e. specific methods. As, without the latter's explicit reference to the proactive responsibility for organising and facilitating learning, the specific emphasis on the educational aspect of youth work methods is liable to be lost from the youth work curriculum.

The following methods straddle the distinction, and could be 'stand alone methods' or specific methods within modes of delivery.

Project based

Project work can be defined by the group and by its purpose or both. Examples of project work are many and varied. Often they are designated as fixed term, perhaps due to funding, but are not necessarily so, and the numbers of young people will be more restricted as opposed to centre based work for example. Advantages of project work are that resources can be targeted to need, and

provision can be tailored accordingly. Examples include Duke of Edinburgh's Award, Lesbian, Gay, Bisexual and Transgender Support Group. Project work as a mode of delivery should not be confused with the setting up and delivery of specific projects within an existing mode of delivery like a graffiti arts project for the young people to renovate their local youth centre. Project work which is fixed term should ensure that an appropriate exit strategy is in place.

Trips, outings and offsite activities

Youth work offers a number of trips, outings and offsite activities as part of its existing centre based or detached work. These are not purely recreational and should be built in to a participative framework. For example, who booked the venue, gave out the consent forms – the young people or the adults? The youth workers should at least 'be working towards' the young people booking their own trips. They should be educational but in the broad sense. The experience of being in a new environment can be and often is the stimulus for a new and different kind of conversation.

Residential or overnight

Clearly a progression from the notion of single day activities away from one's locality, the residential or overnight experiences offer the greater potential for sharing a lived experience. Out of the normal environment, living together for a short period of time provides a myriad of opportunities for reflections on and analysis of one's own and each other's lives as they are lived. This can be anything from an overnight stay in the youth centre, to an international exchange.

One-to-one

Although youth workers do not as a rule form exclusive one-to-one relationships like counsellors, one-to-one work is an important mode of delivery. It may be that informal one-to-one work would develop out of centre based provision where a particular worker would offer support and guidance on a particular issue to a young person on a regular basis over a period of time, perhaps over an issue of bullying or in trying to give up smoking. Perhaps the one-to-one is a one off but equally significant, when a young person one week is particularly upset at being 'dumped' by their boy or girl friend and the youth worker offers a shoulder to cry on and some comforting words. One-to-one work can take place more formally through referral and arrangements to meet be more organised. For example where a young person is having trouble at school and the youth worker is brought in to work through some of the issues. This can be similar to a mentoring role.

Youth forums

Youth forums have taken on a greater profile within the participation agenda in recent years, with the rise in expectations on local authorities to be 'listening to and involving' all aspects of the community. Many local authorities now have youth forums or councils with whom they can 'consult'. Youth forums have for many years however been an important part of youth work. They can be an important mechanism for formalising the participation of young people in decisions which relate to organisation and delivery of the projects. Forums also allow the facilitation of the devolvement of power to young people in a framework of accountability to young people as well as adults (Baker, 1996). In recent years the 'real' power of forums has been advanced considerably through the development of youth banks which 'are run by young people for young people [and] provide small grants for young people's good ideas to benefit their community' (Youth Bank, 2006).

Specific methods

Specific methods relate to the educational input provided by the 'pro-active' role of youth workers. These methods can be planned and delivered in response to specifically identified needs or issues, as ways of stimulating learning through conversation, dialogue and discussion, to initiate and develop a group work process or as mechanisms for promoting participative practice. It is the specific methods which provide vehicles for learning. As we saw in Chapter 2.2, these are

often described as activities. They are the products of youth work, the more tangible aspects of practice, which are vital for a quality process to develop through.

Some examples of specific methods include Cumbria's (undated: 10) 'magazine and video production', 'life skills courses' (such as cooking, parenting and budgeting) and 'lobbying and campaigning'. Derbyshire (undated: 12) propose 'outdoor education', 'performing arts' and 'games and quizzes', whilst Kingston (2002: 10) include 'ICT', 'music' and 'environmental projects'. What is common to all these specific methods is that they include elements of product and process. Both are essential in order for the youth work to flourish.

Traditionally the specific methods of youth work have been simply referred to as activities (Spence, 2001). Although it is often made clear that activities are a means to an end and not an end in themselves, this is not explicit within the notion of 'an activity'. It is quite explicit within the framing of 'specific methods' that they are a means to an 'educational' end.

On programmes and programming

The specific methods can link into the formation of a programme, which could take the form of a specific focus for a weekly session, looking at a newspaper cutting about a recent assault to promote a discussion about violence, or a focus for a particular period such as an environmental clean up or a youth club re-decoration project. The programme should not be confused with the curriculum; it is an aspect of it. The programme or selection of particular topics or activities should always be in negotiation with young people and be responding to the relevant needs or issues of the group. This process should not be a question of us 'imposing our own ideas of curriculum or programme (but) to encourage learners to generate their own' (Tiffany, 2001: 102). Neither should it be a cause for a lack of focus on the spontaneous or emerging issues which are independent to any proactively planned session. Youth workers must always be prepared to respond to what is 'most appropriate'.

On Experiential Learning

Experiential learning is a key concept in the youth work curriculum, and as we found in Chapter 2.3 it has its origins in the work of Dewey (1996, 1997). Experience was at the heart of his educational philosophy and his emphasis on social interaction and the development of real life 'situations' at the centre of learning are very relevant to contemporary youth work practice.

Experiential learning is implicitly incorporated into youth work curriculum documents, through an emphasis on relationship building and the development of social situations, and the interactions that develop from them as a source of learning and social education. 'Whatever methods are in use should be underpinned by social education principles. These may vary from basic befriending to highly complex relations . . .' (Leicestershire, 2000: 7). It is, however, also incorporated more explicitly by many, with reference to David Kolb's theory of experiential learning (1984) by, for example, Wiltshire (2005) Hampshire (2003) Luton (2003) Cheshire (2005) South Tyneside (2005) and Nottinghamshire (2006). Common to this explicit application is an exclusive emphasis on a four stage cycle of 'Plan, Do, Reflect and Analyse or Learn'.

This is however, as we shall see, a problematic interpretation of Kolb's theory:

Kolb and experiential learning

Kolb's theory is explicitly based on the work of Dewey, Kurt Lewin and Jean Piaget and he attempts to provide a comprehensive account of experiential learning. We are familiar with Dewey's work from Chapter 2.3, with his emphasis on the centrality of experience in learning. But we must spend a little more time elaborating on the work of Lewis and Piaget.

Lewin

Lewin (1951) also stresses the importance of 'concrete experience' as the locus of learning. His work was primarily concerned with organisational change and he developed his concept of 'action research' based on the importance of 'here and now' concrete experience to validate and test any abstract concepts. Importantly he utilised the feedback principle from electrical engineering and built this into his theory of social learning and the problem solving process. It was Lewin, in fact, who developed the four stage model of experiential learning for action research (Figure 3.5.1).

Piaget

Piaget is the third important theoretical strand in Kolb's theory. He was concerned exclusively with cognitive development, and he developed a four stage cycle to account for what he regarded as the critical stages of this development.

According to Kolb, Piaget's view is that 'Development from infancy to adulthood moves

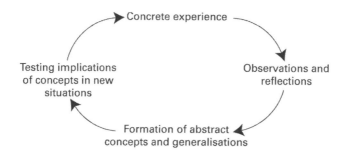

Figure 3.5.1 Lewin's experiential learning model (cited in Kolb, 1984: 21)

from a concrete phenomenal view of the world to an abstract constructionist view, from an active egocentric view to a reflective internalised mode of knowing' (1984: 23), that is, development is a progressive move from immersion in experience to a gradual abstraction, manipulation and conceptual understanding of experience.

Importantly within Piaget's developmental model of learning, at each of his four developmental stages, there is a tension between two fundamental principles of accommodation and assimilation. Accommodation is the process of adapting oneself to the demands of the environment, for example through imitation. Assimilation is modifying or adapting the environment to fit into existing concepts or what Piaget would call 'schema'. The former is an adaptation of oneself to the demands of the world, the latter is an 'internal' adaptation and a reconfiguring of the world or at least how one sees it. Through accommodation the learner changes to fit the environment. Through assimilation, to some extent it is the world that changes or at least the learner's comprehension of it. Importantly, all experience, regardless of the stage of development, is a balanced tension between these two processes. For Kolb, all three

models 'require the resolution of conflicts between dialectically opposed modes of adaptation to the world:

> *The Lewinian model emphasises two such dialectics – the conflict between concrete experience and abstract concepts and the conflict between observation and action. For Dewey, the major dialectic is between the impulse that gives ideas their moving force and reason that gives desire its direction. In Piaget's framework, the twin processes of accommodation of ideas to the external world and the assimilation of experience into existing conceptual structures are the moving forces of cognitive development.*
> (1984: 29)

Kolb's theory

Kolb claims, despite some of the differences of emphasis, that, 'Common to all three traditions of experiential learning is the emphasis on development toward a life of purpose and self-direction as the organising principle for education' (1984: 18). On this basis he incorporates many of the aspects of Dewey, Lewin and Piaget's theories into his own model of experiential learning (Figure 3.5.2).

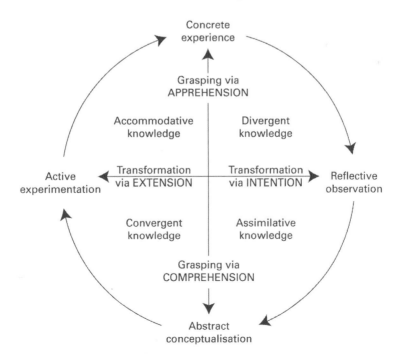

Figure 3.5.2 Structural dimensions underlying the process of experiential learning and the resulting basic knowledge forms

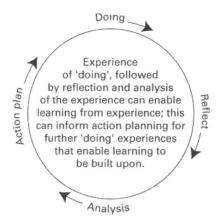

Figure 3.5.3   Application of Kolb's learning cycle within a youth work curriculum (Wiltshire, 2005)

Problems with Kolb's theory

There are clearly differences between Kolb's theory, Figure 3.5.2, and the common application of Kolb: 'Do and Reflect, Analysis and Plan', Figure 3.5.3. Most notably it is only the periphery, the outer circle, which is generally incorporated. This outer circle is actually almost identical to Lewin's model (Figure 3.5.1). Importantly Lewin's model was not a model of experiential learning but an attempt to structure the process of advancing learning in an organisational setting. It is a research method, although perhaps a very active one, and one that integrates experience. But it does not account for experiential learning per se and it was never designed to account for the totality of learning by experience.

To fully understand Kolb's theory, as well as the more familiar outer ring, one must appreciate the central element of his model, what Kolb refers to as the dialectic tensions of the opposing methods of relating to and incorporating experience, the 'abstract detachment' and 'concrete involvement', or accommodation and assimilation; and not least because when considered in its entirety, Kolb's theory appears contradictory. The element of Kolb's theory which describes learning as a sequential model, and which passes through the four successive stages of action, reflection, analysis and planning, is at odds with learning conceived of as an active and dynamic process of interplay between dialectically opposing forces. It cannot be both a separate and sequential process and an active dialectical process.

The element of Kolb's theory of experiential learning which conceives of learning as a

sequential model, as we have seen, is from Lewin. The reflection in Lewin's model is a separate enterprise. That is because it is concerned with organisational learning and the reflective phase is an opportunity for those involved in the organisation to sit down reflect upon and discuss the process of change they are involved in. Together as a group, they analyse the events and work out changes for the future.

At times Kolb's conception of learning does appear to emphasise separate stages of action, reflection and analysis which need to be passed through sequentially in the acquisition of knowledge or separate functions to be applied after an experience. The quote below emphasises Kolb's identification of separate functions of the learning process and the inability to integrate them:

> *New knowledge, skills or attitudes are achieved through confrontation among four modes of experiential learning. Learners, if they are to be effective, need four different kinds of abilities – concrete experience abilities (CE) reflective observation abilities (RO) abstract conceptualisations abilities (AC) and active experimentation (AE) abilities . . . Yet this ideal is difficult to achieve. How can one act and reflect at the same time? How can one be concrete and immediate and still be theoretical. Learning requires abilities that are polar opposites, and the learner, as a result, must continually choose which set of learning abilities they will bring to bear in any specific leaning situation.*
>
> (1984: 30)

Kolb, in the above quote, appears not to comprehend how a holistic approach to learning can be reconciled with these opposite functions, and thereby emphasises a sequential model.

However, at other times, Kolb appears not to believe that the tension within the dynamics of experiential learning is insurmountable and reference is made to how learning is an integration of these separate functions in the learning process: 'All the models above suggest the idea that learning is by its very nature a tension and conflict filled process' (1984: 30). And '. . . experiential learning is also concerned with how these functions are integrated by the person into a holistic adaptive posture toward the world' (1984: 32).

It is not clear what emphasis Kolb places on Lewin's sequential model, as much of his commentary on his own model (despite the inclusion of the Lewin's model in his own) at times strongly emphasises the interactive and holistic nature of experiential learning. This is also particularly evident in the inner part of his model, which primarily follows Piaget. The following quote is clearly a reflection of this: 'It (experiential learning) is an holistic concept . . . as a function of dialectic tensions between basic modes of relating to the world' (1984: 31). He also cites: Bruner (1966) who claims at the heart of the creative process is the dialectic tension between 'abstract detachment' and 'concrete involvement' (1984: 31). Kolb goes on to emphasise this aspect of experiential learning further in his own theory: 'It is an holistic concept . . . in that it seeks to describe the emergence of basic life orientations as a function of dialectic tensions between basic modes of relating to the world. To learn is not the special province of a single specialised realm of human functioning such as cognition or perception: it involves the integrated functioning of the total organism – thinking, feeling, perceiving and behaving' (ibid.).

Experiential dialectics in youth work

The dialectics of experience is important as it places a different emphasis on how we conceive of experiential learning. An example of an application of this dialectical tension of experience in youth work could be illustrated with reference to the experience of young women. Their experience can be seen as a tension between the demand to 'accommodate' themselves to the stereotypical expectations of their gender and femininity, in contrast to the extent to which they conceptualise or 'assimilate' the world as an oppressive environment which restricts their own authentic development irrespective of the environmental demands.

Similarly, the dialectical tension in peer groups could be characterised by the extent to which young people adapt their behaviour to meet the demands of the group, or free themselves through a process of assimilation of information about the experience of peer groups and peer group pressure. They realise that their desires, beliefs or values run contrary to the expectations of the group; discovering that they actually have a choice to conform or not and that this does not necessarily undermine their relationships with their peers.

The infiltration of 'Techne': the product model of learning

At the heart of Kolb's theory therefore lies a contradiction: that is experiential learning is described as both a sequential process of passing through fixed stages and it is also an holistic dialectic process of active engagement with experience. It is difficult to find a plausible explanation for this contradiction. Perhaps the emphasis on the sequential model is out of deference to Lewin, and the appearance of learning as an application of separate functions is not overly intended by Kolb. In fact learning as separate applications through a sequential process is largely inconsistent with experiential learning, certainly as conceived by both Dewey and Piaget. If Kolb is to do justice to the essential nature of experiential learning he must see it primarily, if not entirely, as an active and holistic process of interaction with the world, and not as one which conceives of action, reflection and learning as separate functions.

Another plausible explanation as to why Kolb emphasises sequential learning and quite probably why applications of Kolb have done the same and excluded the essential nature of experiential learning as an holistic process, is the infiltration of *Techne* – the 'analogy of learning as a production line'; an infiltration of the product mentality into an area of human behaviour which is inappropriate. As we saw earlier, with the profound effect the product approach has had on curriculum, Kolb may similarly have been influenced inappropriately by a 'product' approach. Interestingly, Lewin himself quite openly acknowledged that the origins of his feedback model were borrowed from 'electrical

Figure 3.5.4   Kolb reframed as a linear model

engineering' and as we know the sequential aspect of Kolb's theory is derived directly from Lewin.

Kolb's sequential outer circle can be redrawn as a linear model. See Figure 3.5.4. This re-conceptualisation of experiential learning into a linear pattern could be seen as an attempt to demonstrate more clearly the products of learning. However, this would not be consistent with Kolb's ethos as he is explicitly opposed to a product view of learning. He does not see learning as a search for outcomes. 'In all three of the learning models (of Lewin, Dewey and Piaget), learning is described as a process whereby concepts are derived from, and continuously modified by, experience. No two thoughts are the same as experience always intervenes' (1984: 26). 'Learning is an emergent process whose outcomes represent only (an) historical record . . .' (ibid.).

That there are 'products of learning' is not disputed, since realisations, understanding and new knowledge both of one's self and of the world around us, emerge from experiential learning. Importantly, however, it is how one conceives of the acquisition of those products which is fundamental to the youth work process and the resulting curriculum. This re-conceptualisation of experiential learning into a product based model, perhaps in part by Kolb and in full by those who have utilised only a partial reformulation of his model in the youth work curriculum is misconceiving the process of experiential learning and is ultimately detrimental to this process.

Reflection in action

Reflection and action are not necessarily separate things. Moon (2000) suggests that despite Kolb's apparent claim that these are in fact distinct and separate modes he himself seems to describe learning which arises from situations in which reflection and action occur at the same time. Schon (1987) has shown quite clearly in his description of 'Reflection in action' that indeed

the modalities of 'concrete action' and 'reflective observation' (in Kolb's terms) or simply 'having an experience' and 'reflecting upon it' are not mutually exclusive. One can, and often is, aware of reflecting upon action 'in action'. Action and reflection more often combine together to accurately describe learning from experience. According to Schon, reflection is not a separate process applied to an experience after the event, but merely a different way of being in the experience. The problems of the experiential learning cycle derive from this exaggerated separation of the different aspects of learning.

That learning does not necessarily occur with a reflection on, or after, experience, is best exemplified by the Gestalt 'Ah ha principle' (Kohler, 1947). Likened to the analogy of 'when the penny drops', this is learning which appears to just occur, it can be through trial and error, when finally the explanation appears to make sense or 'when it just hits you between the eyes' as a result of 'sudden insight'. But importantly for the Gestaltists, it is holistic, it is 'in the moment' and it is not produced through any processing of a series of sequential inputs.

Experience itself ('the doing' as it is often referred to in youth work curriculum documents) is an interactive process which involves immersion in an experience as well as reflection and analysis of it. It is out of this combination that the learning and ultimately outcomes emerge. If learning is conceived of as something which occurs after the event – through reflection (or in youth work terms a review) this is not in fact 'learning from experience itself' this is learning from 'a reflection on experience'. Furthermore, if emphasis is put on reflection after the event as the primary source of learning, the opportunity for experiential learning itself may well be lost. The review, in fact, is often a way of ensuring that the facilitator has a knowledge of what has actually been learnt during the experience, and is not a means of ensuring learning has occurred at all.

It is not being suggested that it may not be beneficial to reflect upon experience after the event, and that indeed there maybe value in that and learning may arise from it. However, if experiential learning is conceived of as solely a means of passing through separate, sequential stages, this both misconceives how Kolb intended it, and it certainly undermines our knowledge, understanding and application of experiential learning. If the learning from experience is restricted to reflections upon and after experiences, as Smith, H. suggests, workers would be failing in 'seizing learning opportunities as they arise' (2002: 19).

Beyond Kolb

In relation to experiential learning it is evident we must think beyond Kolb. Whilst it is certainly the case that he, perhaps more than most, put experiential learning back on the agenda and gave it back some of its educational legitimacy, his own rationale is both problematic and internally contradictory. Learning is rarely arrived at through sequential linear stages, nor in fact does Kolb 'at times' appear to suggest that it should. The popular application of Kolb through the promotion of the four stage learning cycle is fundamentally flawed; not least because Kolb's own theory must also be seen as a promotion of an active dialectical process of a synthesis of accommodation and assimilation.

Kolb's theory is limited in another key respect. Importantly, as Illeris points out 'Kolb is only concerned with what I understand as the cognitive dimension of learning' (2002: 37). Experiential learning is much broader than it is defined within Kolb's theory. As Illeris rightly concludes, it is 'crucially important that the concepts of 'experience' and 'experiential learning' span all the dimensions of learning, cognitive, psychodynamic and societal' (ibid.). Illeris emphasises the importance of these two, previously ignored spheres. The psychodynamic, affective or emotional realm of learning is of utmost importance: 'How the situation is experienced, which emotions and motivations are attached to the process, and thus what psychological energy is mobilised' (2002: 20). Similarly, what Illeris refers to as the 'historic – societal' aspect of learning should not be ignored. Illeris draws on the work of Wenger (1998) and Gergen (1994) and the 'social constructionists' who emphasise 'situated learning' and the development of meaning and reality in a context of social interaction.

For Illeris, experiential learning is a holistic integration of these three dimensions (cognitive, emotional and social) and it is on this basis that a viable experiential learning for youth work should be conceived.

Section Four
Policy and Practice

Curriculum and Transforming Youth Work*

The initial contexts for this chapter are the publications by the NYA: Merton and Wylie (2002) *Towards a Contemporary Youth Work Curriculum* and the DfES (2002) *Transforming Youth Work: Resourcing Excellent Youth Services*. Both publications contain a curriculum framework which for all intents and purposes is identical as it is based on the same three basic elements, content, pedagogy and assessment. The question of whether or not this should be of concern depends ultimately on what conception of curriculum is contained within the documents, and whether or not it represents authentic curriculum for youth work. Unfortunately, there are clear causes for concern, which need further exploration. For the purposes of discussion the model will be referred to as Merton and Wylie's as they have laid claim to it (2004).

The 'Transforming Youth Work' curriculum model

Content

The first area, content, it has been argued, is 'relatively uncontentious as many curriculum documents in practice utilise the notion of curriculum areas, which broadly summarise young people's issues, interests and concerns' (Ord, 2004a: 51). However, as we saw in Chapter 2.1 the notion of content is not necessarily unproblematic within the process of youth work. It is viable when used in the specification of broad areas of content or as issues to be explored, although it certainly is problematic when content is translated into 'specific content', begins to equate to a syllabus and ultimately translated into outcomes or objectives.

In their description of content Merton and Wylie propose that: 'The core areas of skill,

knowledge and understanding within a youth work curriculum comprise four elements, that of 'emotional literacy', 'creativity and enterprise', 'health and well being' and 'active citizenship' (2002: 23). Whilst it could be argued that these do not encompass the totality of the young people's experience, to a large extent this aspect of their conceptualisation of content is not distinctly different from the notion of 'content areas'.

However, importantly, content is defined as, 'a set of learning outcomes derived from themes or topics' (Merton and Wylie, 2002: 7; DfES, 2002: 27). Merton and Wylie do therefore make the mistake of advocating the translation of the content areas into specific outcomes. These learning outcomes approximate directly to objectives and this begins to expose the curriculum model being proposed by Merton and Wylie and the DfES. It is a product model based on the pre-specification of objectives.

Pedagogy

The second element of curriculum proposed by Merton and Wylie (2002) and the DfES (2002) is 'pedagogy'. This again indicates further divergence between the conception of curriculum being proposed and the curriculum embedded in youth work practice. Pedagogy is a concept that is transposed primarily from teaching, and it relates specifically to the theory or rationale of teaching. Pedagogy equates in part therefore to the methodology of teaching and learning. Pedagogy does not appear in any of the curriculum documents produced in the field. It does have some quite separate links with informal education and youth work through the work of Freire (1972), but this bears no relation to the work of Merton and Wylie.

The use of pedagogy has a strong association with formal education and classroom teaching, and Merton and Wylie's use of the concept may well be a deliberate attempt to give added credibility to the 'educational' basis of youth work. However, an analysis of what is meant by Merton and Wylie as the 'pedagogy of youth

---

*This chapter is a revised and updated version of two papers written by the author (Ord, 2004a, 2004b) previously published in the journal 'Youth and Policy' which formed a critique of current curriculum policy. It also includes references to a rejoinder to the first of these papers by Merton and Wylie (2004).

work' gives further cause for concern. Pedagogy is defined as: 'ways of teaching and learning so that these outcomes can be achieved' (Merton and Wylie, 2002: 7 and DfES, 2002: 27). It is without doubt therefore that what is being proposed, as part of government policy of *Transforming Youth Work* as well as by the NYA, is a strict product based methodology for the youth work curriculum. The rationale or methodology, 'the pedagogy', is strictly defined in terms of the means by which it can ensure the achievement of pre-specified outcomes.

Merton and Wylie (2002) elaborate further on what is meant by pedagogy:

> *Youth work has a pedagogy which is based on learning by doing, often in small groups; people tackling real life problems and finding real life situations, planned, done and reflected on; lessons learned and applied elsewhere. It is essentially educational group work.*
> (Merton and Wylie, 2002: 10)

Whilst the above quote is not anathema to youth work, an explicit reference to 'process' is missing and Merton and Wylie's description of pedagogy of youth work as educational group work, does not sufficiently account for process of youth work. Indeed by utilising the term pedagogy they conveniently avoid using the concept of process in their description of the curriculum. This could be seen as intentional since in utilising the term process they would be undermining the product model, and the specificity of outcomes, that is implicit in their description.

We saw in Chapter 3.2 that group work was in fact an essential element of the youth work curriculum. However, group work is not synonymous with youth work, neither does the utilisation of group work necessarily mean one is employing youth work methods, for example teachers use group work. Youth work employs a particular type of group work that is developmental (Button, 1971, 1974). Importantly as a result of the developmental nature of group work in the youth work curriculum, one cannot necessarily predict with any reliability the eventual outcomes, prior to the onset of the process. Basing the process of youth work on pre-specification and achievement of outcomes can, and will, undermine the process.

Merton and Wylie expand on their 'pedagogy' by utilising the familiar aspects of Kolb's learning cycle of: 'Do', 'Reflect', 'Analyse' and 'Action Plan'. However as we saw in the previous chapter, Kolb is often misinterpreted and likewise Merton and Wylie only utilise the familiar sequential circle of Kolb's model. This, as we have seen, not only excludes elements which imply a dynamic, creative, dialectic process to learning, it employs an interpretation of Kolb which approximates to an outcome and product based approach.

Assessment

Further confirmation of the incorporation of product based methodology into Merton and Wylie's model of curriculum is found in the final part of their model, 'Assessment'. This is defined as: 'performance criteria so that judgements can be made about whether or not these learning outcomes have been achieved; and an outline of processes which can be applied' (Merton and Wylie, 2002: 7; DfES, 2002: 27). Importantly assessment is about ends, but they are not ends which one would be at liberty to discover at the end of a project, based on broad educational aims, which would have informed and governed a process, consistent with a process model. They are ends which must be specified at the outset. This is quite clear: 'Such broad goals need to be expressed in a set of more specific outcomes if they are to be helpful in the planning and in practice. 'The more clearly we can specify the ends, the better we will be able to choose the means for achieving them' (Merton and Wylie 2002: 2; DfES, 2002: 11).

Within Merton and Wylie's commentaries on assessment there are elements which are laudable. They recognise that 'judgements' are necessary in determining any outcomes. They note the importance of 'progress', as an important context within which judgements about outcomes are made. They also recognise the inherent difficulty in establishing this progress: 'Measuring distance travelled and achievement in the area of soft skills, such as those developed by youth work is particularly difficult' (2002: 12). In addition they comment on what they refer to as the problem of 'attribution': how do we know with any certainty that the learning is as a result of the youth worker's efforts and not due to some other unforeseen influence? 'We have to be convinced within a reasonable level of certainty that it was the intervention and no other factor that caused the difference' (2002: 13).

One of the ironies and frustrations about the formulation of curriculum by Merton and Wylie is that they appear to be unaware of the contradiction in their approach. On the one hand they describe quite accurately the dilemmas and difficulties at the heart of the assessment of outcomes, which are a direct consequence of the process of youth work, whilst at the same time advocating a model of curriculum which runs contrary to that process.

In response to specific criticisms of their model of curriculum Merton and Wylie have expressed concern that their approach has been misinterpreted: 'We do not think, as he (Ord) suggests, that what we are proposing is a strict application of the outcome model . . . such a mechanistic, routinised approach would be the kiss of death to youth work' (2004: 65). Indeed, they go on to say that: 'We think it would be foolish for youth workers to nail down the outcomes with great specificity of detail they are after through a relationship that entails negotiation, give and take and from which outcomes will emerge' (ibid).

Despite their protestations, it is evident, however, that their model is an outcome based model, which correlates directly with the theory of curriculum as product. The descriptions of the model, as we have seen, are specifically outcome focussed. It has been shown in fact that all three aspects of the model: the content, pedagogy (or methodology) and the assessment are defined specifically in terms of outcomes or ends. Merton and Wylie may wish to reassert their commitment to youth work principles (Merton and Wylie, 2004) in the light of, and in response to, explicit criticisms (Ord, 2004a) but the model proposed is quite clearly a product model; not least because it contains a linear conceptualisation of learning, see Figure 4.1.1.

NYA and government policy

It is argued (Ord, 2004a; 2004b) and it is evident from the references to curriculum documents throughout this text that the Merton and Wylie (2002) and DfES (2002) re-conception of the youth

work curriculum, deviates significantly from the curriculum that has been developed in the field. It contains within it a pre-eminence placed on outcomes for young people, and which runs contrary to the processes of youth work.

Interestingly, the current climate in youth work is revisiting some of the issues initially raised at ministerial conferences. Whilst the concept of curriculum is now to a large extent embedded into the operations of the statutory youth services throughout the country, the new developments within *Transforming Youth Work* (DfES, 2001, 2002) have brought back into sharp focus the tensions relating specifically to 'curriculum as product', and an emphasis on the outcomes of youth work.

In addition, the relationship between the NYA and DfES has also been brought into clear focus within the current climate of *Transforming Youth Work*. Burke commented on the dynamics at the NYA's inception, around the time of the ministerial conferences, and the scepticism about whether or not the NYA would become the 'government's poodle or the field's rottweiler' (Burke, 1991). Close inspection of the present publications from both the NYA and the DfES gives rise to suspicion and would appear to make valid the concerns over the autonomy of the NYA and the relationship between the NYA and government policy, given the near identical match in conceptions of curriculum.

Merton and Wylie are insistent that in fact the model is theirs: 'The similarity of the texts used by the DfES and the NYA is because the DfES copied material supplied to it by the NYA, not the other way round' (2004: 64). This does, however, raise as many questions as it in fact answers, as they admit further that: 'large elements of the various documents produced by the DfES were generated within the NYA' (ibid.). This appears to confirm that the relationship between the NYA and government is sufficiently close to at least raise suspicions as to how independent the NYA are. For example, how would the NYA steer a course between youth

Figure 4.1.1 Merton and Wylie's (2002) 'Product Based' curriculum

work and government if there is a difference of opinion, as there appears to be in relation to curriculum?

Indeed, Wylie himself seemed to write more authentically about process in the youth work curriculum before he became Chief Executive of the NYA, as reference to Wylie (1997) *Developmental Youth Work 2000* exemplifies. In this paper he advocates a holistic notion of curriculum: 'The youth work curriculum includes the totality of the experiences, opportunities and challenges provided both directly and indirectly, for and by young people, through an organisation's method, structure and programme' (1997: 4). This conceptualisation 'places no emphasis on outcomes within his description of curriculum' (Ord, 2004a: 56). It is also developmental and draws on the Gloucester model of participation. Undoubtedly, Wylie's 1997 curriculum differs markedly from the version incorporated into *Transforming Youth Work* (2002).

Furthermore, in DES (1987) *Effective Youth Work* (which Wylie (2004) informs us that he is the author) he again gives credence to the open ended and unfolding nature of the youth work process which is absent from the more recent curriculum model. Smith describes *Effective Youth Work* as 'one of the last English government reports to promote open youth work' (Smith, 2003b: 1).

It would appear Merton and Wylie are pragmatists, as indicated by their admission that 'If it is to win sufficient resource from the public purse, youth work needs to articulate its purposes and methods clearly and it cannot choose the ground on which to do so' (2004: 66). Perhaps the course of the NYA is necessarily steered very close to current government policy. However, if one's pragmatic approach begins to undermine one's principles, which in curriculum, it would appear to be the case, then there must be cause for concern. The scope of the NYA to support, develop, and advocate on behalf of youth work would be hampered if it merely became a vehicle for government policy. As will become evident, the NYA are in fact in an unenviable position of trying to square a circle between supporting policies which run counter to youth work principles, but at the same time maintain a coherent supportive framework for the work, a job that often appears at times untenable.

Curriculum, accountability and 'New Public Management'

The change in curriculum policy at the NYA, as evidenced at least by the changes in the views of its chief executive Tom Wylie, coincides with the election of New Labour and the new agenda of *Transforming Youth Work*. This new agenda focuses heavily on accountability, and this can be seen as a continuation of New Labour's agenda of 'improving' public services, which has seen considerable changes to the working practices of education, health and welfare services since their election in 1997. This programme of change is premised on a particular form of accountability, one which is based on the pre-specification of outcomes and which when converted into targets, form the basis of the accountability. According to this rationale, without clear predictable outcomes specified prior to the activities of public sector work, like that of teachers or health workers, and now likewise youth workers, they cannot be fully accountable, and their practice cannot improve. The need for a product based model of the youth work curriculum can therefore be seen as a necessary part of this policy process.

Again the parallel with the original attempts to introduce the curriculum in 1989 by Howarth are evident. That formed part of a similar drive, from within the Thatcher government, to improve efficiency and accountability of public services, by introducing for the first time private sector business practices to the public sector. Perhaps part of the original antipathy to the notion of curriculum by youth workers at the time was the implicit assumption that youth workers would be expected to be more accountable, and that this accountability would not be on their terms.

Seen in the context of accountability, Merton and Wylie's model can now be fully comprehended. It is a model which is quite clearly orientated towards accountability. The principle behind this model, and the reason why it needs to avoid any notion of process within it, is that this model must allow specificity of inputs to outcomes, which a process approach does not. The necessary conditions of an acceptable youth work curriculum to a New Labour approach to accountability in public services must be product based, be linear in its conception and have a specific link between input and outcome (or output).

This approach to public sector 'improvement', often described as New Public Management (NPM) introduces a step change in the working

Figure 4.1.2   Systems approach to management (adapted from Cole, 2004: 75).

practices of a number of public sector organisations. This change is illustrated by an emphasis on efficiency and effectiveness, but is however most clearly defined by its commitment to a principle of accountability based on target setting. So whether that is formal education and its targets for the number of GCSE grade Cs, for example, or health professionals and their targets for waiting list times, all public sector work has increasingly, over the last two decades, been interpreted in terms of its ability to meet government specified targets. This has been far from universally welcomed, and for those who are opposed to it, it has been branded as 'managerialist' (Clarke et al., 2000). Managerialism is a pejorative term which implies a belief that the business practices of the private sector have been inappropriately imported into the public sector (Denhart, 2003).

New Public Management and the 'management' of youth work

There is little disagreement about the origins of NPM, that it is from private sector management theory and practice, the difference, which is considerable, is about the appropriateness or otherwise of its importation into the public sector. The theory of management which underpins NPM is a systems approach to management, illustrated by Figure 4.1.2 (adapted from Cole, 2004: 75). A distinction is made between open and closed systems models. However, both models are concerned with the conversion of inputs to outputs. The differences being that an open system is said to 'receive inputs or energy from their environment . . . (and) discharge their outputs to the environment (ibid.).

The comparisons between this model and the Merton and Wylie/DfES model are quite evident, see Figure 4.1.3.

The content is injected into the youth work session, converted through the delivery of educational group work into outcomes in terms of increased knowledge or skills, which are subsequently assessed. For example, in a sexual health awareness session, the content of knowledge and skills about how to use condoms is incorporated into a group work session and converted into increased awareness in young people about contraception, as well as a concomitant output of a reduction in teenage pregnancies.

When shown in their diagrammatic form and the comparisons made explicit between the systems management models and the curriculum proposed by Merton and Wylie, the reality appears to be that a model of curriculum has emerged because it fits into a managerial conceptualisation of youth work, not because it enhances our ability to comprehend youth work practice or for any other 'educational' reason.

This application of a systems approach to youth work has been elaborated by Ford et al. (2005) as part of the Ford Management Partnership (2003; 2005) one of whose stake holders is the NYA. They are integrated into the government's agenda of 'transforming youth services' and 'delivered a management development programme for youth work managers in England . . . on behalf of the DfES' (Turner, 2006: 100) and which trained a significant proportion of the senior youth workers and youth officers in England in 2003 and 2004. They work on the premise that: 'Most organisations use an open systems model to understand and monitor their performance. This

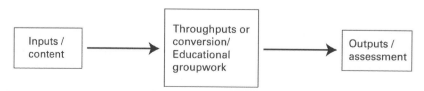

Figure 4.1.3   A comparison between 'systems management model' and Merton and Wylie's model of curriculum

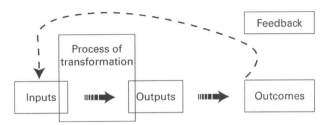

Figure 4.1.4 A performance model of management (Ford, Hunter, Merton and Waller, 2005: 163)

involves identifying input, the process of transforming input into output, and the outcomes these can lead to' (2005: 163). Their approach elaborates upon basic systems theory by incorporating a feedback loop (see Figure 4.1.4). It is entitled a performance model but it is basically concerned with the conversion of inputs to outputs, and is an adaptation of systems management theory. For Ford et al.:

Inputs are what goes into providing the service, usually the people, the plant and pounds including staff's knowledge and skills . . . The process is the variety of ways we work with young people (the heart of most youth work). The outputs are a measure of the activity that has taken place, such as the volume of service, range of activities and levels of achievement . . . The outcomes are the results our services have on the lives of the young people who use them. This might include progression to training or employment . . .

(2005: 164)

It should be remembered that this is a management model and not a model of practice per se. For example, the inputs as pounds spent or number of staff employed is to be distinguished from the notion of educational input which, as has been previously identified, is the responsibility of the proactive educator. However, as the model is designed to 'monitor performance', it has important implications for how practice is conceived, and for the basis upon which judgements about practice are made.

The problem of this approach is twofold. Firstly it conflates quantity and quality, and secondly it inappropriately incorporates linear causality to the process of youth work. These difficulties are most apparent in the conception of outputs and in the link between outputs and outcomes.

Youth work is a qualitative process, and a judgement of the efficiency or effectiveness of that process must be made on a basis that accurately conceives of that process. Crude calculations like

those recommended by Ford et al., such as 'The volume of outputs divided by the cost of the inputs gives you a measure of the efficiency of the activity' (2005: 164) does not allow for the subtlety of the process. The process is founded on the relationships between youth worker and the young people; as such it is not the number of staff 'inputed' into youth work that is important but the type and quality of the youth worker and their ability to engage with the young people concerned, as well as the quality of the relationships and interactions between the workers and young people.

Importantly, the relationship between the outputs and outcomes is also problematic. As Ford et al., themselves admit, their model 'involves . . . the process of transforming input into output, and the outcomes these *can* lead to' (my italics) (2005: 163). By their own admission therefore there is no necessary link between outputs and outcomes. This is an important point and goes to the heart of the difficulties of applying a causal analysis to a process of human interaction.

By their own admission this brings into doubt the relevance of outputs in any judgement about youth work practice. What is important are the 'outcomes' as well as an appreciation for the process from which they emerge. For example, what are the outputs in educational conversation? What is the relationship between output and outcome in an educational medium which is driven by conversation? A ludicrous but logical extension of their rationale would be the more conversations a youth worker had the more outcomes one would expect. So a youth worker must never pause, observe, listen, perceive because this would undermine the number of conversations they could have and therefore the potential to produce more outcomes. Clearly this is ridiculous but it is necessary to entertain such possible implications of this application of causal and mechanistic thinking to youth work practice.

It is exactly because the 'qualitative' aspects of human interaction contained within the youth work process cannot be quantifiably measured that this approach to monitoring performance is flawed.

Ironically Ford at el. acknowledge that: 'Youth work is a developmental process. It works through the relationship between youth worker and young person on a negotiated agenda of activities towards a broad curriculum' (Ford et al., 2005: 211). Furthermore they acknowledge that: 'There is a tension between this developmental approach and culture and the instrumental policy framework within which youth work is required to deliver pre-set results' (ibid.). What they have not done, despite this acknowledgement, is to articulate a framework for the management of youth work which adequately incorporates a conceptualisation of the process of youth work. Their approach has an instrumental and technocratic view of its operations. One should not be fooled by the terminology of 'process of transformation' as this is little more than systems theories' 'throughputs' and incorporates the crude analogy of the production line's conversion of inputs to outputs.

Contingency theory of management

Ford et al. assure us that 'Most organisations use an open systems model to understand and monitor their performance' (2005: 163). This does not necessarily mean that it is either correct, or the most appropriate. As will be seen shortly the setting of targets is universally utilised to 'improve performance' and targets do not in fact necessarily improve anything. It is possible that in fact a different approach is called for, one which accounts for the unique requirements and circumstances of the practices to which it is designed to manage. On this basis it is perhaps more suitable to take a 'contingency approach 'rather than a 'systems approach' to the management of youth work. Handy (1999) suggests a contingency approach which emphasises 'appropriateness of fit' between the circumstances of the practice to be managed and its management. A contingency approach according to Cole, 'deals in relativities . . . It is essentially a situational approach to management' (2004: 83). It would certainly seem to suggest that a contingency approach to management of youth work would be more likely to take account of the 'process' of youth work. It would advocate a conception of management which evolved out of the unique circumstances of the environment to be managed – solutions to problems and resulting management practices would be 'contingent' on the circumstances and unique situations of the practice concerned.

On Targets

It should not be forgotten that the driving force behind performance management in the public sector is accountability. Whilst its introduction is novel in youth work it has been around in formal education for a number of years, since the Education Reform Act 1988 and the introduction of the national curriculum. Its influence is apparent in what Bernstein (1996) calls the 'performance' mode of pedagogic practice (cited in Kelly, 2004: 71). This approach is the dominant ethos of the national curriculum. Kelly describes this as a combination of a content and objectives approach, whereby content selection is the starting point. The objectives approach is then the methodology for the delivery, whereby the content is broken down into 'bite sized pieces', from which attainment targets are derived.

This model has a number of negative implications, not least those associated with content and objectives (or product) approaches which we have already considered previously. What Kelly describes as 'The worst of both, all of the inadequacies which we have identified as features of both models – in particular, the inequalities, the potential disaffection and alienation of the content model, and the behaviourism, the instrumentalism and the loss of a genuine concept of education of the objectives model' (2005: 71). In addition it also introduces the spectre of targets into education, which as Kelly rightly describes: 'To plan by targets is to place all of the emphasis on quantity rather than quality' (2005: 59).

New Public Management (NPM) and impact of targets

Despite all the changes in the new climate of youth work, heralded by New Labour to date, it is the introduction of targets that have the potential to do the most harm, and undermine the process curriculum of youth work.

Targets are essentially politically motivated. They serve the political purpose of evidencing 'improvement', but this improvement is only based on the specification of the narrowly defined target and importantly only equates to an improvement in that particular area even if the target is genuinely achieved. The problem is workers responsible for the achievement of the targets cannot be seen to be failing to achieve them. This has the combined effect of skewing provision to ensure that the maximum time and effort is spent working towards the target, and secondly, if necessary fabricating evidence to ensure that they are in fact met. Targets in youth work have not been in existence for long enough for them to have worked through the system, but it is without doubt that sooner or later representative bodies such as APYC (Association of Principal Youth Officers) or CYWU (Community and Youth Workers Union) will be debating the pressure put on their members to achieve targets, the effects this has on the quality of practice and perhaps even the inevitable fabrication of evidence. For example, youth workers being held responsible for the 'anti-social behaviour' of young people in the local community, who have been banned from youth clubs because they don't wish to take part in the 'programme' or workers fabricating aspects of the youth achievement awards to ensure the requisite number of 'passes'.

The problems associated with targets are already evident in professions like the health service with considerably more experience of the effects of targets. For example, where the retiring chair of the British Medical Association Dr Ian Bogle ferociously attacked the current government policy, saying, 'I am absolutely appalled by the cheating going on and by the Government having put human beings in such a position that they feel that to preserve their jobs (they must do it) . . . The pressures are obscene and the Government should be ashamed of itself for the consequences' (Bogle, cited in Hinsliffe, 2003 online). He goes on to suggest that provision has been skewed to such an extent that clinical need, the primary driver of health care, is no longer the most important factor: The driving force is the meeting of particular targets. For example: 'That targets for suspected cancer cases to be diagnosed within two weeks have drained resources from the treatment of confirmed cancer patients' (ibid.).

Bogle appears to have been vindicated, following recent criticisms of Stoke Mandeville hospital by the Healthcare Commission, the 'Health Inspectorate'. The commission directly attributed the deaths of 65 people following two outbreaks of the 'super bug' Clostridium Difficile to 'senior managers mistakenly prioritising government targets such as maximum waiting time (over basic hygiene)' (Lister, 2006: 4). Ironically however, it is the managers that are singled out for criticism, not the failings of the system of managerial targets within which hospitals have to operate.

Similarly, problems as a result of the introduction of targets has occurred in the police force: Davies, N. comments critically on the 'fiddling of figures' to ensure that crime figures are falling. He cites cases where 'offenders in police stations who agreed to have extra offences added to their list of crimes to be 'taken into consideration' (TIC) by the court . . . were guaranteed that their admissions would not incur any extra penalty' (2003 online). This served to write off unsolved crimes. He cites examples of cases in Nottinghamshire, Bedfordshire and Kent where the crime figures were consistently manipulated. For example: 'The Bedfordshire inquiry went on to find that 42 per cent of all the previous year's detections were achieved by using TICs, prison write-offs and claims that offences needed no further police action, three techniques which were riddled with evidence of 'a deliberate manipulation of facts to maximise detection figures" (ibid.).

It would appear that Michael Howard MP was right when he criticised 'The (*present*) government's obsession with targets for public services' (2003 online) saying 'They have distorted priorities, they have stifled local initiative, they have contributed to the feeling of disillusionment among doctors, nurses, teachers and police officers. They encourage cheating and they have actually diverted time and attention away from the task of improving frontline services.' (ibid.). There is a considerable degree of irony here though, given his previous involvement in the Thatcher government, which introduced private sector involvement in the public services in the first place.

NPM and its impact on youth work

Youth work had until relatively recently been immune from the influence of NPM. Its arrival was heralded with *Transforming Youth Work: Resourcing Excellent Youth Services (REYS)* (DfES, 2002). The most immediate impact of the resulting step change has been the arrival of targets for youth work. The most notable examples of which are:

- 25 per cent of the target population 13–19 reached (to reflect the cultural diversity of the community).
- Of the 25 per cent reached in the 13–19 target population, 60 per cent to undergo personal and social development which results in an accredited outcome.

(DfES, 2002: 16)

The *REYS* targets were amended after lobbying by the NYA and APYCO, and in a letter to Principal Youth Officers by Margaret Hodge (2003). The following targets have been in operation since 2004:

- 25 per cent contact with the resident 13–19 population (to reflect the cultural diversity of the community).
- A participation rate in youth work of 15 per cent of the resident 13–19 population.
- 60 per cent of participants in youth work gaining a recorded outcome.
- 30 per cent of participants in youth work gaining an accredited outcome.

The first target can, on initial appearance, seem to be innocuous and in some ways it can be applauded. Should youth work not be open to as many young people as possible? Should it not reflect the cultural diversity of the locality, and provision not be dominated by one group or another? Indeed REYS (DfES, 2002) appeared to be offering the resources to back up this expansion of access by recommending a minimum level of funding of £100 per head of the 13–19 population, a figure which, however, never materialised. As Barrett confirms, 'just 38 of England's some 150 authorities hit or exceeded the £100 per head youth service spending target in 2003–04' (Barrett, 2005).

'The devil' however is, as ever, 'in the detail', so what exactly is meant by 'reached'? Does this mean that 25 per cent of young people in a given locality must have met youth workers? What must this meeting contain? Must it be meaningful, and if so to the youth worker or the young person, and if so how are we to tell? Must the 'reaching' result in the formation of a relationship with youth workers? Have they been influenced by youth workers? Or have they learned something as a result of contact with youth workers?

The answers to these questions have been addressed in some respects by the NYA through the publication *Recording Young People's Progress and Accreditation in Youth Work* (Flint, 2005), within which Flint defines the terms of contact, participation, recorded outcomes and accredited outcomes, contained in these targets. They are, however, not explicitly referred to as targets, rather they are referred to as the 'four benchmarks' or 'performance indicators'. Perhaps the NYA, or the DfES will think workers will be less averse to them if they are not described as such, but let us not be under any illusions that they are, in fact, targets.

We must therefore critically reflect on these four targets in turn.

Target for 'contacts'

Flint (2005) explains that the notion of 'reaching young people' (DfES, 2002) has now been superseded by 'contact'. On behalf of the NYA she defines a contact as, 'The youth worker knows the name and face of the young person and is consciously building a relationship with them'. In addition they may 'attend events occasionally', 'seek information or advice' or 'may be involved in issue based session/s with a group at a school' (Flint, 2005: 2).

The notion of a contact approximates to the early stages of the participatory ladder that is integral to the youth work curriculum. There is an implicit assumption that a great many of the 'contacts' will continue on to become participants, but for some this will not be either necessary or needed. The notion of maximising contact is in some respects to be welcomed. For example the more young people who know about the activities or services on offer in a given locality, the more likely they are to access them. If a young person is known to the youth worker they are more likely to approach them if they are in need. However, this publicising aspect is explicitly excluded from the notion of a 'contact',

for example, school assemblies are excluded from the definition. Importantly also within a 'contact' youth workers are 'consciously building a relationship' and so a contact is quite explicitly at the start a youth work process.

This target does avoid the worst effects of maximising of youth work contacts, by emphasising the need for an aspect of relationship building, but a return to large scale leisure events which attract large numbers of young people enabling youth workers to get to know a significant proportion 'of names and faces' could be a consequence of this target. However, this is further mitigated by the second target relating to participation, that 15 per cent of the resident 13–19 population are expected 'to participate' in youth service provision.

Target for participation

It should perhaps be welcomed that at least if youth workers are going to be set targets they are for something that is distinctively youth work, which participative practice clearly is. Participation is, as we have seen, one of the essential elements of the youth work curriculum. In relation to this target, Flint defines participation as, 'A young person with whom the youth worker has an on-going relationship, and . . . is involved with or attends youth work sessions or activities on a regular basis and is participating in a youth work curriculum in some way or takes part in a concentrated experience . . . such as a residential' (2005: 2). This definition is a little vague and does not do justice to the active nature of participation, the degree of engagement and power with which a genuine 'participant' in youth work is responsible for. Indeed, the participants within Flint's definition could be relatively passive, and never progress very high up the participative ladder.

A further problem within Flint's definition of participation is the concept of curriculum contained within it. It follows the partial and product based curriculum previously proposed by the NYA and DfES. Implicitly therefore curriculum is something which is partial and separate, injected into sessions by youth workers. This in turn is used to define the difference between a contact and a participant. This is a false distinction. Does the worker behave differently when they are making 'contacts', to when they are working participatively? No – youth work is always informed by certain values and procedural principles which define its curriculum. Furthermore as there are very often young people who are defined as contacts in the same sessions as those who are participants one cannot therefore use the curriculum (product based or otherwise) to specify the difference between the two.

Flint and the NYA admit themselves that 'judgement' is required in deciding on the difference between a participant and a contact: 'The decision about whether a young person is participating in youth work is essentially a matter of judgement' (Flint, 2005: 14). There is, however, not a tight, definable distinction between contact and participant. They are not mutually exclusive. A line has been drawn in the participation ladder which is not quantifiable, not least because the same participant can move up and down the ladder and switch between levels. In principle, therefore, one could switch from being a participant to being a contact, but this is nonsensical as one can't undo a relationship. It is true that a young person cannot participate in youth work until they have made contact with a youth worker or they have made contact with them, but that is not to say that the transition from one to the other is quantifiable in the sense in which it is being proposed.

There is an extent to which the NYA on behalf of the DfES is quantifying the unquantifiable. By the NYA's own admission, 'Only the worker on the ground can judge the level of involvement and engagement a young person has with youth work . . . further definition cannot be given that will cover the variety of circumstances in which young people engage with the curriculum . . . and participation cannot be further defined by a number of sessions and/or a length of time of attendance' (2005: 14). The NYA have squared the circle by producing quantitative targets for a concept which is necessarily qualitative in nature – the fact that a judgement is required to assess the level of involvement is evidence of this, that is, a judgement is required because it is not quantifiable. This anomaly demonstrates an irrationality underpinning these targets which makes the whole enterprise highly questionable.

Target for recorded outcomes

That the participation target is unquantifiable is implicitly acknowledged by the third target

which relates to recorded outcomes of: '60 per cent of participants in youth work gaining a recorded outcome'. Flint specifies that recorded outcomes must show 'actions taken by (a) young person, their progression and distance travelled . . . and be clear about the achievement, learning gain and end product'. Also it must 'be meaningful . . . it must confirm the achievement of a declared objective that is significant for that individual young person' (2005: 2). This is quite obviously a demand on youth work to quantify its benefits or outcomes.

How problematic this demand is depends on how it is conceived of, in particular how is it expected that outcomes are to be arrived at? Are they allowed to emerge out of a process of youth work, or are they expected to be pre-specified and planned for, as such recorded outcomes themselves at least have the potential to be part of an authentic youth work curriculum. The extent to which there is an expectation on youth workers to have specified content, plan the input and transmission of that content to the young people, and convert that content into specific outcomes, returns us to the original questions about both the dominance of a product approach to curriculum, as well the problems we have seen with this approach.

The setting of targets for recorded outcomes also inevitably begins to introduce some of the problems of targets themselves; like the skewing of the provision in order to ensure they are met. The size of the target will be an important factor in this as well as what actually counts as a legitimate outcome. However, with the recorded outcomes target, like with many other targets, there is a prioritisation of quantity over quality. Who should say that 100 outcomes with middle class, able bodied, white, male high academic achievers is necessarily better than 10 outcomes with a group of young people who are from a vulnerable or disadvantaged group in society with whom it may take much longer to achieve success? There is clearly a qualitative difference.

Another potential negative effect of the recorded outcomes target is that it may affect who youth workers work with. There may well be a tendency to work with the more compliant, those that one can most easily show progression with, and those with whom it is easy to build a relationship. Furthermore, it is detrimental to practice to set targets for outcomes which require that each of the recorded outcomes must be with different young people. Once one individual has completed an 'experience' or 'achieved' something which has been recognised by a youth worker and entered as a recorded outcome, the onus will be on the worker to ensure their focus shifts onto other young people. The young person cannot count as a recorded outcome for statistical purposes until the following year, so the incentive on the workers if they prioritise their targets (which inevitably they will have little choice not to) is to switch their focus to other individuals or groups. This is clearly inconsistent with a process approach and potentially ignores the needs of the young person concerned.

In addition to the problem with the target itself, the recorded outcomes target begs a number of questions about the whole notion of outcomes in youth work which we will spend sometime looking at in the next chapter, but before doing that we must take a critical look at the last of the targets; that of accredited outcomes.

Target for accreditation

The benefit of recorded outcomes is that they do not need to be established through a formal accreditation programme, unlike accredited outcomes, which Flint (2005) defines as: 'A young person must have successfully completed one or more modules of a nationally recognised award or a local award which carries accredited status' (2005: 6).

It is the accreditation target, however, which has the most profound impact on youth work practice. Although accreditation is certainly not anathema to youth work, Huskins (1996) had previously developed an accreditation programme known as Youth Achievement Awards which allowed progression through four awards, achieved through increased participation, and the Duke of Edinburgh has for many years been a significant vehicle for the development of young people. Accreditation was however a relatively small and peripheral aspect of the totality of youth work. This target is an unnecessary importation of accreditation into mainstream youth work practice which is neither wanted, nor needed.

Why has this occurred? The reason is twofold: Firstly, it is, as far as the government is concerned, the best means by which accountability for any of the so called changes, or benefits, that youth work claims to have brought about – its outcomes, can be verified and justified.

It is argued that if the achievement or learning merits the awarding of an externally validated certificate it is more likely to be authentic. That this should be required is in part based on the unquantifiable nature of the three previous targets, and we have seen that the contact and participation targets require a judgement, likewise with the recorded outcomes which require a 'subjective judgment . . . to be made in assessing what constitutes a significant objective for each young person' (Flint, 2005: 2).

The context for the second reason for this importation of accreditation into youth work is New Labour's 'Welfare to Work' policy. New labour see 'joblessness' as a primary determinant of poverty and welfare reforms are as much geared towards getting people into work as they are to reform benefits (Exell, 2001). It is presumed no doubt in the corridors of Whitehall that it is all very well that youth workers are facilitating changes in young people, particularly those on the periphery of society with limited formal qualifications, but how is this going to enable them to get a job? The 'wisdom', or otherwise, of the importation of accreditation lies in the perceived increase in employability of the young people who receive them. This is clearly evidenced by the explicit criteria for an accredited outcome: 'Have currency/credibility outside youth work . . . and where possible, a link to employment, education or training' (Flint, 2005: 6). Perhaps government was in part influenced by the esteem that the Duke of Edinburgh gold award has, but this is unique not least because a limited number of young people achieve it, and invariably they are not under 19 years old.

The very real problems of incorporating accreditation schemes into youth work provision have not been considered. There is a distinct lack of fit between the informal approaches of youth workers and the formality of many accreditation programmes. The spontaneous and developing nature of the youth work process cannot be married with the following of a syllabus of an accreditation framework. It is to be welcomed that the target was reduced from its onerous 60 per cent to 30. However, the introduction of a formal accreditation syllabus will inevitably have a detrimental effect on the convivial nature of youth work, and therefore negatively effect who will choose to be involved. It is perhaps the case that the development of local accreditation awards mitigates against some of the more restrictive elements of some accreditation programmes. However, it should be remembered that these awards have been developed in the main to enable authorities to meet their targets, despite any claims that they are worthwhile and valuable in their own right.

There is a dilemma that underpins any attempts to increase the level of accreditation in youth work, and thereby undermine its potential, and it is also true that workers can often be surprised at the genuine meaning attached to young people's receiving of certificates, especially for those young people with low self-esteem and for those who have achieved little in their lives. However, the dilemma is that their worth is correlated with their previous lack, and therefore they must be given out relatively sparingly in order to preserve their worth – if everyone gets a certificate they become meaningless. This also correlates with the employability that accreditation is thought to aid; it is probably the case that the Duke of Edinburgh Gold award is held in some esteem by employers but that is in no small part due to the fact that so few attain it.

Further criticisms of targets

Bloxham (1993) commented on the 'technocratic' concentration on outcomes in youth work, interestingly well before the effects of the *Transforming Youth Work* targets, but similarly suggesting that the 'bureaucratisation' of youth work, far from improving practice, actually reinforces poor practice. She cites Mintzberg (1979), suggesting that increases in managerial controls affects 'The standardisation of work processes and standardisation of outputs . . . are in direct contradiction with traditional youth work practice (and) that not only does it fail to improve the work of incompetent staff, it also damages the work and motivation of competent staff' (1993: 8). Bloxham goes on to explain how poor workers merely re-describe their poor practice in terms of the required outcomes. For example, 'workers re-describe football as developing teamwork and constructive use of conflict' (1993: 9).

Although the targets are relatively new, the research into detached and outreach work by Crimmins et al. (2004) undertaken on behalf of the Joseph Rowntree Foundation, has already uncovered some of the predicted deleterious effects. Spence (2004), who was part of that research team, notes that the targets are already

having a detrimental affect on practice. Workers are already admitting to 'creative accounting', and she notes a shift in focus on what is regarded as 'objectively important', where the observable and measurable changes such as the acquisition of cooking skills was taking precedence over some of the more important but less substantive changes in personal development, like a young person's ability to maintain eye contact.

The impact of these targets is that they inevitably skew provision, in particular, through the need to meet the accreditation targets. Individual youth centres are now being given accreditation targets to meet. For example a youth and community centre in a suburb of Plymouth known as the Rees Centre, which is open to young people between the ages of 13–19 on four nights per week, was set a target of 129 accredited outcomes in 2004/05 (Rees Youth and Community Centre, 2005). Inevitably youth workers in those situations will be forced to choose to work with those young people with whom it is deemed will be willing and able to commit to an accredited learning programme.

Those young people who are more suited to a formal accredited programme are not necessarily those who are in the most need. As such the skewing of provision through accreditation targets runs counter to the needs based approach of youth work. There is no means for allowing a process to develop out of which needs emerge and a programme be developed through which they can be met. The curriculum, which stresses accreditation, being promulgated from the DfES is little more than an off-shoot of formal education, which runs counter to the person centred, process based curriculum of youth work. The problem is, as Spence notes, 'Although TYW takes recognisable youth work concerns as its key themes, (e.g. participation, citizenship, curriculum) it mobilises these concepts to set targets and specify outcomes which are related to, but do not derive from youth work itself' (2004: 262), although in the case of the accreditation the relationship is even more spurious.

Targets, accountability and youth work

Whilst the rhetoric of NPM might focus on improving performance, the reality is it is principally concerned with accountability.

Stenhouse noted this with the rise of the objectives approach and the rising dominance of curriculum as product:

> What are your objectives is more often asked in a tone of challenge than one of interested and helpful inquiry. The demand for objectives is a demand for justification rather than simply description of ends. As such, it is part of a political dialogue rather than an educational one. It is not about curriculum design, but rather an expression of irritation in the face of the problems of accountability in education.
>
> (1975: 77)

The targets set for youth work are an explicit attempt to make it more accountable. The information on the performance of each local authority will be collated by the NYA in the annual returns (Flint, 2005) and presumably be available to the DfES. The opposition to these targets is not because youth work is against accountability per se, however 'accountability can only be worthwhile if its criteria reflect the realities of practice' (Spence, 2004: 270). One of the problems is that the relationship between accountability and outcomes has become too close, they are mutually exclusive, and they are becoming synonymous. There is a conflation of qualitative education benefits with the quantitative demands of accountability. What is needed is a separation of accountability from pedagogy; one does not choose ones pedagogy based on its best fit with a system of accountability. Nor does one change the practice of youth work to fit a system of accountability (Ord, 2004b).

Accountability and the process of youth work

The process of youth work does raise important problems in terms of the accountability of youth work, and Stenhouse (1975) noted similar problems with the process curriculum for formal education. Certainly the youth work process is not compatible with how accountability is framed within current policy with an emphasis on targets, which only consider the legitimacy of measurable outcomes, and which invariably are required to be specified in advance and be attributable specifically to identifiable inputs.

Tony Jeffs, commenting on the problems of accountability and measurable outcomes for youth work, claims 'there is a need . . . to trust informal educators and give them freer rein to plan their work. It is an act of faith' (Jeffs cited in Burke, 2004). Jeffs has a point, but it is however only half the story, as importantly it is not an act of 'blind faith' as Jeffs seems to imply, but an act of faith in the process. It is the process which youth work should be accountable for and not the process of youth work changed, or overridden to fit a model of accountability.

An element of this rationale already exists in the 'Ofsted's revised framework for inspection', in that services are held to account for the quality of the relationships which staff have with young people. This forms part of their assessment of the 'Quality of Education Provided', in how they '. . . establish and sustain positive relationships with them . . .' (Ofsted, 2001a: 8). Some recent examples include:

Quality of Education Provided (point 2)

> In most provision youth workers had good relationships with young people.
>
> (Bradford Ofsted Report, *Ofsted*, 2002a)

Quality of Education Provided (point 4)

> Staff were caring, patient and committed to the development of young people. Their relationships with young people provided a firm basis from which they could challenge and encourage.
>
> (Cornwall Ofsted Report, *Ofsted*, 2001b)

Quality of Education Provided (point 4)

> Experienced and tenacious staff, including many who work part time have, over time, developed very good relationships with young people.
>
> (Manchester Ofsted Report, *Ofsted*, 2003)

Quality of Education Provided (point 3)

> Relationships with young people were always good. Outreach and detached youth workers were particularly skilful in engaging with vulnerable young people and developing a level of trust that enabled them to offer support and guidance to those at greatest risk of social exclusion.
>
> (Wirral Ofsted Report, *Ofsted*, 2001c)

Some reports also make reference to relationships when assessing the 'Educational Standards Achieved', for example in the inspection of Wirral Youth Service:

> In all projects and units, their relationships with youth workers and with each other were very good.
>
> (Wirral Ofsted Report, *Ofsted*, 2001c)

Accountability for inputs

Youth work can be accountable for the quality of its educational input, the quality of the process of the learning environment, the preparations youth workers make in enabling and facilitating discussions, the extent to which they develop participative practice, as well as the creative methods employed in providing vehicles for learning.

Youth workers can of course be accountable for their outcomes, but the problem remains that not all their outcomes are visible (Williamson, 2004). The problem with outcomes however, is as much a problem with an insistence on their pre-specification, as it is with the outcomes themselves. The problem with the implementation of curriculum as product is as much a problem of planning as it is with evaluation. That is a problem which results from a belief that outcomes can only be legitimately derived from specifically planned intentions. Some of the problems of outcomes for youth work are mitigated if at least youth work is permitted to utilise their **emergent outcomes** as a legitimate basis for their work. It is to outcomes however that we must now look in more detail.

On Outcomes

Traditionally, youth workers have perhaps not been the best at articulating the benefits of their practice. This could be because youth workers are always immersed in the process. It is always to some extent unfinished business as the process of learning and developing is never ending, and therefore it is difficult to find end points. Often the most obvious end point is when young people move on and stop attending but then there are always other young people who become a focus of concern and attention. Sometimes it is simply a question of a lack of time to reflect on the benefits of particular activities or practices. Also reflection and analysis is often done in the moment (Schon, 1987), action taken, amendments to plans made, learning identified and applied, and then the process moves on.

There is little doubt that the changes implemented to the conception of youth work are not all negative. As Kelly points out in his observations about product approaches to formal education, despite his substantive criticisms, he identifies 'That the objectives movement has rightly drawn our attention to the importance of being clear about the purposes of curriculum' (2005: 74). Similarly, the current climate in youth work has rightly drawn our attention to the need to be clearer about outcomes.

As Dave Phillips, NYA development officer, states, 'The challenge is to get workers that are passionate about how they work alongside young people to become equally passionate about how they record their work' (2005: 10). It is in everyone's interest, youth workers, funders, the local community, politicians and especially young people that we are clear what the outcomes of the work are. Phillips goes on to suggest however that 'A prerequisite for any recorded outcome must be a conversation between a young person and worker in which the young person can recognise the learning that has taken place and agrees that it is meaningful to them' (ibid.).

This, however, conflates 'learning' with 'the conscious recognition or acknowledgment of that learning'. What if a young person has stopped doing something that they were either too ashamed to admit, or are in denial of, like bullying or shoplifting but through a period of engagement in a youth project they had stopped. Perhaps their attention was directly or indirectly drawn to the consequences of their behaviour, perhaps they had taken on a role model who would clearly not approve of the previous behaviour. Must a condition of a youth work outcome be a conscious recognition by the young person of that change? Clearly not, since a behavioural change is still a behavioural change regardless of the degree of awareness the person has about the change that has been made. That is not to say there would not be advantages to having a conversation about the change, at an appropriate time, but to equate the change with the recognition of the change is a fallacy. To think that all learning and development is as a result of conscious and intentional decision making is fallacious. With some aspects of learning and development in personal and social education, for example with the effects of role models, there are unconscious and conscious processes at work.

One possible motivation for Phillips' committing this fallacy arises from a desire to overcome the problem which arises from the lack of necessary causality between input and outcome in youth work; as we can never know with any certainty whether a youth worker's intervention had that particular effect and produced that particular outcome. Young people themselves therefore can solve this problem by substantiating the claim – there is the proof. The problem even then is however, how do we know they are not simply telling us what we want to hear? The fact is, as Merton and Wylie (2002) were right to point out, the outcomes of youth work are derived from a judgement. Any causality is at best an 'inferred' and not a direct causality.

The lack of specificity of input to outcome

The source of the problem in identifying outcomes and the difficulty in establishing causality is the lack of specificity between input and outcome in youth work.

This is perhaps best illustrated by the following illustration. It is widely accepted that youth work is concerned with personal and social development, an example of which may be the influence of kindness. Few would argue, that as a rule, if you genuinely show kindness, care and attention to someone consistently and reliably over time this will have a beneficial effect on how the recipients of that behaviour will feel about themselves, they are more likely to think of themselves as worthy of care and their sense of wellbeing will probably improve. They will also probably behave towards others 'with kindness', and the quality of their relationships with others will improve.

It is a different thing to argue that as a result of specific acts of kindness one can specify outcomes in terms of a person's wellbeing. If one makes this assumption one is guilty of the fallacy of arguing from the general to the specific. It is certainly the case that each individual act of kindness played a part in the overall behavioural change but it is impossible to say which one was most important, if in fact, there was one. It is also difficult to say at which stage in the process the changes or learning had taken place.

The first description is a general rule relating to a process of interaction and of the process of development which has broad outcomes. Importantly, one can only even begin to be specific about the outcomes in terms of the degree of change and make judgements about end products after the event. The product model of the youth work curriculum in requiring the prior specification of input and in the prior specification of the resulting product or outcome fails to account for the complexities of people, and the complexities of learning associated with the personal and social development. Personal and social development is necessarily complex and the process of youth work reflects this.

A distinction must be drawn between the 'open-ended/person-centred educational process' contained in the youth work curriculum in practice, with the 'outcome based model' proposed by Merton and Wylie. Youth work is not about producing specifically predetermined outcomes, it is about the personal and social development of young people, the outcomes of which emerge out of a process of engagement.

The relationship between outcomes and process is further illustrated by what Smith (1988)

refers to as the 'incidental' nature of learning, that is the learning or outcomes in youth work develop out of a process but are indirect. They are a consequence of the process, but he concurs are not necessarily specifically attributable to any particular part of it. Learning results from purposeful activity, but does not directly result from a single or series of specific inputs. The learning is not accidental but 'incidental'. The acquisition of social skills is like this, for example, in how young people learn to appreciate each other. It is learning which will derive out of a process of interaction over time. Even if each individual involved could attribute their learning to a specific incident within that process, where perhaps their need was met specifically by someone's intervention, in truth the change is most likely to be due to a complex interplay of a number of factors and incidences. Even if this was the case it is another thing to suggest that one could have anticipated such an eventuality and planned the activity accordingly, having previously specified this as a desirable outcome.

The process 'paradox'

Within the notion of process, outcomes are often best described as 'emergent'; they emerge out of the process as they are not necessarily related to any one particular intervention or series of interactions. This is in part due to the nature of the outcomes themselves, particularly those related to personal and social development. These outcomes are 'aspects of a person', they are not things which can be taught directly, like the learning of skills which has been shown is more suitable to a product based approach.

One of the problems with the product approach to curriculum, evident in Merton and Wylie's model, is there is a conflation of the outcomes of personal and social development with the notion of skills. Learning in personal and social development as we have seen is not linear, and the outcomes invariably cannot be reduced to specific inputs. This is exemplified in relation to 'confidence'.

Whilst it makes sense to say a youth worker is working towards building the confidence of the young people they are working with, how would we apply Merton and Wylie's concept of curriculum as Content, Pedagogy, of Educational Group Work and Assessment to this legitimate youth work aim? What would the content be like?

What miraculous educational group work session could 'produce' confidence? A youth worker could do the sorts of things that are intended to 'build confidence', and over time, all things being equal, they should. But there is an important distinction. Confidence is not a tangible 'thing' which is taught. It is not produced through the subtle manipulation of group dynamics. It can not be assessed like the skill of DJ-ing.

Confidence is not a skill at all, though it is often implicitly, and sometimes explicitly wrongly referred to as one (Berry, 2001; Huskins, 2003). That is part of the problem. Confidence is a human attribute, or characteristic, not a skill. According to Ryle (1949) this would be described as a 'category mistake': A conceptual error 'made by people who did not know how to wield the concepts (and) arose from (an) inability to use certain items in the English vocabulary' (1949: 19).

Category mistakes have important implications as they fundamentally affect our understanding, as, in this case, it results in a misconception of what it is to be a person. It makes sense to say in a given situation one is feeling confident or not. One may say one is either a confident 'person' or not. One can learn to be more confident, but one does not acquire that confidence like one acquires skills. The same models or methods of teaching the acquisition of skills cannot be applied to learning in personal and social development. The benefits of personal and social 'development', which are characteristics of a person, cannot fit into a model of learning skills.

Confidence emerges out of the youth work process; it is not reducible to its inputs. Indeed, if one tried explicitly to build someone's confidence it is quite possible that it would do the reverse, by putting someone on the spot, singling them out and focusing on their deficits. Brent (2004) gives a good example of the emergence of this type of outcome in youth work in his description of 'The smile'. He describes how a young girl who he calls Kelly changes during her time at the youth club. Initially she is a 'shadowy appendage of her boyfriend. She looks miserable and unhappy . . . Gradually she gets to talk a bit . . . she starts confiding to one staff member' (2004: 70). Kelly begins to explain her problems concerning her school, home life, eating; 'Problems for which we have no solutions.' Youth workers attempt to formally intervene to find her a flat, but this does not appear to be the real issue and it is quickly forgotten. Over time, she begins 'to smile', a transformation appears to have taken place and 'she throws herself into the life of the centre'. 'There has been no product, no target met, no plan completed, yet all the evidence points to there being a profoundly important personal outcome for Kelly' (2004: 70). To what can the smile be attributed? This is the important point. It makes sense to talk of youth workers taking an interest in her wellbeing, offering her support etc., in a broad youth work sense, within the concept of a process of engagement. It certainly does not make sense to start reducing the outcome to any one or a number of interventions.

This conception of the process is evidenced further by the recent analysis of self-esteem contained in *Self-Esteem and Youth Development* (Richards, 2003). This is a collection of papers from the seminar held at the Brathay Institute which contains analysis of, and responses, to Emler's research, *Self-Esteem: The Costs and Causes of Low Self-esteem*' (Emler, 2001).

Guidance is offered against the search for immediate outcomes in relation to objectives such as self-esteem:

> *When we adults attach ourselves too strongly and focus too closely on the behavioural outcomes then we fall into the trap of missing the relational opportunities offered by process work which is fundamental in enhancing self-esteem.*
>
> (Smith, B., 2003: 83)

Likewise in relation to facilitating changes in self-esteem the importance of the relationship is highlighted:

> *. . . the major factor that enables positive change to take place is the quality of the relationship between teacher and pupil, young person and youth worker.*
>
> (Peel, 2003: 57)

The lack of specificity of process to its outcomes, is exemplified by the examples of the smile, the analysis of confidence, and the recent work on self-esteem. This indirectness of end product to youth work input has always been seen implicitly as a problem. Smith (citing Brookfield, 1983) is quick to assure critics that the indirectness is not accidental and that the learning arises from 'much that is purposeful and deliberate' (Brookfield, 1983: 12–13). The youth work and informal education field has always been defensive about this state of affairs and the educational merits implicitly have been downgraded as a result of this lack of specific relationship between input and outcome, as is evidenced by the currency of terms like 'woolly' to describe the work.

In the analysis of confidence, or in the example of Kelly's smile, the focus is on 'the person', not the end point of increases in self-confidence or the production of a smile. The relationship is developed, the engagement with the person is genuine, interventions and interactions purposeful and meaningful and over time outcomes emerge. Importantly, it is only possible to achieve those outcomes if one does not focus directly on them. Clearly the interventions and interactions must be the kind of things that would ultimately support the development of those characteristics but the outcome is incidental to the process of achieving it, and it occurs specifically because one does not focus directly on its achievement. This is the **paradox** at the heart of the youth work process.

This kind of philosophical paradox is not new. A number exist which appear to underlie the circumstances of 'being human' (or our phenomenology), which illustrate this point. For example, John Stuart Mill was the first to identify a paradox in relation to the achievement of happiness:

> But I now thought that this end (one's happiness) was only to be attained by not making it the direct end. Those only are happy (I thought) who have their minds fixed on some object other than their own happiness . . . Aiming thus at something else, they find happiness along the way . . . Ask yourself whether you are happy, and you cease to be so.
>
> (Mill, 1909: 94)

Similar paradoxes exist in relation to success, self-realisation, hedonism etc. The point is that in certain aspects of our humanity, whether it be happiness, wellbeing, success or confidence, the achievement of it arises incidentally, as a result of engaging in a process. The process is instrumental in bringing about the end point but the focus is not on the end point in its achievement.

Thus the youth work process can be seen as paradoxical; not as loosely articulated and lacking in clarity, but in actually accurately describing something uniquely and necessarily human. If Brent (2004) had specifically set out to make Kelly smile, or achieve 'a profoundly important personal outcome for Kelly', it would have been impossible to achieve as focusing on

that end would have derailed the process, not least because a lack of genuineness would have been apparent to Kelly.

Far from being a weakness, the 'indeterminedness' is a necessary condition of 'process' learning in much personal and social development. In fact as well as being indeterminate, paradoxically for the process to be successful, it is often necessary to specifically *not* focus on the end point or the desired outcome to enable its achievement.

Perhaps Tiffany summarises this well when he suggests:

> Being obsessively focused on predetermined aims, however worthy, can make us blind to the very evidence we need to consider in order to be objective about relationship. Our quest for quality can, ironically, divert our attention from the very process that allows it to happen.
>
> (2001: 103)

Outcomes in curriculum documents

Outcomes are an important feature of youth service curriculum documents, although their incorporation differs considerably. For many their articulation is a means of communicating the broad benefits of youth work, consistent with a process approach, for others they are specific learning outcomes which are specifiable prior to engagement and equate to a product model of curriculum.

Process outcomes

In some curriculum documents it is evident that outcomes remain broad. As such they approximate to aims rather than objectives.

Rochdale's curriculum (2004: 11) 'has a range of core learning outcomes that can be used or adapted'. This is a list of 20 outcomes which include:

- Develop insight into their own attitudes and beliefs.
- Make informed choices and decisions and take responsibility for their actions and consequences.
- Express themselves clearly and understand their feelings and emotions.
- Become more aware of others and how people affect each other.

Merseyside similarly have a list of seven 'key learning outcomes' which include: 'Taking control and being responsible for their own lives' and 'Understanding how they work with others and how their behaviour affects others' (2004: 11). Hull Youth Service also have a list of seven learning outcomes which include: 'Experienced raised self-esteem and confidence' (2003: 19).

Finally Cheshire (2005: 2.2) have identified three objectives:

- To improve wellbeing of young people.
- To contribute to the achievement of young people.
- To support and develop the voice of young people.

These objectives, which in reality equate more accurately to aims, are described as the 'Cheshire way'. It is argued that they encapsulate the five outcomes of *Every Child Matters* (DfES, 2003), and this broad approach to outcomes is the only method by which Cheshire youth service articulate outcomes in their curriculum.

The identification of general outcomes which are worked towards in the 'process' of youth work can be subsequently specified in more detail, and recorded if necessary, 'after the event'. They emerge out of a process of engagement and cannot be specified in any detail prior to the development of that process. The facilitation of the general outcomes can be planned for but the detail emerges during the process. *Process outcomes are therefore emergent.* So a worker always has in mind as a procedural principle that young people's confidence is an issue to contend with and they are always mindful of the need to bolster it where necessary. But the details of any outcomes in relation to confidence emerge during the process of engagement with the young people.

As we saw in Chapter 2.4 the best example of a process approach is taken by the Isle of Wight (2000). Theirs is one of the few documents to have explicitly incorporated the notion of procedural principles in the framing of their curriculum (although they do not refer to them as such). Their curriculum areas do not contain guidance on the outcomes to be expected but on key questions which guide and interrogate practice and the process of working with young people on those particular topics or issues.

Isle of Wight do use the concepts of input, in terms of staffing, funding and resources, and

output in terms of 'the ability to deliver benefits to young people . . . developing specific skills, gaining knowledge and exploring their own attitudes, values and beliefs' (2000: 30). However, the use of these terms, more often associated with a managerial and product based approach, is inconsequential as they explicitly frame youth work around a process which is described as 'educative, participative, empowering (and promotes) equality'.

Finally, another way of incorporating outcomes which is consistent with a process approach has been devised by West Sussex (2000; 2005). Within designated curriculum areas they have guidance on 'good practice' as well as the identification of 'desirable outcomes'. For example in relation to gender issues:

- *Good practice is embodied in youth work which:*

- *Challenges gender role stereotyping.*
- *Creates opportunities for young men to discuss their inhibitions about expressing their emotions.*
- *Creates environments where women are respected.*
  (2005: 20)

Desirable outcomes are divided into 'Knowledge and Understanding', for example, 'Understands the full range of opportunities available to them'; 'Skills', for example, 'Can challenge sexist language and behaviour' (ibid.) and 'Attitudes and Values', for example, 'Feels comfortable taking part in a broader range of activities than traditionally encouraged' (ibid.).

Knowledge, skills and attitudes?

The approach to outcomes, which distinguishes between three 'central features of knowledge, skills and attitudes', was recommended by the *Big Red Book of the Youth Work Curriculum* (1990). It has been incorporated into a number of youth work curriculum, for example by Brighton and Hove (2005), Southend-on-Sea (2006), South Tyneside (2006), Tower Hamlets (2004) and Oxfordshire (2005) as well as West Sussex (2000; 2005) although in some cases this has been expanded to 'knowledge and understanding', 'skills', and 'attitudes and values'. This conceptualisation equates to the intellectual, physical and emotional spheres of learning. Southend describes this separation of outcomes into 'learning domains' and it may have its uses to begin to distinguish some of the differences in terms of possible outcomes but it should be applied with caution as it does not account for the entirety of practice.

Many of the outcomes of youth work are holistic and cannot be compartmentalised into the separate realms. For example, confidence and self-esteem, which are often seen as important outcomes of the process of youth work do not fit into any of those categories. Although it underlies or influences each of the separate realms, greater confidence might enable a young person to approach the learning of new skills differently, their attitudes to themselves and others would be significantly different with improved confidence, and one's self-knowledge may change with a growth in confidence. In addition the same outcome could be located in each of the different realms depending on how it is framed. A young person's ability to use the internet could be described in terms of increased knowledge and understanding of ICT, increased skills in ICT or indeed described as a change in attitude or value in an appreciation of the importance of ICT as a means of communication.

An approach to this conceptualisation of outcomes should be consistent with the approach adopted by Milton Keynes who suggest the following can be used as examples of:

> . . . *what young people get out of their participation in youth work, but they are not proposed as exhaustive categories:*

- *Knowledge* or *understanding about themselves; their identity, values, sense of self.*
- *Skills* in *making and managing positive relationships with peers or adults.*
- *Positive* *attitudes* *towards equality and diversity.*
> (their emphasis, 2005: 4)

Product outcomes

Some curriculum documents have been irrevocably affected by the dominant ethos of curriculum as product, and their articulation of curriculum has a clear commitment to a product approach. In these documents youth work is conceived of as a number of distinct and separate sessions in which each session is planned with a specific, previously identified objective, input is planned in order to best achieve that objective and evaluation is carried out to assess the

achievement of that previously specified learning outcome or objective.

Buckinghamshire (2004) for example, utilise both the NAOMIE Planning cycle (of needs identification, aims, objectives, methods, implementation and evaluation) alongside an emphasis on SMART objectives (specific, measurable, attainable, realistic and timetabled) in order to ensure that workers clearly plan for the specific products of their work. The use of such planning mechanisms, in particular the emphasis on SMART objectives, clearly runs counter to the fluidity and creativity of a process approach, and inevitably brings into play a number of the problems we have already highlighted with an exclusively product approach to curriculum.

North Somerset has similarly adopted a product based rationale to their curriculum. They have sub-divided their curriculum areas into between three and five 'subjects' and learning outcomes are derived from those. For example, the area of equality of opportunity is broken down into three 'subjects': Cultural awareness, understanding and awareness of race, gender, disability and other ways in which people are discriminated against, and lastly challenging stereotypes (2005: 13). This specification of content is not necessarily contrary to a process approach, as the delivery of the ideas and issues contained within this, particularly the identification of content, could be framed around procedural principles devised to explore the issues.

However, North Somerset's approach to the planning and delivery certainly appears to be exclusively product focused. This is evidenced most clearly by the 'session recording sheet' in the appendix to the curriculum (2005: 29–31). The session recording sheet makes no mention of the developing nature of the work. All the headings relate to that session: 'What do we hope to achieve?, What is planned?, What did you learn?' (ibid.). No mention is made of previous work, in terms of how this follows on from previous issues, or how this work might be continued. Reference is made to how 'it be improved' but this is specifically in relation to how this individual session might be improved and not how the work as a whole might be improved, or how the issues raised might link to the future.

The youth work in North Somerset's curriculum appears to be conceived largely as a series of separate and isolated learning inputs. It is certainly recorded as if this is the case. Recording of process based youth work must necessarily take account of both what precipitated the session (the past) as well as how this session is conceived of relating to the future. In addition, importantly, it must leave a significant proportion of any write-up to what emerged (often unexpectedly) through the process of discussion, dialogue and learning, not just on the outcomes which were specifically planned for.

Coventry also adopts a product approach for their curriculum. They define curriculum as: 'A planned educational programme designed to achieve a range of specified outcomes' (2004: 6) and go on to suggest that 'Effective youth work is conscious and deliberate and therefore must be planned' (ibid.). Also within the planning guidance, 'Curriculum Profile', workers are requested specifically to 'Describe the main objectives for this piece of work along with the *key learning outcomes* that you anticipate young people gaining through their involvement in this piece of work' (2004: 42, their emphasis).

In many ways it is not surprising that some youth services have been strongly influenced by the product model of curriculum given as Grundy (1987), amongst others, points out it is the dominant ethos, often to the exclusion of all others. In fact, many of the youth service curriculum documents have been influenced at least to some extent by the technocratic product model, which focus exclusively on the educators' ability to 'produce' intended learning outcomes. Planning cycles are prevalent and workers are explicitly encouraged to plan their work to enable them to achieve identified learning objectives.

Even some of those authorities, who appear to specify their outcomes in a manner consistent with a process approach, often have an additional expectation for the setting of project specific outcomes. For example, Rochdale maintain 'Where there is a curriculum theme being addressed within a project, learning outcomes should therefore be defined in order to measure young people's progress, their distance travelled' (2004: 11). What is of equal importance therefore, whether or not the overall framing of the curriculum is orientated to a product or process model, is the reality of youth worker's practice.

Youth work is a devolved practice where workers operate independently and largely autonomously. The question remains how do youth workers plan and deliver their own work?

'Planning' for outcomes?

Planning is not synonymous with a product model of curriculum. The process model does not advocate unplanned work. The question is whether workers are planning for the achievement of specific outcomes or planning to facilitate opportunities for learning to occur. The former focuses on specified knowledge or understanding, the latter on the promotion of dialogue, discussion and the asking of questions, within the context of an educational purpose. The crux of the matter is, within youth workers' own delivery, in individual centres and projects, are workers planning exclusively for the achievement of pre-specified outcomes or are they helping to organise activities or projects (participatively with young people) which will encourage and facilitate learning; the products of which will only become apparent during and after the event? The extent to which the curriculum is process or product based is as much a question of planning.

The recording of outcomes therefore, is not necessarily problematic in itself, especially without the contamination of targets, as they communicate the benefits of the work to the wider public and improve practice, giving workers a clear indication of what works. The extent to which they are problematic is dependant on the degree to which they are to be specifically planned for. If a product curriculum approach is applied consistently the youth work being delivered will be so far removed from its essential processes that it begins to approximate to formal educational instruction and becomes something other than youth work.

Before moving on to a discussion about the current youth policy and its influences on youth work and its curriculum, we must pause for a moment and clarify some outstanding issues in relation to outcomes in youth work, which often underpin some of the problems, that is, progression, measurability and youth work over time.

On Progression and Time

Of fundamental importance in the youth work process is the concept of time. Youth work necessarily takes place over time, in part because it needs time to develop. The relationships need to deepen. Trust needs to be established and clearly this cannot be acquired overnight, particularly when working with young people who find trusting adults difficult. Time needs to be taken to form relationships and then for those relationships to provide the platform for the process to develop.

So a group of young men may begin over time to drop the bravado and macho posturing which is common in their peer group and begin to reflect and explore their behaviour in the light of the vulnerabilities which they have until now consistently masked. Similarly a group of young women may begin to assert themselves as a result of a bourgeoning realisation that the roles they had previously accepted were not 'givens' but are nothing more than gendered constructions.

The 'process' by which these scenarios emerge is through the skilful intervention of effective youth work, 'being with' young people consistently, in a respectful relationship based on mutuality. We enter into conversations which sometimes offer support, sometimes challenge, but fundamentally is based on what Davies (2005) described as the principle that youth workers are there 'for young people'. The youth work process cannot be understood and therefore youth work itself cannot be understood without reference to a concept of time – not the time spent with youth workers in terms of the number of sessions or hours in some crude calculation; but genuine appreciation of a 'process of development through and over time'.

Progression and 'distance travelled'

Because of the time dependency of the youth work process the notion of progression is important when considering youth work outcomes. As a result the concept of 'distance travelled' by a young person has developed considerable credence in youth work. It is utilised explicitly in the curriculum of Suffolk (2002), Rochdale (2004) and Nottinghamshire (2005) who 'use case studies . . . to measure the distance travelled by young people as a direct result of the work we undertake with them' (2005: 34). Distance travelled is also incorporated by Flint (2005) on behalf of the NYA, as an important consideration when making judgements about recorded outcomes. The notion of distance travelled appreciates where a young person was at the start of the project and this becomes a bench mark against which any behavioural or attitudinal change can be gauged.

Whilst distance travelled is no doubt a valid consideration when attempting to ascertain the benefits of youth work it should also be considered that changes in young people's lives can occur in both directions, progressively or regressively, for good or ill. Distance travelled provides a useful means for measuring progressive development, but for some young people preventing decline is an equally important outcome which is much less quantifiable. This may be possible to evidence when, for example, a young person comes off drugs or stops committing crime, but in a sense that is also a positive change. Genuine 'preventative work' is in essence unquantifiable. How can one show the effects that would have occurred if a youth worker had not been working in a particular community for a period of time? As Tim Price, an Exeter youth worker suggests, (cited in White, 2005) 'You would have to close down the youth service for a couple of years to see if the figures went up or down'.

In addition, the thorny issue of young people's subsequent achievement, either after they have left the project or in later life, is the clearest example of the unquantifiable outcomes. Spence (2004) notes that little research evidence exists on the longitudinal benefits of youth work, and notes that this is an area which needs evidencing. Merton et al.'s (2004) research does collate some evidence of the benefits and outcomes of youth work, both in terms of personal and social development as well as the building of social capital, but they also acknowledge that one of the issues that need to be tackled '. . . (is) the development of a range of tools for measuring the benefits of what youth work achieves' (2004: 12). Anecdotally, youth workers can point to young people they 'know' would not be where they are without the intervention, support, opportunity and challenge offered by their work, but this has little influence on the 'measurability criteria' of policy makers.

Measurability

In the previous chapter we saw the problems being created for youth work by the increasing demands placed upon it to be accountable for its outcomes. Implicit within this assumption however is a belief that outcomes are measurable. The NYA (Flint, 2005) at least in part disagree with this belief by insisting that a judgement is needed to ascertain whether or not outcomes which are to be recorded have in fact been achieved or not, and furthermore that outcomes are in fact contextual and the worker in place is the best person to make that judgement. Much of this is the case and it is important that the NYA make this clear within their broad support for government policy.

There is an inherent difficulty in the measurability of any outcomes, as there is no control group with which to make a comparison. These are real events and circumstances in young people's lives. One can make a good case for having an influence over young people's lives and many will testify to this but one ultimately cannot prove it, in a similar way to the fact you cannot prove a negative. Measurability is inherently problematic.

One of the clearest examples of intangibility of outcomes is in relation to role models. Van Vark (2005) explores this complex issue, citing the Baroness Jay and Tessa Jowell MP, and she suggests that few would disagree that young people need positive role models. Van Vark also gives examples of the recent questions raised over the influence of the Spice Girls over young women and of the need to promote positive role models for young black men. It is widely accepted that all young people are at an impressionable age where positive influence is of vital importance.

Whether that influence be directly through the emulation of youth workers themselves, where young people look up to and respect what Young

(1999) refers to as the 'consistency' and 'moral integrity' of youth workers which underpins their ability to be good role models, or whether that influence is through the promotion of external or indirect role models, for example what Wandrum (cited in van Vark, 2005) attempts, in creating a 'hall of fame' for black teenagers to aspire to, she '. . . is keen to encourage black teenagers to consider a range of careers'. 'It is always music and sport' she says, 'you have to broaden their horizons' (ibid.).

Few would disagree with the laudable intentions of both direct and indirect role models and they are an accepted part of the process of youth work. They are, however, completely intangible and un-measurable, and one cannot imagine it being a legitimate element of a 'recorded outcome'. It is therefore of concern that such aspects of youth work which are less tangible, quantifiable and measurable will be undermined in the current climate. It is, as Williamson suggests, important that: 'the intangible and un-measurable outcomes of decent youth work . . . are not subordinated or forgotten' (2004: 15).

Measurability, outcomes and money

Underpinning the emphasis on measurability of outcomes is the overriding importance placed on the monetary valuations. White explains that politicians are overwhelmingly concerned with a cost benefit analysis: 'The money society spends on youth work salaries and the rest (are) 'inputs'. The benefit society gets back as a result of that spending is the 'output', and there you have youth work's 'value added'. This should appear in the national accounts' (2005: 16–17). The problem, of course, is as White admits, it would appear in the accounts 'if it wasn't so hard to measure' (ibid.).

Wylie (cited in White, 2005) suggests two ways in which youth work could be measured. Firstly, through a calculation of the costs of crime, an evaluation could be made of youth work based on an estimate of the number of young people who have been diverted from crime. Secondly, through the costs estimated from the benefits of volunteering. Merton (cited in White, 2005) also offers a cautious suggestion that the effects of increased employability could also be used. Whilst all of these examples could be utilised to give 'an impression' of the monetary value of youth work, this would be at best only an impression.

The fact remains that youth work is not quantifiable in the sense in which politicians would like it to be, in the same way as making a judgement about the value for money which a service it has inspected is judged to be providing. A monetary value on youth work like on any human endeavour is often spurious and demeaning. It clearly costs money to provide youth work, but the benefits of youth work, its value like that of education in the broadest sense, go far beyond costs and are not reducible to its mere monetary valuation. What is the cost of human happiness or endeavour? One is reminded of a Cree Indian saying, 'Only when the last tree has been chopped down and the last animal been killed will you realise you cannot eat money'.

The overwhelming concern with the monetary valuation of youth work (as well as most other aspects of public life) in contemporary governance, is another example of the effects of the inappropriate and unwanted concern with Techne over Phronesis in conceptualising human life. We encountered this in earlier criticisms of the product curriculum and it is relevant here again where aspects of human life are conceptualised as if they were products and tasks on which a monetary value can be placed and then presumably be traded in the market. As we have seen, 'Phronesis' is the term Aristotle (5th Century BC) used to refer to the form of human reasoning associated with the experiential realm and questions about how one would live a good life. It is opposed to 'Techne' which is the form of reasoning which refers to the making of products. Modern governance suffers from the mistaken assumption that 'Techne' or technological reasoning can be applied to all areas of human life.

'Being' and time

There is another aspect of time which is fundamental to the youth work process and this is perhaps best described as a process 'in time', or time as a symbolic process. As Heidegger (1927) rightly points out human beings are 'beings in time'. They are beings who are aware of themselves in time like no other creatures. They know they had a beginning in their birth and will have an end in their death. They also have a developing sense of awareness of both, where

they came from, their past, what and who they are now in the present, as well as who they will become in the future. For Heidegger, importantly, this results 'in our being itself', being 'an issue or a concern' to us. As a result ultimately therefore human beings are faced with a search for meaning. They must make sense of *their* world.

Youth workers work directly with these aspects of process. For example, young people discover aspects of themselves and their past and perhaps come to terms with both who they are and where they have come from. They explore issues in the present and respond to what is relevant in their daily lives as well as helping them to formulate plans for the future. Importantly, this is not simply in practical ways, they are symbolic, as Young points out: 'Youth workers conversations with young people are essentially about one thing, the development of young people's ability to 'make sense' of themselves and the world'. Youth worker's conversations with young people, therefore, provide those much needed opportunities for young people to deliberately and consciously examine their experiences and the meanings they compose for their lives' (1999:90). This is a further reminder of why, in fact, any outcome must always be seen in the context of young people's own lives and how they understand and come to terms with aspects of their own existence.

The importance of narratives

In terms of outcomes the 'meaning making' aspect of the youth work process, the ongoing process of young people making sense of their lives, is best made explicit and articulated within the youth work curriculum through the use of narratives. Narratives are the unique personal stories which both interpret and communicate, both to ourselves and others, the sense we make out of our lives both retrospectively to understand the past, and progressively to project ourselves into the future. They help to define who we are and what we will become. Narratives are therefore inextricably linked to our self-concept and our self-identity (Young, 1999; Giddens, 1991).

Narratives do feature explicitly in some curriculum documents. For example, Hampshire give 'an example of a young person's journey' (2003: 20–1) which reflects upon both issues from the past and concerns for the future.

Another important way in which narratives can be communicated is through case studies, and Sunderland (2003b) identify case studies as one of the best ways to evidence recorded outcomes. Narratives are an essential element of the youth work curriculum. They are person centred, holistic, defined by the young person themselves and retain the integrity and authenticity of a process approach to youth work.

Curriculum and Recent Youth Policy

Children's Act 2004: *Every Child Matters*

The green paper *Every Child Matters* (DfES, 2003) and the subsequent Children's Act 2004 has had, and continues to have, a significant influence on curriculum policy and practice. Many, if not all, youth services are at least modifying, if not wholly restructuring, their curriculum in terms of this new policy. As Bracey, principal youth officer for Southend-on-Sea admitted: 'We all agreed it (our curriculum) needed a major rewrite to bring it up to date to reflect the *Every Child Matters* agenda . . . the challenge for us is to demonstrate how youth work contributes to improving the five outcomes' (8–14 March 2006: 44).

Every Child Matters (ECM) is defined by its five outcomes, which were produced out of a consultation with young people. They are:

- Being healthy.
- Staying safe.
- Enjoying and achieving.
- Making a positive contribution.
- Economic wellbeing.

The *Every Child Matters* agenda has been incorporated into curriculum documents in a number of ways ranging from integrating the five outcomes into existing frameworks, in the cases of Brighton and Hove (2005) Wakefield (2006) Southend-on-Sea (2006) and Kingston (2005), or Manchester, for example, who have developed a number of 'entitlements' in response to the five outcomes, which they describe as the 'Process enabling the worker, in partnership with the young persons, to establish key priority areas of challenging, learning and development opportunities' (2005: 8). For example, in relation to 'Staying safe', they maintain: 'When something happens that threatens you we will try our best to provide immediate help, and support you in

making any decisions or taking actions that might be needed' (2005: 12).

Alternatively, some authorities have completely revamped the whole document with little apparent retention of what went before, as appears to be the case for Sunderland (2005).

The ease with which the outcomes have been incorporated is perhaps evidence of the relatively unproblematic nature of the outcomes themselves. In fact, Rochdale (2004) claim there is a 'clear fit' between their five curriculum themes and the five ECM outcomes: whereby 'self and relationships' equates with 'staying safe', 'equality' with 'enjoying and achieving', 'health' with 'being healthy', 'social issues' with 'economic wellbeing', and 'citizenship' with 'making a positive contribution'. Whilst this argument appears to be a little difficult to sustain in its entirety there clearly are parallels. Cheshire (2005) have devised what they call the 'Cheshire way' which focuses on three primary objectives of 'well being', 'achievement' and 'youth voice' which they maintain contribute to all five of the ECM outcomes. Hounslow (2005) are confident that their 10 curriculum themes contribute 'to the likelihood of them' achieving the five outcomes.

Not all authorities have altered their curriculum, however, and there are some notable exceptions. For example, West Sussex (2005) Issue No.5, is a development of their original 1989 document, but is entirely consistent with it and makes no mention of the ECM five outcomes or any other current youth policy. Similarly Devon (2006) is largely consistent with their (2002) version, and there is little mention of ECM. Their acknowledgement of ECM is through a separate document *Every Child Matters: The Youth Work Contributions to the Five Outcomes* (Devon, 2005). This charts the contribution the service makes to the five outcomes through case studies of particular projects throughout the county. It describes seven projects ranging from young parents work to graffiti art and explains the contribution these projects make to the five outcomes. The test for Devon, West Sussex and the other services that have not wholly altered their curriculum will be the judgements made on their documents by the Joint Area Review and Ofsted inspections.

What the above shows is that the outcomes themselves have not necessarily altered how youth work conceives of its practice or the outcomes of it. In addition, the lack of opposition to the appearance of the *Every Child Matters* outcomes compared to its sister policy *Youth Matters* (DfES, 2005a) which has generated considerable opposition, as well as to its predecessor *Transforming Youth Work* (2002), is further evidence that the ECM outcomes at least approximate to some of the key purposes of youth work.

The 'five outcomes' themselves approximate to aims not objectives, as they are largely the kind of outcomes which are on-going, and to some extent unachievable and never ending. Being healthy and staying safe, for example, are not things that are achieved as single entities, they are facets of living which need constant attention. Even 'economic stability', although it might at first appear definitive, in that if a young person acquires secure employment, this outcome is 'ticked off'. In actuality, their ability to budget, manage their spending etc., is on-going. The fact that no job is a job for life means that to some extent, the instability of the job itself, results in the outcome at the very least needing constant monitoring. Similarly, though the job itself may be secure, it may be questionable whether the young person is able to manage the ups and downs of their life in a way which enables them to fulfil the obligations of the employment and actually keep the job.

As such, therefore, the outcomes themselves are not incompatible with a process approach. They would in fact have to be translated into objectives to be suitable for a product model of curriculum. The issue remains, however, as to what model of curriculum would be utilised by individual services to *produce* or *work towards* these outcomes. For example, within a product approach, are youth workers expected to plan every session to meet one or other of the five outcomes, or is it accepted that the five outcomes will emerge out of the process of youth work?

How youth workers interpret the outcomes is also important. Will they 'go looking' for the outcomes and if so, how far will this skew provision. How accountable will the workers be in terms of these outcomes? How many of the outcomes will each young person be expected to meet? And how often will they be expected to have evidenced them; in every session, once a year? Will each youth work session be expected to contribute to all of the outcomes or will particular projects 'specialise'? It is not the outcomes themselves which are necessarily problematic, but their application and most importantly their links to accountability.

Another question remains, as to whether the framing of these outcomes is conceived of as the sum total of the focus of the work, or as the National Curriculum has become (Lawton, 1996) conceived of as a minimum, from which individual schools (or in youth work's case individual projects) expand upon and respond to individual need accordingly. Some documents clearly do not see the five outcomes as covering the entirety of the content of youth work. For example, Reading (2006) give as much importance to 'promoting equality' and 'celebrating diversity' as they do the five outcomes. In addition, the fact that the five outcomes are general and broad, and importantly no targets are derived from them, allows flexibility and creativity in response to them.

Children's Trusts and inter agency working

The second key feature of the Children Act 2004 is the establishment of Children's Trusts, which amount to a radical restructuring of all services to young people. Compulsory by 2008, Children's Trusts offer a challenge to youth work and its curriculum. This policy can be seen as a logical extension of the commitment to 'joined up' government which has since its inception been a mantra of New Labour. The context for this latest policy initiative was the death of Victoria Climbié from physical abuse and neglect despite being in contact with a number of agencies. The lack of specific responsibility for Victoria located in any one of the agencies concerned, together with the lack of coordination between the agencies, was one of the reasons given for this 'systemic' failure to prevent the death of this eight year old girl (Lord Laming, 2003).

The Children Act 2004 is a deliberate attempt to enforce the cooperation and integration of a number of disparate services, which historically have been largely separate in local government, from social services to education.

An important date in the road towards integration was 1st April 2006. This saw the advent of local authorities' Children and Young People's Plans for integrated services. As Roe, Head of Strategic Planning for Hampshire County Council said: 'We are on the brink of moving forward into a whole new world. The boundaries between professions will be broken down . . . The plans must set out the timetable for fully establishing children's trusts by 2008' (cited in Plummer, 2006: 14).

As we have seen from the young people's work force development plans for a common qualifications framework, there is a very real danger that the integration will become a homogenisation. Indeed, at a conference prior to the publication of *Youth Matters*: 'One youth worker asked Margaret Hodge (who was the then Minister for Youth) what his service's place was in the post green paper landscape, and was told this was symptomatic of a flawed attitude. Youth workers must look at the whole, rather than adopting a 'silo' approach, she said. They must think children and young people not services' (Barrett, 2004). Not only does this fail to appreciate the differences in approach and methodology of the various services but also has the capacity of the smallest and least powerful professions like youth work being subsumed by the larger and more powerful, like social work.

Comments by Paul Clark, director of children's services for Harrow, exemplify this problem. Harrow has restructured services into a 'Transitions Group' which includes a youth offending team, youth workers, leaving care services, Connexions etc. Whilst this is not problematic in itself and could lead to effective partnership work, what is more worrying is that the role of youth work is potentially being devalued and undermined. Clarke asserts that, 'The divisions between whether someone is a Connexions worker or a youth worker will be less important in the long run' (in Goddard, 2005: 13). He refers to workers as 'Transitions workers', not social workers or youth workers. He even suggests that 'we may have a detached youth work group in transitions that will be a mixed group from all the teams' (ibid.). What this exemplifies is a lack of understanding about the methodology of youth work. Detached work is a method of work, a mode of delivery which, though it implies a setting – the streets, a shopping parade or a local park, is more importantly a particular way of working with young people, based on the building of relationships, group work, starting where the

young people are, and adopts the procedural principles of the youth work process. When Clarke makes the assumption that anyone can do detached work, it shows a fundamental ignorance of youth work. Connexions could, in theory, take an aspect of their service out on to the streets but they would not be doing detached youth work.

This state of affairs has led to anxieties about both the place and role of youth work within new structures and practices. As Wylie, chief executive of the NYA acknowledges: '. . . if you put all the pieces together you could have anxieties, and vigilance is needed to ensure youth work is not overlooked' (Rogers, 2005).

The problem lies in a lack of appreciation for differences in methodology of the various professions. Whilst it may be true that the ultimate goals and purposes are similar, if not the same, which is evidenced by the ease with which the different professions have embraced the five outcomes, the methods by which various professions conceive of the best way to meet the outcomes are different. Indeed, Clarke explicitly makes this mistake: 'They (the different professions working with young people) are dealing with young people at a point of change in their lives, and they have a shared agenda about achievement, health and so on' (op cit).

This is further exemplified by looking at how a youth worker approaches a young offender compared to how a youth offending team (YOT) worker or social worker would. For the YOT worker, to a large extent, the offence, and their offending behaviour, is the primary focus. They would not have had contact without it, the action plan would be geared around both attempting to steer them away from further crime and pointing out the consequences of committing this and other offences. At least to some extent they will be labelled a young offender, and the worker inevitably perceives the young person through this lens. Similarly, the young person engages with the worker as an offender.

In youth work, the approach, the methodology adopted, is different. The young person is a person, an individual first and an offender second (if, in fact, they are thought of as an offender at all). This is precipitated by the starting point being the building of a relationship of mutuality and trust. It is a methodology which ensures the youth worker is there for them and is not prioritising the needs of others, whether that is the judicial system or the needs of victims. This methodology might only be achieved through voluntary participation, where the young people have a choice to engage or not.

The important point is both methodologies, or approaches, are valid. The police, courts and YOT workers have an approach which prioritises the formal consequences of actions. Both need each other, the youth workers need the police as guardians of the formal boundaries 'if necessary to arrest the young person' if they stray too far beyond the boundaries of acceptability, and the formal bodies like police need youth workers to work with the whole person, engage with their lives and the real issues. The approaches are complementary, but to a large extent mutually exclusive. They are parts of a whole which cannot be homogenised. It is the difference in methodologies which is the reason why an amalgamation of approaches is untenable.

The ECM agenda therefore is not necessarily problematic in itself – but a problem arises if one assumes that if the end points or ultimate aims are the same the means by which one attains those aims is also identical. It is the 'how' of youth work which is fundamentally important, the overarching values and procedural principles which inform the dynamic and evolving process are unique to youth work. Outcomes may be similar but the process of how we get there is significantly different. It is the process of youth work, its methodology and how its practice unfolds which makes it distinct and as such is at risk of being undermined and subsumed by a dominant ethos which does not appear to understand the subtleties of youth work practice.

It is imperative that the 'process' of youth work is articulated and acknowledged. This is why commentators like Barry (2005) are mistaken when they point out that what they think was wrong with the curriculum debate in the Journal *Youth and Policy* (Ord, 2004a; Jeffs, 2004; Merton and Wylie, 2004; Ord, 2004b etc.) was that it '. . . focused on the methods rather than the outcomes of youth work – the 'how' rather than the 'what' (2005: 21). It is the 'how' – the methodology, which is what defines youth work and distinguishes it from other professions' practices. Furthermore, recognition of this distinctive methodology is either failing to be comprehended or is being ignored in contemporary policy debates and initiatives.

The real story of the ECM 'five outcomes'

Only now does the real story of the ECM five outcomes become apparent. They are no more than a subtle but very effective political device for enabling the amalgamation and homogenisation of services. When the original idea of the integration of services, which in practice means the amalgamation of education and social services within local authorities, was first suggested the dissent was considerable. Even when these objections were collated as 'official responses', for example from the Association of Directors of Social Services (Cozens, 2003), the desire to preserve the distinctiveness of their own profession is clear.

However, post ECM and the Children Act (2004) workers and services are 'falling over themselves' in their desire to express how well they can meet these outcomes. The ease with which they achieve this undermines any criticisms they may wish to offer as to the feasibility of integrating services. It could be argued that the five outcomes are classic New Labour 'all style and no substance'. The five outcomes may in themselves be 'insubstantial', but their ability to promote and support the reform of existing services towards integration is not.

Other problems of integrated services

Common Assessment Framework

Another potential problem for the practice of youth work within the integrated services of children's trusts is the application of the *Common Assessment Framework* (CAF) (DfES, 2006b, 2006c). It is unclear exactly how this assessment framework will apply in practice, for example which of the professions will be responsible for carrying out the assessments and who will be given the responsibility of the 'lead professional'; and of course there may well be local variations. But the CAF does have the potential to work contrary to the practices of youth work, not least because youth work does not formally assess need in this manner prior to engagement. The young people's needs often emerge out of the development of a trusting relationship. Young people's needs, as we have seen, are critically reflected upon throughout the 'process' of youth work. Youth work is not 'a service' which is delivered in response to a particular identified need, in the same way that other welfare services operate.

A dilemma exists therefore for youth work: does it opt out of the CAF and therefore potentially relegate itself to the role of a second class profession within integrated services, as it may well be deemed incapable of assessing and therefore working with vulnerable young people. Or does it work within the CAF and potentially undermine the 'informal' nature of engagement, by working with formal assessment procedures.

Information sharing

There is an expectation within Children's Trusts that information will be shared across agencies about individuals and families. Whilst it is evident that there are distinct advantages to this process, for example in avoiding duplication since 'lack of information sharing' was also identified as one of the many faults leading to the death of Victoria Climbié (Lord Laming, 2003). Some youth work, however, perhaps detached work, or work with vulnerable or minority groups, works well precisely because it operates in isolation. Perhaps the projects are seen by the participants as outside the mainstream and having an independence which enables young people to develop trust in the youth workers.

Whilst the guidance from government suggests that, 'In most cases you will share information about them with consent' (DfES, 2006c: 3), they acknowledge that 'there may be circumstances when you need to override this' (ibid.). It is likely that the information sharing expectations of Children's Trusts will be undermining at least some of youth work's potential for developing trust and enabling engagement.

Ultimately, it is not the five outcomes which are necessarily problematic within the ECM agenda. The five outcomes when perceived as ultimate aims or end points with an explicit acknowledgement that they are best achieved, at least by youth workers through a process based curriculum, is not overly problematic. What is problematic is that within the integration, or dismantling, of the different professions the distinctive methodology of youth work may be lost.

Current policy developments: *Youth Matters*

The scope of *Youth Matters* (DfES, 2005a) and its follow up *Youth Matters: Next Steps* (DfES, 2006a)

goes far beyond curriculum, and as such beyond the scope of this book. But as *Youth Matters* does have important implications for both the curriculum of youth work and its methodology, some of these specific implications will be addressed as well as some of the wider concerns.

The 'proposals (in *Youth Matters*) aim to address four 'key challenges':

- How to engage more young people in positive activities and empower them to shape the service they receive.
- How to encourage more young people to volunteer and become involved in their communities.
- How to provide better information, advice and guidance to young people to help them make informed choices about their lives.
- How to provide better and more personalised support for each young person who has serious problems or gets into trouble'.

(DfES, 2005a: 5)

Searching for positives

The positives are unfortunately limited. As Wylie notes, the green paper does have a focus on 'Youth' which is in 'itself a recognition – by government – of the need to balance its concern for the years of childhood with a policy framework which addresses the changing vulnerabilities and the greater sense of self-determination, which characterise adolescence' (2006: 65). Cole acknowledges that '. . . many of the underlying principles are sound, although familiar. Making services for young people more integrated, efficient and effective . . . narrowing the gap between those who do well and those who do not . . .' (2006: 14). Also the notion of young people's 'empowerment' returns to the policy arena, and Davies welcomes: 'The commitment to increase young people's leverage on provision, including creating an opportunity fund giving young people some genuine control over resources' (2006: 22).

The concerns

There is, however, much to concern us about *Youth Matters*. One of the primary concerns is that it does not embrace youth work. As Davies points out: 'Ultimately *Youth Matters* isn't much (if at all) about youth work . . . many of the perspectives underpinning *Youth Matters* are deeply at odds with youth work as a distinctive practice' (2006: 22–3). For example, Davies notes the denial of the 'centrality of sociability in its own right to the teenage world which so shaped the thinking of both (previous government reports of) Albemarle and Thompson' (ibid.).

Youth Matters can be seen as another step in a direction started by *Transforming Youth Work* (DfES 2001, 2002) which as Smith (2003a) noted at the time indicated a shift from traditional youth work which was based around relationships to a more formalised 'delivery' emphasising outcomes and accreditation. He summarised this shift as a move from youth work to youth development. Another example of this shift away from distinctive aspects of practice appears with regard to participation, in relation to which, Young notes, *Youth Matters* also falls short: 'Participation is limited to consultation or specific projects with limited spheres of influence' (2005: 74).

A deficiency model and a targeted response

Indeed it is probably not the case that this shift in practice, or at least the attempts by policy makers to alter practice, began with *Transforming Youth Work*. Davies (1979) notes a worrying shift in the late 1970s which he describes as a move from social education to life skills training. However subsequent policies, in particular those of New Labour, culminating in *Youth Matters*, are an ever more stringent attempt to restrict and curtail the expansive 'universal' aspect of youth work into ever more specifically predetermined responses to perceived 'individual' need. *Youth Matters* like many of its predecessors operates from a 'deficiency model' of young people (Davies, 2005; Jeffs and Smith, 2006), that is a model which over emphasises young people as problematic individuals and is overly concerned with the need to find specific solutions to their 'problems'.

What is also evident, in addition to the deficit model, is the promotion of a targeted response to the perceived problems. In this respect *Youth Matters* is consistent with previous New Labour policies which emphasised the need to respond to NEET young people (those Not in Education, Employment or Training) through, for example the Connexions Strategy (DfES, 2000). What is potentially problematic about a targeted

approach is that it runs counter to the principle of voluntary participation, as targeted work very often involves a lack of choice as to whether or not to attend. Targeted work is not anathema to youth work, as voluntary participation is not a necessary or a sufficient condition of youth work. But what is required is a balance of universal and targeted work (Merton et al., 2004). Youth work practice would be much the poorer, and young people's ability to benefit from engaging in youth work would be much reduced if youth work over emphasised targeted work.

Marketisation of youth work

The Opportunity Card which establishes young people as consumers, in an attempt to coerce providers to make the 'places to go and things to do' relevant, is spurious in the extreme. It threatens to 'drive a coach and horses' through the network of youth projects, not least in the voluntary sector. As Jeffs and Smith (2006) note this aspect of current policy runs counter to the whole notion of the development of civil society, a significant part of which is the development of a network of support groups and educational endeavours which are 'bottom up' and 'grass roots' in their origin. The context for this policy is again the continued domination of New Public Management, which sees the establishment of an internal market as essential in the achievement of efficiency and effectiveness of service provision in the public sector (Power, 1997). The only result that this restructuring of provision according to the buying power of the consumer will have is it ensures the provision accords with a private sector philosophy, which over emphasises the ability of the market to meet individual or social need. A claim which is anything but widely accepted, or validated.

Ultimately *Youth Matters* has a very strong social control as opposed to educational agenda. It is concerned with finding 'things to do and places to go' for young people, as well as encouraging volunteering, in order to keep them out of trouble and off the streets, as well as emphasising an overly individualised and problematised conception of young people needing rehabilitation.

Where is the education?

Another major concern about *Youth Matters* is its distinct lack of emphasis on education. Whilst there has been some debate in youth work circles about the relative merits of social education as opposed to informal education as a legitimate educational basis for youth work (Smith, 1988) there is a unanimous agreement that youth work's primary role is educational.

Traditionally youth work has had branches in both the 'recreation/leisure', and 'social care/ welfare' camps. Its associations with recreation and leisure stem in part from it occurring in out of school leisure time, as well as its focus on leisure activities as a means of providing social education. Its legitimate associations with social care and welfare agendas results from its dealing with the welfare needs of young people which youth workers attempt to meet, often in conjunction with, or referral to, other services. However despite this, youth work has its roots firmly planted in education. Rosseter makes the point clearly: 'First and foremost youth workers are educators. All other roles they may fulfil at certain times are secondary' (1987: 52). It is the educational ethos which defines it and the majority of curriculum documents make this clear, as exemplified by North Somerset: 'the youth work role is an educational one, enabling young people to learn about themselves, their community and the wider world' (2005: 4).

Perhaps never before has a government green paper on youth and youth work been so remiss in its reference to this educational role. Even *Transforming Youth Work* had an educational curriculum (though perhaps admittedly not a particularly youth work friendly one) at the heart of its policy. Jeffs and Smith echo this point and deplore the 'extent to which education is being ejected from the youth work tent' (2006: 27). A clear illustration of this appears in the inability to incorporate the educational role of youth work in how *Youth Matters* frames activities. There is a clear emphasis on activities but it is within a distinctly different methodology. Activities are not as we saw emphasised in the process curriculum, a means to an end, vehicles for learning or methods of engagement through which a group process can ensue. They are either ends in themselves or portrayed as a regressive means of containing young people or keeping them off the streets.

Conclusions on recent policy

Perhaps the irony in the new agenda, whether that be *Transforming Youth Work, Every Child Matters, Youth Matters* and latterly with *Youth Matters Next Steps* (DfES, 2006a) is that whilst 'the long overdue recognition of youth work's important contribution' (Turner, 2006: 49) that many had desired, has finally arrived, it is in a manner which fails to comprehend youth work's principles and its practices: its curriculum, and this in turn threatens the very notion of youth work itself.

Transforming Youth Work paved the way for this new agenda, tabling youth work as a unique and important contributor to youth policy, but at the same time it proposed a curriculum which formalised and structured the work in a way which undermined the process approach to working with young people. *Every Child Matters* is perhaps the least threatening of the three, as though it pre-specifies outcomes to be worked towards they are broad enough not to be inconsistent with the locally agreed content areas and themes, and does not preclude a process approach to their achievement. The threats contained in *Every Child Matters* relate more directly to the potential for youth work to be subsumed by other more dominant professions in the integration of services. It is with *Youth Matters*, with the Opportunity Card and the 'marketisation' of youth work facilities, its stress on activities and its focus on targeted work, rehabilitating and supporting 'problematised youth', that provides the greatest threat to youth work .

It will be quite evident to readers that, given the policy pressures on youth work from central government, the curriculum of youth work is even more important now than ever before. It is through an authentic locally agreed curriculum framework, which identifies the values, purposes, process, methods and possible outcomes, that at least some, if not all, of youth work's distinctive practice can be retained. It is therefore to the use of curriculum that we must now turn our attention.

Section Five:
Curriculum in Context

Use of Curriculum

A distinction is made between two types of 'use' of curriculum; firstly the use of the curriculum in terms of how useful it is in facilitating learning, and secondly the usefulness of the concept as a whole. The former is concerned with the learning which results from the curriculum, which can be justified or assessed in terms of its outcomes or practical use. Whilst the latter, on the other hand, is concerned with the use to which the 'concept of curriculum' itself and the framing of youth work in terms of curriculum can bring. Too much emphasis on the former as we have seen can be problematic, for example with the utilitarian curriculum of the New Right. Utility should not be the guiding principle of a democratic curriculum (Kelly, 2005). Much of this book has been concerned with the use of curriculum in facilitating learning and in delivering the process. It is the latter: The use of the 'concept of curriculum' that this chapter is concerned with.

Curriculum as a concept is useful in many respects. It should be remembered that youth work does not have, as in formal education, a defined national curriculum, (despite attempts by Merton and Wylie, 2002; DfES, 2002) to propose a framework for one). What youth work has is a locally agreed curriculum. This is an important context, and there lies the opportunity to articulate the curriculum: youth work's values, purposes and methods. The value of a curriculum can be analysed according to how it influences practice on three distinct levels: through its communication of practice, through its development of practice, and through its legitimation of practice.

Communication of practice

Curriculum provides an important means by which youth work can communicate its worth, not least because as Young notes 'the future of youth work (and the youth service) rests, not on its ability to successfully pursue the agendas and objectives of other agencies, but on the clear articulation of its 'own 'core' purposes (Young, 1999: 120). Williamson concurs that 'the capacity

to explain the role of youth work (both to those who control the purse strings and to young people) is critical (2005: 80).

The role of the curriculum in youth work is to articulate and communicate the values, purposes, processes, methods and outcomes which define youth work.

This does not require any changing of either theory or practice, the fact remains that youth work as a whole has been poor in both articulating and communicating its practice: It has been 'poorly explained and promoted' (Williamson, 2005: 75). As a result much can be achieved by seizing the opportunity which curriculum affords it to communicate both its principles and practices. Williamson goes on however to suggests that youth work should actually adopt the language of current policy, as by 'framing the language of the practice of youth work in such terms immediately strikes a chord and secures a more favourable response' (2005: 81). This is a dangerous game and one must be very careful in reframing practice for the following reasons. Firstly one must be careful that in fact the reframing is consistent with the original ethos. Secondly one can not continuously change the terms of reference of practice and maintain credibility, and thirdly there is considerable ownership and historical continuity in the existing framing of youth work which could be lost with any change. Finally and perhaps most importantly it is not the actual framing of youth work which is the problem it is that historically youth work has been opposed to the wider communication of it through the use of the concept of curriculum.

One of the principal benefits of the communication of youth work through curriculum, is in the context of *Every Child Matters* (DfES, 2003) its emphasis on inter agency collaboration and the dismantling of departmental and inter professional boundaries, as well as the broader agenda of partnership working. In this environment the curriculum becomes a powerful means of articulating practice in the uncertain professional environment which invariably has the tension of combining collaboration and competition under the same roof. It should be noted that many in existing local authorities often have little knowledge or understanding of youth work, even in allied professions like teaching or social work.

Many of the curriculum documents belie this desire and commitment to communicate the work. The title in fact of Rochdale (2004) is *What is Youth Work? Curriculum Document*. Bournemouth also expressly states that:' The document will explain to our partners and other agencies the process by which youth work practice enables young people to develop and learn' (2005: 2). There is little doubt that the potential for communication is great, whether that be with stakeholders, fellow professionals, local or national politicians, young people and even potential funders.

Legitimacy of practice

The curriculum is not just a means of communicating practice. It is also a way of establishing the legitimacy of that practice, by communicating key aspects of both its principles and practice. Therefore in an environment in which youth work is under threat the curriculum becomes a medium for establishing the 'givens' of practice and there by enhancing both its credibility and status. Whilst this may not be the primary motivation for the development of curriculum, in the current climate it is certainly a useful by product. Indeed given the threat to the educational basis of youth work through *Youth Matters* it is imperative that curriculum continues to fulfil this role (DfES, 2005a; 2006a).

Curriculum is also an important means of agreeing and thereby legitimising local priorities. The educational priorities articulated within the curriculum become a defence against the vagaries of the local political climate, and help prevent the use of youth work to 'fire fight' the 'problem' of young people in the area. For example: Bradford (2006), presumably following the racially motivated riots, have cited Community Cohesion as one of their four core curriculum areas. Whilst this is a responsive example, the response is one which is framed in legitimate youth work practice. This is an example of a priority that is not contested, there would be few that would disagree with the setting of this as a priority following the riots, and indeed it would have

been remiss not to. The curriculum is however an important means of agreeing contentious areas of practice. Ord (2004b) cited the example of West Sussex where it was expressed that now race and racism was identified as an aspect of the youth work curriculum it was now much easier to undertake such work in an apparently 'racially unproblematic' area.

Development of practice

It was argued by Ord (2004a, 2004b) that curriculum was a 'bottom up' democratic enterprise and that the documents that were produced in each locality were through negotiation and consultation with all aspects of the service. This was contested by Jeffs (2004) who argued that they were 'motivated by fear . . . that without it they would lose their claim to be an educational service [and] . . . workers would drift ineffectually devoid of any clarity' (2004: 57). Ultimately Jeffs argues the curriculum documents were: 'Cooked up to meet the expectations of the inspectorate, politicians and mangers – people up the chain of command' (ibid.).

What Jeff's (2004) critique fails to appreciate is the distinction between the original political impetus for curriculum and the eventual production of the documents. As we saw in Chapter 1.1, on the historical emergence of an 'explicit' curriculum, following the ministerial conferences, there was an expectation from Ofsted that each authority would have its own document. This however, only provided a context for their production. The individual curricula are on the whole produced primarily by workers for workers. For example, Kingston Youth Service has produced four distinct documents (1992, 1996, 2002 and 2005) and no outside pressure or influence was brought to bear on content, direction or focus. This point is an important one and lays the foundation of the curriculum as a means for the 'development of practice'.

One of the primary purposes of establishing or revising a curriculum are the benefits it brings in communication, dialogue and agreement about practice amongst the workers in a given locality. This is a genuine opportunity which curriculum affords and one which ought to be taken. Given youth work's commitment to participation both in principle and in practice one would expect the development of curriculum within localities to be participative.

West Sussex appear to have adopted these principles in the development of their first document: 'When a curriculum for the West Sussex youth and community service was first instigated in 1987, it was clearly obvious that if it was to be implemented successfully, all colleagues with an involvement in the statutory youth service should, if they so wished, have the opportunity to contribute to its development' (1989: 1). 'To this end a Curriculum Consultative day was held' (ibid.) from which a 'working party' and 'specialist sub groups' were formed. A draft was produced and the working party made it explicit that they '. . . would welcome any comments that you [workers] may have' (ibid.).

In practice curriculum has embraced this developmental role in a number of different ways. Cheshire (2005) contains separate sections on theory and practice in order to educate the reader, as well as a programme of ideas and further reading including resource books and website links. Another example of this is the communication of good practice contained in Sunderland's tool kit (2005), as well as the case studies of best practice within Greater Merseyside (2004) which provides guidance for workers. In addition the sharing of good practice does not solely occur within local authority boundaries, as curriculum has on occasion become the focus of debate amongst authorities. Isle of Wight acknowledge six other authorities inputting into their updated 3rd edition (2000) and Bournemouth acknowledge research from Dorset, Wiltshire, Cornwall and Somerset. Some services have even combined to produce a document which covers a number of separate services, as is the case for Greater Merseyside (2004) which combines the boroughs of Sefton, Knowsley, Liverpool, Wirral, St Helens and Halton.

However with the increasingly pressurised world of modern local government time is not always on the services' side and things are often expected to have been done 'yesterday'.

Some authorities have specified the consultation or involvement of staff in the production of the revised editions. For example Bournemouth (2005) acknowledges consultation with staff and young people on two occasions in November 2004 and June 2005 in the production of their document. Buckinghamshire (2004) state that they hold an 'annual curriculum conference'. The extent to which this is merely ticking the box or affords genuine consultation is difficult to ascertain, however it is hard to believe that this consultation could approximate to genuine participation; which in turn asks the question about the extent to which the curriculum is owned by the workers.

Genuine participation is unfortunately not always the case. Some anecdotal evidence from part time youth workers and less senior youth workers, would suggest that those who are outside the curriculum development loop or 'inner circle' may feel excluded from the process. Key decisions are taken about 'framing the work', key priorities and issues of content, and then workers are consulted, feeling sometimes that this is a paper exercise as the document is all but written.

This is understandable given the increasing pressure to have a viable curriculum in place. One could imagine that, for example, if a service was being inspected after the Children Act (2004) there would almost certainly be some criticism in the final report about the service not having responded to the ECM five outcomes, though in reality everyone, including the inspectors, would know that they would have had precious little time to complete the task with any degree of involvement by the staff. Similarly in a service which has had specific criticism levelled at it about its lack of adequate curriculum framework, as was the case for example with Halton Youth Service (Ofsted, 2004). The degree of urgency with which the council would like to see this criticism responded to, would not be conducive to a quality participative process.

It is imperative that services continue to provide a genuine commitment to the process of curriculum development as well as the establishment of the curriculum 'product' in the form of a glossy document. A lack of participation in curriculum production represents a lost opportunity. It is divisive and misses an opportunity for growth and knowledge sharing which curriculum development offers. Where genuine participation is afforded to workers curriculum production and dissemination becomes a dynamic educational medium where practice is discussed debated, and learning is enhanced. This process of discussion about what the curriculum is and how the work will be framed is particularly important given the significant proportion of part time youth workers within the youth service. These workers have probably not had the opportunity to study youth work in the depth afforded the full time workers through their qualifying course. So the curriculum is particularly important for this group of workers. However, it is not only the finished article as a means of communicating the principles and practices of the work which is important. The process of producing the curriculum is educational for all workers and needs to involve all levels if it is to retain its vibrancy and be genuinely owned by all; and not just be a document which sits on the shelf until the 'inspector calls'.

Curriculum and the 'community of practice'

If curriculum is to fulfil its potential both as a developer of practice and as a communicator of practice it must actively seek to be one of the vehicles through which the 'community of practice' is developed and enhanced. Community of practice is a term coined by Lave and Wenger (1991). It is a social theory of learning and seeks to explain how people learn in social settings, what they call 'situated learning'.

It conceives of learning as 'social participation' and is opposed to traditional concepts of learning which sees knowledge as abstract, learned in isolation and then applied in practice. Relationships, identity, meaning making are both integral to and essential for learning and knowledge according to Lave and Wenger. Learning is a combination of 'community: learning as belonging', 'Identity: learning as becoming', 'Meaning: learning as experiencing' and 'Practice: learning as doing' (Wenger, 1998: 5). According to Wenger we are all involved in communities of practice all the time, at work, school, family life, etc. All have distinct and yet overlapping communities of practice associated with them.

Communities of practice are independent of organisational structures and systems, and because of their informality they generally 'cut across' them. The importance of communities of practice according to Wenger is that through them:

Individuals develop and share the capacity to create and use knowledge. Even when people work for large companies (or organisations) they learn through participation in more specific communities made up of people whom they interact with on a regular basis . . . they are a company's most versatile and dynamic knowledge resource and form the basis of an organisation's ability to know and learn.
(Wenger, 1998b: 1)

Individual youth work organisations, agencies and services will have their own, perhaps even a large number of, communities of practice, within which workers locate themselves, find meaning and are continuously learning and developing their practice. Given this, it is vital that the youth work curriculum engages with the communities of practice within the organisation for the following reasons. Firstly, as the communities of practice are the primary locus of meaning making and learning in any organisation, if those responsible for the development of the curriculum are not actively engaged with the relevant communities of practice it has the potential for the curriculum to be less meaningful to the members of the organisation as it has not incorporated the extant meanings already in operation.

Secondly, the communities of practice offer an important resource for the communication of the curriculum and it is unlikely that the curriculum will become embedded unless those networks are engaged with. Thirdly, and perhaps most importantly, the curriculum has the potential to provide a symbiotic developmental role whereby both the communities of practice and the curriculum itself are developed. It is the curriculum that can provide the vehicle for this. Wenger suggests that although the communities of practice develop 'naturally' this does not mean that they do not require 'nurturing'. Indeed communities of practice can be most active and perform at their optimum when they have a particular activity to engage in. Curriculum development would provide an ideal activity for this process. In Wenger's terms the curriculum would become a 'creative artefact', for the development of the communities of practice, which would in turn develop the curriculum into a 'living curriculum'.

Curriculum and Culture

Culture is an all pervading but unique aspect of human life. Culture is perhaps founded in the ability of humans to use language, it is characterised by norms values, attitudes, beliefs and customs which imbue social life; and manifests itself through the myriad aspects of human life including music, art, science etc. Importantly as a result of culture who we are is not determined exclusively by biology, as it is with animals, but through what we learn as a result of the particular society or culture we grow up in. This is not however a passive relationship, there is a tension or dynamic between the individual's adaptation to their culture as well as the individuals themselves precipitating cultural and social change. Curriculum reflects and is influenced by culture and it has a responsibility to acknowledge both aspects of this dynamic: As a result Lawton suggests both 'culture and curriculum should be concerned with "what might be" as well as "what is"' (1996: 25).

This results in a key dynamic in the youth work curriculum. On the one hand youth work assists young people to learn about, and adapt to, the existing social reality, for example negotiate relationships or make career choices, within existing states of affairs. On the other hand, youth work encourages young people to engage in a critical dialogue regarding that social reality and its effects on the lives of individuals and communities, ultimately attempting to influence and change this status quo. For example, developing an understanding about the social circumstances within which relationships are negotiated, like our gendered lives; or understanding the political circumstances within which career choices are made. This overtly 'political' aspect to youth work should not be underestimated, and it is often this important aspect of the curriculum which is missing from contemporary conceptions of practice. Youth work is concerned with social change as much as it is concerned with individual change.

Lawton (1978) describes the two opposing sides of this tension as equating to two differing aspects of curriculum: the society centred curriculum and the child centred curriculum. The former places a pre-eminence on the importance of 'society's needs' within the curriculum and is primarily concerned with how it can best mobilise individuals to meet those needs. This is opposed to the child (or person) centred curriculum, which places at its centre the needs of the individual, which as we have seen is what in part underpins the process curriculum. Although this distinction is useful, it does not fully account for the aspect of 'social critique' that is evident within curriculum and culture as the person-centred curriculum does not explicitly have a commitment to social change.

This cultural dynamic or tension in the youth work curriculum equates to the age old distinction between youth workers as agents of social control as opposed to its conceptualisation as an educational means of achieving individual and collective liberation. This tension has always imbued practice. It would be naïve to think there was an emancipatory golden age when issues of social control were not impacting on practice. For example Davies (1999a) shows that the origins of statutory youth work were in the concerns for unaccompanied youth during both the first and second world wars. Jeffs also notes: 'There is, it must be stressed, nothing inherently progressive or 'empowering' about a great deal of practice: much of which unthinkingly accepts 'problems' as defined by those in power and responds accordingly . . . [thus workers respond] to teenage pregnancy and truancy as 'serous social problems' rather than, in many instances, as rational responses to an irrational world' (2001: 42). However within current policy formations of youth work and its curriculum, especially within *Transforming Youth Work* (2002) and continued within *Youth Matters* (DfES, 2005a) there has been a noticeable shift towards the society centred, and away from the emancipatory and person-centred curriculum.

This manifests itself in two distinct but related ways; how it conceives of young people's development and the function or purpose of the curriculum.

The function of curriculum is best understood through a distinction proposed by Ross between on the one hand what he describes as the rise of the 'utilitarian or vocational' curriculum and the other two distinctly different approaches the 'academic' curriculum and the progressive or process curriculum. The academic curriculum 'seeks to develop critical thinking through the controversies and arguments within traditional subjects' (2000: 123). This is, it is argued, the dominant pedagogy of traditional higher education, which conceives of learning as the acquiring of expertise and mastering the discipline. The progressive or process driven curriculum is participative and experiential, and conceives of the teacher as facilitator and the learning is person centred and self directed (Stenhouse, 1975).

The utilitarian or vocational curriculum which is opposed to both the academic and the process approach is exclusively concerned with the use to which the curriculum is put. Ross maintains that the utilitarian curriculum dominated the New Right agenda of the Thatcher era and has to a large extent influenced educational policy since. The adoption of utility as the guiding principle of curriculum brought with it a threat to the previously dominant liberal ethos.

Curricula founded on principles of utility are predominantly based on objectives or product approaches. Golby (1989) identifies this as the 'technocratic tradition' one that is founded on 'rational planning' akin to the approach taken by Tyler (1949). The outcomes of the curriculum are of utmost importance in this approach with particular emphasis on 'transferable skills and 'employability'. The needs of society predominate and there is a distinct lack of reflection upon the society which makes these demands or a critique of the status quo, which this approach inevitably supports.

It is quite apparent that current curriculum policy in youth work is following similar patterns. The emphasis on accreditation as a means of increasing employability is perhaps the starkest example of this.

It should be noted that no curriculum will be entirely devoted to one side of this dynamic, particularly not the curriculum of a public funded educational system, whether formal or informal. This tension between the need for stability and the learning about existing culture will always be played out with the need for a social critique which focuses on progression,

development and change. In this respect Williamson (2001) is right to point out that youth work operates within a triangle of young people's needs, the progressive values of practice and the policy priorities which are increasingly orientated towards the maintenance of the status quo.

Sociology of the youth work curriculum

Hurley and Treacy (1993) apply a sociological analysis of the educational role of youth work and thereby clarify the distinction we have introduced between a critical curriculum and a curriculum that seeks to maintain the status quo. They apply 'the two broad sociologies of education: functionalism and conflict theory' to elucidate this issue. Functionalism proposes that society operates according to a consensus, inequality is believed to be inevitable and society to be meritocratic. The education system functions as part of this consensus. Thus: 'schools and educational institutions help young people discover their talents so that when they join the workforce they will enter an occupation suitable to them and needed by society' (1993: 5).

On the contrary conflict theorists do not believe a consensus exists. They believe inequality is neither necessary nor inevitable and its continuation merely serves the interests of those who benefit from the inequality. Conflict theory has its origins in the works of Marx (1844) and his conception of the exploitative relationship between capital and labour. Marx's own 'surplus theory of value' which attempts to explain this exploitative relationship has now been somewhat discredited (Wolff, 2003). But conflict theory has been developed to articulate a 'class struggle', which it is proposed underpins economic and social life. This is driven primarily by 'a class based analysis of the worker's struggle for better wages and conditions of work, versus the capitalist's drive for ever greater profits' (Wolff, 2003: 3).

Importantly as a result of this 'class' conflict society has an inherent problem with social control. Conflict theorists see the role of education as a means of achieving this control. Although not offered by Hurley and Treacy, an extension of conflict theory to an analysis of youth work should incorporate the key social divisions of gender, race, disability, age etc. as equally valid root causes of conflict. For example

The sociology of radical change	
Radical structuralist	**Critical Social education**
Radical humanist	Radical structuralist
Interpretive	Functionalist
Personal development	**Character building**
The sociology of regulation	

Subjective (left) — Objective (right)

Figure 5.2.1 Sociological models of youth work adapted from Burrell and Morgan's framework (cited in Hurley and Treacy, 1993: 7)

from a feminist or anti-racist perspective the origins of conflict along divisions of sex or race are not necessarily seen along the lines of class. This additional aspect of conflict theory can be incorporated without affecting the legitimacy of Hurley and Treacy's overall framework.

Hurley and Treacy's (1993) 'sociological models of youth work'

Hurley and Treacy then develop this initial distinction of functionalism and conflict theory to propose four distinct sociological models of youth work, each of which are derived from the four distinct sociological paradigms, functionalist and interpretative, radical structuralist, radical humanist (Burrell and Morgan, 1979).

'Character building' model of youth work

The character building model is firmly located in the functionalist paradigm. As we have seen functionalism emphasises the need for order, stability and the maintenance of the status quo. This perspective is exemplified by Emile Durkheim: 'Society can only survive if there exists among its members a sufficient degree of homogeneity; education perpetuates and reinforces this homogeneity by fixing in the child from the beginning the essential similarities that collective life demands' (1956: 71, cited in Hurley and Treacy). The character building model of youth work which is derived from, or located within, this sociological perspective is one which does not ask any questions of the society in which the individuals are located. The status quo is

accepted as legitimate, and the means of maintaining the status quo is to a large extent achieved by the continuation of the norms, values and beliefs contained within the consensus. Therefore according to Hurley and Treacy: 'In this context functionalists see the need for a new social institution, youth work, to support the school, the family, and the church to develop the individual's capability to distinguish 'right from wrong' and to live by the moral codes of society. This role for youth work is ideologically a conservative one' (1993: 11). The character building model of youth work is one which is necessarily opposed to social change.

Characteristic of this model of youth work is a belief that 'youth work is complementary to family and school . . . it recognises that young people must be prepared for specific roles in society [and] . . . it recognises that young people need to have their energy and drive directed in a constructive fashion' (1993: 15). In practice character building youth work programmes 'will concentrate on inculcating existing moral and social values of society and act as a means through which rule breaking and disorder is prevented . . . [Emphasising] 'Education for life programmes, health education, relationships, faith education, alcohol and substance programmes etc.' (1993: 17). Where any political education takes place within this perspective it focuses on 'existing structures and how they work'. This model is often but not exclusively associated with uniformed groups.

'Personal development' model of youth work

The personal development model is located within an interpretive paradigm.

The interpretive perspective's starting point is everyday social life, with an attempt to 'interpret' and understand it. 'Interpretive' sociology is concerned with understanding the essence of the everyday world primarily from the viewpoint of the actions directly involved in the social process' (1993: 20). It is consistent with a functionalist perspective as 'the paradigm adopts a consensus approach to society because they fail to question the social realities' (ibid.), failing to grasp wider issues of conflict and relations within society which perpetuate that conflict.

Unlike functionalism which is an objective or macro approach, believing it is objective structures such as the family or school which define individual social life, interpretivism is a subjective or micro approach believing that 'everyday activity is the building block of society' (Hurley and Treacy, 1993: 21). They emphasise the meanings individual 'social actors' give to their actions, and these 'meanings are personal to the actor, they are not given by the culture or society, rather they are constructed from culture by the actors involved' (ibid.). Interpretivists do not deny the influence of social structures such as family or education but that the starting point for understanding social life must be the 'consciousness and intentionality' of individuals.

The personal development model of youth work therefore pays little attention to the wider social issues beyond the individual needs of young people. It perceives of young people as being in a period of transition and 'youth work contributes to the smooth transition through this phase by providing a variety of opportunities to acquire the skills necessary to take on the responsibilities of adult life' (Hurley and Treacy, 1993: 27). A key focus of this model therefore is the developmental tasks of adolescence: 'acquiring a positive self image, stable relationships and the social skills necessary to participate within existing social structures' (1993: 28).

In practice the personal development model emphasises an exploration and clarification of young people's own values especially 'related to health, sexuality, faith etc and to understand the consequences of the choices they make for themselves' (1993: 28). This model attempts to develop in young people a 'sense of control over their lives and believe that they can succeed if they try hard enough' (1993: 30). Participation is encouraged within existing structures as young people 'are prepared for an active role in society' (ibid.).

This model is also essentially a conservative one in that it is opposed to social change, conceiving of youth work as a means of working with individuals to make the most of themselves and their lives within existing social structures.

'Critical social education' model of youth work

The critical social education model is a 'conflict model' and is located within a radical humanist paradigm, 'defined by its concern to develop a sociology of radical change from a subjectivist standpoint. The approach places most emphasis upon radical change, modes of domination, emancipation, deprivation and potentiality' (Burrell and Morgan, 1979: 32 cited in Hurley and Treacy, 1993: 32). 'One of the basic notions underlying the whole of this paradigm is that the consciousness of the individual is dominated by the ideological superstructures with which a person interacts, and that these drive a wedge between oneself and ones true consciousness' 1993: 32). Its starting point therefore is a critical approach to the self, seeing it as 'socially constructed'. It is concerned with notions of 'alienation' and 'false consciousness' which prevent human fulfilment. The cause of which is located in ideology and the maintenance of the inherent conflict in society: for example within patriarchy and the continued belief in the dominance of men over women, and within heterosexism and the continued belief in the 'naturalness' of heterosexuality over homosexuality.

The starting point for a critical social education model of youth work is that 'Structural factors impede the development of groups of young people [and] . . . inequalities which exist in society impact adversely on the life chances of groups of young people, particularly the disadvantaged' (1993: 41). It focuses primarily on 'consciousness raising strategies' and attempts to encourage realisations that the 'dominant value system is an inherent part of young people's problems' (ibid.). In practice the critical social education model of youth work is focused on 'self managed groups' of young people, within which power is transferred, and issues of concern can be explored. Work with girls and young women from a feminist perspective is a typical example of this.

'Radical social change' model of youth work

The radical social change model is located within a radical structuralist paradigm which whilst similarly being concerned with 'radical change', it is however from an 'objective standpoint'. Its starting point is the structure of society not the social relations within society. It is broadly Marxist in origin and follows the Marxist belief that consciousness is determined by economic relations. Put simply the exploitative nature of capitalism is the determining factor in human consciousness and the resulting social relationships. It is essentially class based and therefore proposes that one does not understand, or change society, by investigating the relationships between people but by changing economic relations. Radical structuralists both 'seek to explore ways in which cultural beliefs and practices, which support capitalist society are created, perpetuated and reproduced through the education system' (1993: 46), as well as aiming 'to rise above the level of critique and discuss strategies for change' (ibid.). One of the means of influencing, although not in itself changing, the structure of society is through 'cultural change' and it is in this respect that radical structuralists are committed.

In practice therefore 'Young people may be regarded as potential agents of cultural revolution. From this radical perspective revolutionary change in the socio-cultural system is a necessary though not sufficient condition for transforming economic and political systems from capitalist into full socialised societies, in which human potential is no longer systematically distorted and wasted' (1993: 55). Youth work from within this perspective is exclusively political in which young people will 'have developed the skills to act . . . and be viewed as political activists' (1993: 57), the ultimate aim of which is institutional change and transformation.

Towards a 'critical' youth work curriculum

It is probably naïve to think that within a public funded, and, therefore at least implicitly, a government backed youth provision, one could maintain a radically structuralist perspective, certainly not explicitly, within the curriculum.

There may be workers from within this perspective who choose to work subversively, or perhaps who work voluntarily or through small scale non-government funded groups, but this perspective is not one which is prominent in the youth work curriculum. Similarly it is hard to see the legitimacy of the character building model in an authentic youth work curriculum. It contains a passive view of young people, and is overly concerned with young people 'fitting in' rather than promoting choice, and the development of either the individual or the society is absent. It is not entirely absent however, as it can be seen to be operating through the enforcement of ground rules, and ultimately through the implementation of 'bans' in youth clubs. As Jeffs and Banks (2001) rightly point out youth workers do inevitably at times work 'as controllers'.

The two sociological models which underpin the youth work curriculum are therefore those of the 'personal development' and the 'critical social education' models. There will be workers who locate themselves more in one, than the other. For example: feminist workers, who are committed to combating sexism and the emancipation of both women and men from the constraints of their 'gendered lives', will clearly favour the critical social education model. Similarly however the developmental tasks of youth cannot be ignored from the youth work curriculum. The transition of young people from childhood to adulthood, though a problematic concept (White and Wynn, 1997) does provide a 'framework' for a number of key tasks, which need to be completed; like identity formation, the negotiating and maintaining of adult relationships, as well as the practical ones like finding a job. Youth work related to these transitions will be located within the personal development model.

The documents produced in the field vary in the extent to which they adopt a critical or conservative ethos. Some are explicitly critical for example: 'Youth work in North Somerset inspires and challenges young people to change the world' (2005: 3). Similarly Wandsworth propose that 'Youth work encourages young people to be both critical and creative in their response to their world' (2001: 12). For some however this is less explicit.

One of the main threats to a critical curriculum is, as we have seen, from the current policy agenda. The models of youth work implicit within this new agenda, whether that be *Transforming Youth Work* (DfES, 2002) *Every Child*

Matters (DfES, 2003) or *Youth Matters* (DfES, 2005a) oscillates between 'character building' and 'personal development'. Those who advocate that the new agenda is unproblematic, e.g. Merton and Wylie (2002) could perhaps, quite rightly point to some of the common ground within both youth workers' and government's commitment to the personal development model; where youth work is seen as a supportive role in assisting young people to find their way in the world. However this is not sufficient for an authentic curriculum. Youth work is necessarily critical and aspires towards social as well as individual change and transformation. It is committed to challenging and confronting inequality and not accepting that it is inevitable. The lack of a critical perspective in the current policy agendas is its defining weakness and what sets it apart from authentic youth work. Seeing youth work in terms of critical social education clearly allows youth workers to distinguish between current policy and youth work practice and enables them to articulate what are the distinctive and crucial differences.

Some of the more problematic curriculum in practice are therefore those which have whole heartedly adopted the new agenda and altered their whole curriculum accordingly, as we saw for example with Sunderland (2005a). Whilst they do not necessarily become incompatible with youth work, they are worryingly 'uncritical'. They are in danger of depriving young people of their potential for fulfilment by ignoring wider critical questions about how 'who we are' is at least in part defined by social forces, and how these forces impact on how we inevitably see ourselves and perceive each other. Youth work is first and foremost about these key questions which concern individual's lives as well as the society and wider world in which they live.

It is the purpose of the youth work curriculum, to frame these key questions by articulating the educational values, purposes, methods and if necessary the 'emergent' outcomes of the distinctive educational practice of youth work, and thereby assist in the support, preservation and development of it.

References

Adams, J. (2001) Group Work. in *The RHP Companion to Working with Young People*. Lyme Regis: Russell House Publishing.

Aristotle (5th Century BC) *Nichomachean Ethics* (Translated with Introduction and notes by Terence Irwin,1999). Indianapolis: Hackett.

Arnstein, S. (1969) A Ladder of Citizen Participation. *AIP Journal*, 216–24.

Baker, J. (1996) *The Fourth Partner: Participant or Consumer?* Leicester: Youth Work Press.

Banks, S. (1999) *Ethical Issues in Youth Work*. London: Routledge

Banks, S. (2001) Professional Values in Informal Education Work. in Deer Richardson, L. and Wolfe, M. (Eds.) *Principles and Practice of Informal Education*. London: Routledge Falmer.

Barnett, R. and Coate, K. (2005) *Engaging the Curriculum in Higher Education*. Berkshire: OUP.

Barrett, S. (2004) Youth Services Are Part of the Package. *Young People Now*, 1–7 Dec. 15.

Barrett, S. (2005) Youth Service Spending Needs Monitoring. *Young People Now*, 14–20 Sep. 13.

Barry, M. (1996) The Empowering Process. *Youth and Policy*, 54: 1–12.

Barry, M. (2005) Curriculum by any other name . . . *Youth and Policy*, 86: 19–32.

Berne, E. (1964) *Games People Play*. Harmondsworth: Penguin.

Bernstein, B. (1996) *Pedagogy, Symbolic Control and Identity: Theory, Research, Critique*. London: Taylor and Francis.

Berry, M. (2001) *Challenging Transitions*. London: Save the Children.

Bessant, J. and Evans, M. (1996) Gendering the Youth Work Curricula in Australia: A Case Study. In *Youth and Policy*, Autumn (1996) Volume 54.

Biddulph, S. (1984) *The Secret of Happy Children*. London: Thorsons.

Blacker, H. (2001) Learning From Experience. in Deer Richardson, L. and Wolfe, M. (Eds.) *Principles and Practice of Informal Education*. London: Routledge Falmer.

Blenkin, G.M. and Kelly, A.V. (1987) *The Primary Curriculum*. 2nd edn. London: PCP.

Bloom, B.S. et al. (1956) *The Taxonomy of Educational Objectives. Handbook 1, Cognitive Domain*. London: Longmans.

Bloxham, S. (1993) Managerialism in Youth and Community Work: A Critique of Organisational Structures and Management Practices. *Youth and Policy*, 41: 1–12.

Boagey, J. (2006) Blackberries From Mexico to Help Bring a Global Theme to Youth Work. *Young People Now*, 14–20.

Boagey, J. et al. (2006) *Blackberries from Mexico: Youth Work, Young People and the Global Society*. Leicester: NYA.

Bobbitt, F. (1918) *The Curriculum*. Boston: Houghton Mifflin.

Boud, D., Cohen, R. and Walker, D. (1983) *Using Experience for Learning*. Buckingham: OUP.

Bournemouth Youth Service (2005) *Curriculum Policy*. Bournemouth Borough Council.

Bracey, M. (2006) Last word. *Young People Now*, 8–14 Mar. 44.

Bradford Youth Service (2006) *Youth Work Curriculum Framework*. Bradford Met. Borough Council.

Bradford, S. (2005) Modernising Youth Work: From the Universal to the Particular and Back Again. in Harrison, R. and Wise, C. (Eds.) *Working with Young People*. London: OUP/Sage.

Brent, J. (2004) The Arch and the Smile. *Youth and Policy*, 84: 69–73.

Brighton and Hove Youth Support Service (2005) *Curriculum Framework*. Brighton and Hove City Council.

Bristol Youth Service (2002) *Youth Work Curriculum Framework*. Bristol City Council.

Brookfield, S. (1983) *Adult Learning, Adult Education and the Community*. Milton Keynes: OUP.

Bruner, J. (1960) *The Process of Education*. Cambridge: Harvard University.

Bruner, J. (1966) *Towards a Theory of Instruction*. Cambridge: Harvard University.

Bruner, J. (1966) *Man: A Course of Study*. Cambridge, MA: Educational Development Center.

Bruner, J. (1996) *The Culture of Education*. Cambridge: Harvard University.

Buckinghamshire Youth and Community Service (2004) *Curriculum Policy*. Buckinghamshire County Council.

Burke, J. (1995) *Outcomes, Learning and the Curriculum.* London: The Falmer Press.

Burke, T. (1991) A New Breed of Agency. *Young People Now.*

Burke, T. (2004) Has Informal Learning had its Day? *Young People Now*, 8.

Burns, R.W. and Brooks, G.D. (1974) Processes, Problem Solving and Curriculum Reform. in Eisener, E.W. and Vallance, E. (Eds.) *Conflicting Conceptions of Curriculum.* Berkeley: McCutchan Pubs.

Burrell, G. and Morgan, G. (1979) *Sociological Paradigms and Organisational Analysis.* London: Heinemann.

Burrow, L. (1971) *Discovery and Experience: A New Approach to Training, Group Work and Teaching.* London: Oxford University Press.

Button, L. (1971) *Discovery and Experience: A New Approach to Training, Group Work and Teaching.* London: Oxford University Press.

Button, L. (1974) *Developmental Group Work with Adolescents.* London: Hodder and Stoughton.

Carr, W. (1995) *For Education: Towards Critical Educational Enquiry.* Milton Keynes: OUP.

Cheshire Youth Service (2005) *Youth Work Curriculum.* Cheshire County Council.

Clarke, J., Gerwitz, S. and McLaughlin, E. (2000) *New Managerialism: New Welfare?* Milton Keynes: OUP.

Cole, B. (2006) Youth Policy 1995–2005: From 'The Best Start' to 'Youth Smatters'. *Youth and Policy*, 89: 7–19.

Cole, G.A. (2004) *Management Theory and Practice.* 6th edn. London: Thomson Learning.

Collander-Brown, D. (2005) Being with Another as a Professional Practitioner. *Youth and Policy*, 88: 5–27.

Cornbleth, C. (1990) *Curriculum in Context.* London: Falmer.

Cornwall Youth Service (2003) *Curriculum Document.* Cornwall County Council.

Coventry Youth Service (2004) *Curriculum Framework.* Coventry City Council.

Cozens, A. (2003) Response from the Association of Directors of Social Services to the Consultation on Every Child Matters. Available online at: http://www.adss.org.uk/publications/consresp/2003/greenfin.pdf

Crimmins, D. et al. (2004) *Researching Socially Excluded Young People: A National Study of Street Based Youth Work.* Leicester: NYA/Joseph Rowntree Foundation.

Crosby, M. (2005) Working With People as an Informal Educator. in Harrison, R. and Wise, C. (Eds.) *Working with Young People.* London: OUP/Sage.

Cumbria Youth Service (undated) *Cumbria Youth Service Curriculum.* Cumbria County Council.

Curzon, L.B. (1990) *Teaching in Further Education.* 4th edn. London: Cassell Education.

Davies, B. (1979) From Social Education to Life Skills Training: In Whose Interests. at: http://www.infed.org/archives/bernard_davies/davies_in_whose_interests.htm

Davies, B. (1991) Whose Youth Service Curriculum. *Youth and Policy*, 32: 1–9.

Davies, B. (1999a) *From Voluntaryism to Welfare State: A History of the Youth Service in England. Volume 1.* Leicester: Youth Work Press.

Davies, B. (1999b) *From Thatcherism to New Labour: A History of the Youth Service in England. Volume 2.* Leicester: Youth Work Press.

Davies, B. (2004) Curriculum in Youth Work: An Old Debate in New Clothes. *Youth and Policy*, 85: 87–97.

Davies, B. (2005) Youth Work: A Manifesto for Our Times. *Youth and Policy*, 88: 5–27.

Davies, B. (2006) If Youth Matters Where is the Youth Work? *Youth and Policy*, 89: 21–26.

Davies, N. (2003) Fiddling the Figures at http://www.guardian.co.uk/crime/article/0,995906,00.html

Deer Richardson, L. and Wolfe, M. (Eds.) (2001) *Principles and Practice of Informal Education,* London: Routledge Falmer.

Denhart, R. (2003) *Theories of Public Organisations,* 4th edn. New York: Wadsworth.

Derbyshire Youth Service (undated) *A Framework For Youth Work That Connects Young People.* Derbyshire County Council.

DES (1969) *Youth and Community Work in the 70s.* (Fairbairn-Milson Report) London: HMSO.

DES (1982) *Participation and Experience.* (Thompson Report). London: HMSO.

DES (1987) *Effective Youth Work: A Report by HMI Education Observed 6.* London: DES.

Devon Youth Service (2002) *Youth Work in Devon: A Practical Guide to the Youth Work Curriculum.* Devon County Council.

Devon Youth Service (2005) *Every Child Matters: The Youth Work Contributions to the Five Outcomes.* Devon County Council.

Devon Youth Service (2006) *Youth Work in Devon: A Practical Guide to the Youth Work Curriculum.* Devon County Council.

Dewey, J. (1966) *Democracy and Education: An Introduction to the Philosophy of Education.* New York: Free Press.

Dewey, J. (1997) *Experience and Education.* New York: Macmillan.

DfEE (2000) *Connexions: The Best Start in Life for All Young People.* Nottingham: DfEE.

DfES (2001) *Transforming Youth Work: Developing Youth Work for Young People.* Nottingham: DfES.

DfES (2002) *Transforming Youth Work: Resourcing Excellent Youth Services.* Nottingham: DfES.

DfES (2002a) *Good Practice Guide, on Involving Young People in the Governance of Connexions.* Nottingham: DfES.

DfES (2002b) *Encouraging and Recognising Young People's Involvement in Connexions.* Nottingham: DfES.

DfES (2003) *Every Child Matters.* London: HMSO.

DfES (2005a) *Youth Matters.* London: HMSO.

DfES (2005b) *Putting the World into World Class Education.* London: HMSO.

DfES (2006a) *Youth Matters: Next Steps.* London: HMSO.

DfES (2006b) *Making it Happen: Working Together for Children, Young People and Families.* London: HMSO.

DfES (2006c) *The Lead Professional: A Practitioners Guide, Integrated Working to Improve Outcomes for Children and Young People.* London: HMSO.

Doyle, M.E. (2001) On Being an Educator. in Deer Richardson, L. and Wolfe, M. (Eds.) *Principles and Practice of Informal Education.* London: Routledge Falmer.

Durkheim, E. (1956) *Education and Sociology.* New York: The Free Press.

Eisener, E.W. and Vallance, E. (Eds.) (1974) *Conflicting Conceptions of Curriculum.* Berkeley: McCutchan Pubs.

Eisner, E.W. (1979) *The Edcuatonal Imagination: On the Design and Evaluation of School Programs.* London: Collier Macmilan.

Eisner, E.W. (1982) *Cognition and Curriculum.* London: Longman.

Elliott, J. (1995) Education in the Shadow of the Education Reform Act. in Rudduck, J. (Ed.) *An Education that Empowers, A Collection of Lectures in the Memory of Lawrence Stenhouse.* Avon: Multilingual Matters.

Ellis, J.W. (1990) Informal Education: A Christian Perspective. in Jeffs, T. and Smith, M.K. *Using Informal Education.* Buckingham: OUP.

Emler, N. (2001) *Self Esteem: The Costs and Causes of Low Self Esteem.* York: Joseph Rowntree Foundation/YPS.

Ewen, J. (1975) *Curriculum Development in the Youth Club.* Leicester: NYB.

Exell, R. (2001) Employment and Poverty. in Fimister, G. (Ed.) *An End in Sight: Tackling Child Poverty in the UK.* London: CPAG.

Fabes, R., Payne, B. and Wood, J. (2003) *Who Says Nothing Ever Happens Around Here?* Leicester: NYA.

Flint, W. (2005) *Recording Young People's Progress and Accreditation in Youth Work.* Leicester: NYA.

Ford, K. et al. (2005) *Leading and Managing Youth Work and Services for Young People.* Leicester: NYA.

Freire, P. (1972) *The Pedagogy of the Oppressed.* Harmonsworth: Penguin.

Garratt, D. (2004) Youth Cultures and Sub Cultures. in Roche, J. et al. *Youth in Society.* 2nd edn. London: Sage/OUP.

Gergen, K.J. (1994) *Realities and Relationships.* Cambridge, MA: Harvard University Press.

Giddens, A. (1991) *Modernity and Self Identity.* Cambridge: Polity Press.

Gilchrist, R., Jeffs, T. and Spence, J. (2001) *Essays in the History of Community and Youth Work.* Leicester: Youth Work Press.

Gloucestershire Youth and Community Service (2004) *The Youth Work Curriculum.* Gloucestershire County Council.

Gloucestershire Youth and Community Service (circa 1992) *The Youth Work Curriculum.* Gloucestershire County Council.

Goddard, C. (2005) Ready to Tackle Transitions. *Young People Now,* 14–20th Sep. 13.

Golby, M. (1989) Curriculum Traditions. in Moon, B., Murphy, P. and Raynor, J. (Eds.) *Policies for the Curriculum.* London: Hodder and Stoughton.

Greater Merseyside (2004) *Greater Merseyside Youth Service Curriculum.* Greater Merseyside Youth Services.

Grundy, S. (1987) *Curriculum: Product or Praxis.* London: Routledge Falmer.

Habermas, J. (1972) *Knowledge and Human Interests.* London: Heinamann.

Hall, T. and Williamson, H. (1999) *Citizenship and Community.* Leicester: Youth Work Press.

Hall, T. Williamson, H. and Coffey, A. (2000) Young People, Citizenship and the Third Way. *Journal of Youth Studies,* 3: 4.

Hampshire County Youth Service (1991) *Youth work Policy and Curriculum.* Hampshire County Council.

Hampshire County Youth Service (2003) *Hampshire County Youth Service Curriculum.* Hampshire County Council.

Handy, C. (1999) *Understanding Organisations*. 4th edn. London: Pelican.

Harland, K. et al. (2005) Worth their Weight in Gold. *Youth and Policy*, 86: 49–61.

Hart, R. (1992) *Children's Participation: From Tokenism to Citizenship, Innocenti Essays, No.4*. Florence: Unicef.

Hartlepool Youth Service (2005) *Curriculum Development Policy*. Hartlepool Borough Council.

Havering Youth Support Service (2004) *Curriculum for Youth Work . . . Guidance on Making a Difference*. London Borough of Havering.

Heidegger, M. (1927) *Being and Time*. Trans. Macquire, J. and Robinson, E. (1962) Oxford: Blackwell.

Herefordshire Youth Service (2002) *Community Youth Service Curriculum*. Herefordshire Council.

Hertfordshire Children, Schools and Families (2002) *Youth Service Curriculum Policy*. Hertfordshire County Council.

Hinsliffe, G. (2003) BMA Chief Attacks 'Obscene' Pressure to hit NHS Targets. http://www.guardian.co.uk/medicine/story/0,,987366,00.html

Hirst, P.H. (1969) The Logic of Curriculum. in Hooper, R. (Ed.) The *Curriculum: Context, Design and Development*. Edinburgh: OUP.

Hirst, P.H. (1974) *Knowledge and the Curriculum: A Collection of Philosophical Papers*. London: Kegan Paul.

Hirst, P.H. and Peters R.S. (1974) The Curriculum. in Eisner, E.W. and Vallance, E. (Eds.) *Conflicting Conceptions of Curriculum*. Berkeley: McCutchan Pubs.

Hodge, M. (2003) *Letter to Principal Youth Officers*. 13th Dec.

Hodge, M. (2005) *The Youth of Today*. Speech to the Institute of Policy Research. 19th Jan.

Hooper, R. (Ed.) (1973) *The Curriculum: Context, Design and Development*. Edinburgh: Oliver and Boyd/OUP

Hopkinson, A. (2006) NYA Editorial, *Young People Now*, 1–7 Mar. 20.

Hounslow Youth Service (2005) *Curriculum Framework (Revised and Amended)*. London Borough of Hounslow.

Houston, G. (1993) *The Red Book of Groups and How to Lead them Better*. Rochester Foundation.

Howard, M. (2003) Speech to the Houses of Parliament. http://www.guardian.co.uk/uk_news/story/0,,994028,00.html

Hull Youth Service (2003) *Curriculum Document*. Hull City Council.

Hurley, L. and Treacy, D. (1993) *Models of Youth Work: A Sociological Framework*. Dublin: Irish Youth Work Press.

Huskins, J. (1996) *Quality Work with Young People*. London: Youth Clubs UK.

Huskins, J. (2003) Self Esteem and Youth Development: A Youth Work Perspective. in Richards, K. (Ed.) *Self Esteem and Youth Development*. Ambleside: Brathay.

Illeris, K. (2002) *The Three Dimensions of Learning*. Samfundslitteratur: Roskilde University Press.

Ingram, G. and Harris, J. (2001) *Delivering Good Youth Work*. Lyme Regis: Russell House Publishing.

Isle of Wight Youth and Community Service (2000) *Youth and Community Service Curriculum*. Isle of Wight Council.

Jeffs, T. (2001) First Lessons: Historical Perspectives on Informal Education. in Deer Richardson, L. and Wolfe, M. (Eds.) *Principles and Practice of Informal Education*. London: Routledge Falmer.

Jeffs, T. (2004) The Youth Work Curriculum: A Letter to Jon Ord. *Youth and Policy*, 84: 55–61.

Jeffs, T. and Banks, S. (1999) Youth Workers as Controllers. in Banks, S. *Ethical Issues in Youth Work*. London: Routledge.

Jeffs, T. and Smith, M.K (1998/9) The Problem of Youth for Youth Work. *Youth and Policy*, 62: 45–66.

Jeffs, T. and Smith, M.K (2006) Where is Youth Matters Taking us? *Youth and Policy*, 91: 23–39.

Jeffs, T. and Smith, M.K. (1990) *Using Informal Education*. Buckingham: OUP.

Jeffs, T. and Smith, M.K. (2005) *Informal Education, Conversation, Democracy and Learning*. 3rd edn. Derby: Education Now.

Kellmer Pringle, M. (1980) *The Needs of Young People: A Personal Perspective*. London: Hutchinson.

Kelly, A.V. (1995) *Education and Democracy, Principles and Practices*. London: Paul Chapman.

Kelly, A.V. (2005) *The Curriculum: Theory and Practice*. London: Sage.

Kingston Youth Service (1992) *Breaking the Mould: A Youth Service Curriculum*. Royal Borough of Kingston.

Kingston Youth Service (1996) *Kingston Youth Service Curriculum*. Royal Borough of Kingston.

Kingston Youth Service (2002) *Kingston Youth Service Curriculum*. Royal Borough of Kingston.

Kingston Youth Service (2005) *Kingston Youth Service Curriculum*. Royal Borough of Kingston.

Kohler, W. (1947) *Gestalt Psychology*. New York: Mentor Books.

Kolb, D. (1984) *Experiential Learning, Experience as the Source of Learning and Development*. Englewood Cliffs, NJ: Prentice Hall.

Laming, Lord (2003) *The Climbié Enquiry Report*. London: HMSO.

Lave, J. and Wenger, E. (1991) *Situated Learning, Legitimate Peripheral Participation*. Cambridge: Cambridge University Press.

Lawton, D. (1978) Why Curriculum Studies? in Lawton, D. et al. *Theory and Practice of Curriculum Studies*. London: Routledge and Kegan Paul.

Lawton, D. (1996) *Beyond the National Curriculum: Teacher Professionalism and Empowerment*. London: Hodder and Stoughton.

Leicester Youth Service (2003) *Youth Service Curriculum Framework*. Leicester City Council.

Leicestershire Youth Service (2000) *A Youth Work Curriculum for Leicestershire*. Leicestershire County Council.

Lewin, K. (1951) *Field Theory in Social Sciences*. London: Harper Row.

Lodge, A. et al. (2006) Going Green in Devon. *YouthAction*, Spring.

Lovett, T., Clarke, C. and Kitmurray, A. (1983) *Adult Education and Community Action*. Crookhelm.

LutonYouth Service (2003) *Luton Youth Service Curriculum Framework and Toolkit*. Luton Borough Council.

Mahoney, J. (2001) What is Informal Education? in Deer Richardson, L. and Wolfe, M. (Eds.) *Principles and Practice of Informal Education*. London: Routledge Falmer.

Manchester Youth Service (2006) *Curriculum Framework*. Manchester City Council.

Marsh, J. (1992) *Key Concepts for Understanding Curriculum*. London: The Falmer Press.

Marx, Karl (circa 1844) *Selected Writings*. 2nd edn. McLennan, D. (Ed.) (2000) Oxford: Oxford University Press.

Maslow, A. H. (1954) *Motivation and Personality*. London: Harper Row.

Merton Youth Service (1997) *Youth Work Curriculum for Merton*. London Borough of Merton.

Merton, B. and Wylie, T. (2002) *Towards a Contemporary Youth Work Curriculum*. Leicester: NYA.

Merton, B. and Wylie, T. (2004) The Youth Work Curriculum: A Response to Jon Ord. *Youth and Policy*, 84: 63–7.

Merton, B. et al. (2004) *Research Brief: An Evaluation of the Impact of Youth Work in England*. London: DfES.

Mill, J.S. (1909) *Autobiography*. Norton, C.E. (Ed.) New York: P.F. Collier and Son.

Milton Keynes Youth Service (2003) *Curriculum Policy*. Milton Keynes Council.

Milton Keynes Youth Service (2005) *Curriculum Policy Framework*. Milton Keynes Council.

Ministry of Education (1960) *Youth Service in England and Wales* (Albemarle Report). London: HMSO.

Ministry of Reconstruction (1919) *Report of the Adult Education Committee of the Ministry of Reconstruction*. London: HMSO. Republished R.D. Waller (Ed.) (1956) *A Design for Democracy*. London: Max Parrish.

Mintzberg, H. (1979) *The Structuring of Organisations*. Englewood Cliffs: Prentice Hall.

Mizen, P. (2004) *The Changing State of Youth*. Basingstoke: PalgraveMacmillan.

Moon, J. (2000) *Reflection in Learning and Professional Development*. London: Kegan Paul.

Nemko, J. (2006) *Who am I? Who Are You*. Lyme Regis: Russell House Publishing.

Newman, E. and Ingram, G. (1989) *The Youth Work Curriculum*. London: Further Education Unit.

Night Shift (1990) *The Big Red Book of the Youth Work Curriculum*. Abergavenny: Night Shift.

Norfolk Youth Service (2005) *Youth Work Curriculum Guidelines*. Norfolk County Council.

Northern Ireland Youth Service (1987) *Youth Work: A Model for Effective Practice*. Northern Ireland Youth Service.

Nottingham (circa 2003) *Youth Service Curriculum Framework*. Nottingham City Council.

Nottinghamshire Youth Service (2006) *Curriculum Policy and Framework*. Nottinghamshire County Council.

NYB (1990) *Danger or Opportunity: Towards a Core Curriculum for the Youth Service?* Report of the First Ministerial Conference. Leicester: NYB.

NYB (1991) *Towards a Core Curriculum for the Youth Service: The Next Step*. Report of the Second Ministerial Conference. Leicester: NYB.

NYA (1992) *Planning and Evaluation in a Time of Change: The Next Step*. Report of the Third Ministerial Conference. Leicester: NYA.

NYA (1995) *Planning the Way: Guidelines for Planning Your Youth Work Curriculum*. Leicester: NYA.

NYA (1999) *Ethical Conduct in Youth Work: A Statement of Values and Principles From the NYA*. Leicester: NYA.

NYA (2005a) *Spirituality and Spiritual Development: A Consultation Paper.* Leicester: NYA.

NYA (2005b) *The Edge: NYA Briefing.* Issue 8, winter. Leicester: NYA.

O'Neill, O. (2002) *Reith Lectures: An Introduction.* http://www.open2.net/trust/oneilLon_trust/oneilLon_trust2.htm

Ofsted (1993) *The Youth Work Curriculum.* London: HMSO.

Ofsted (2001a) *Inspecting Youth Work: A Revised Framework for Inspection.* London: HMSO.

Ofsted (2001b) *Report on Cornwall Youth Service Ofsted Inspection.* London: HMSO. https://www.ofsted.gov.uk/reports/servicereports/385.htm#Main

Ofsted (2001c) *Report on Wirral Youth Service Ofsted Inspection.* London: HMSO. https://www.ofsted.gov.uk/reports/servicereports/423.htm#Main

Ofsted (2002a) *Report on Bradford Youth Service Ofsted Inspection.* London: HMSO. https://www.ofsted.gov.uk/reports/servicereports/379.htm#P158_10226

Ofsted (2002b) *Report on Kingston Youth Service Ofsted Inspection.* London: HMSO. https://www.ofsted.gov.uk/reports/servicereports/396.htm

Ofsted (2003) *Report on Manchester Youth Service Ofsted Inspection.* London: HMSO. https://www.ofsted.gov.uk/reports/servicereports/500.htm#P183_6309

Ofsted (2004) *Report on Halton Youth Service Ofsted Inspection.* London: HMSO. https://www.ofsted.gov.uk/reports/servicereports/567.htm

Ord, J. (2004a) The Youth Work Curriculum and the Transforming Youth Work Agenda. *Youth and Policy,* 83: 43–59.

Ord, J. (2004b) The Youth Work Curriculum as Process not as Output and Outcome to Aid Accountability. *Youth and Policy,* 85: 53–69.

Oxfordshire Youth Service (2005) *Curriculum: 2.* Oxfordshire County Council.

Peel, J.C.F. (2003) Self Esteem and Youth Development: The Case for a Person-Centred Approach. in Richards, K. (Ed.) *Self Esteem and Youth Development.* Ambleside: Brathay.

Peters, R.S. (1959) *Authority, Responsibility and Education.* London: Allen and Unwin.

Phillips, D. (2005) Develop a Passion of Recording Youth Work Outcomes. *Young People Now,* 10 Sep. 17–23.

Plummer, J. (2006) A Plan of Action. *Young People Now,* 14.

Plymouth Youth Service (1999) *Curriculum Framework.* Plymouth City Council.

Plymouth Youth Service (2006) *Curriculum Framework.* Plymouth City Council.

Pope, D. (1983) *The Objectives Model of Curriculum Planning and Evaluation.* London: Council for Educational technology.

Power, M. (1997) *The Audit Society.* Oxford: Oxford University Press.

Pring, R. (1978) Philosophical Issue. in Lawton, D. et al. (1978) *Theory and Practice of Curriculum Studies.* London: Routledge & Kegan Paul.

Raths, J.D. (1971) Teaching Without Specified Objectives. *Educational Leadership,* 714–20.

Reading Youth Service (2006) *Reading Youth Service Curriculum.* Reading Borough Council.

Redcar and Cleveland Youth and Community Service (2006) *Youth Work Curriculum Framework.* Redcar and Cleveland Borough Council.

Redfearn, G. (2003) Youth Work against Racism. *Young People Now,* 17–23 Sep.

Redfearn, G. (2005) A Gateway to Employment. *Young People Now,* 13–19 April.

Rees Youth and Community Centre (2005) *Service Level Agreement.* Plymouth City Council.

Richards, K. (Ed.) (2003) *Self Esteem and Youth Development.* Ambleside: Brathay.

Robertson, S. (2004) The Youth Work Curriculum. *Youth and Policy,* 84: 75–9.

Rochdale Youth Service (2004) *What is Youth Work? Curriculum Document.* Rochdale Met. Borough Council.

Rogers, C. (1967) *On Being a Person.* London: Constable and Co.

Rogers, C. with Freiberg, H.J. (1994) *Freedom to Learn.* 3rd edn. Prentice Hall.

Rogers, E. (2005) Youth Workers Reassured Social Care Will Not Take Over. *Young People Now,* 20–26 April, 2.

Ross, A. (2000) *Curriculum: Construction and Critique.* London: Falmer Press.

Rosseter, B. (1987) Youth Workers as Educators. in Jeffs, T. and Smith, M.K. *Youth Work.* Basingstoke: Macmillan.

Rousseau, J-J. (1762) *Emile or on Education.* Intro, translation and notes. Bloom, A. (1978) New York: Basic Books.

Ruddock, J. (Ed.) (1995) *An Education that Empowers, A Collection of Lectures in the Memory of Lawrence Stenhouse.* Avon: Multilingual Matters.

Ryle, G. (1949) *The Concept of Mind.* London: Hutchison.

Save the Children and Dynamix (2002) *Participation: Spice it up!* Cardiff: Save the Children.

Schon, D.A. (1987) *The Reflective Practitioner: How Professionals Think in Action.* USA: Basic Books.

Shenton, F. (2004) *Everyday Participation: A Practical Guide to Everyday Youth Involvement.* London: UK Youth.

Shropshire Youth Service (2001) *Curriculum Document: Youth Matters.* Shropshire County Council.

Smith, B. (2003) No Strings Attached: The Challenge of Detaching Ourselves from the Outcomes of Work with Young People. in Richards, K. (Ed.) *Self Esteem and Youth Development.* Ambleside: Brathay.

Smith, H. (2002) Seeking out the Gift of Authenticity. *Youth and Policy*, 77: 19–32.

Smith, M.K. (1983) *Creators not Consumers.* Leicester: Youth Clubs UK.

Smith, M.K. (1988) *Developing Youth Work.* Milton Keynes: OUP.

Smith, M.K. (1994) *Local Education.* Buckingham OUP.

Smith, M.K. (2000) *Curriculum Theory and Practice: The Encyclopaedia of Informal Education.* www.infed.org/biblio/b-curric.htm

Smith, M.K. (2003a) From Youth Work to Youth Development. *Youth and Policy*, 79: 46–59.

Smith, M.K. (2003b) Introduction to *Effective Youth Work.* http://www.infed.org/archives/gov_uk/effective_youth_work.htm#outcomes

South Tyneside Youth Service (2005) *Curriculum Guidelines.* South Tyneside Council.

Southend-on-Sea Youth and Connexions Service (2006) *Curriculum Framework.* Southend-on-Sea Borough Council.

Spence, J. (1990) Youth Work and Gender. in Jeffs, T. and Smith, M. (eds.) (1990) *Young People, Inequality and Youth Work.* Basingstoke: Macmillan.

Spence, J. (2004) Targeting, Accountability and Youth Work Practice. *Practice*, 16: 4.

Spence, J. (2001) Activities, in Deer Richardson, L. and Wolfe, M. (Eds.) *Principles and Practice of Informal Education*, London: Routledge Falmer.

St Helens Met. Borough Council (2001) *St Helens Youth Service Curriculum Plan.* St Helens Met. Borough Council

Stanton, N. (2004) The Youth Work Curriculum and the Abandonment of Informal Education. *Youth and Policy*, 85: 71–85.

Stenhouse, L. (1975) *An Introduction to Curriculum Research and Development.* London: Heinemann.

Stenhouse, L. (1980) Product or Process? A Reply to Brian Crittenden. Reprinted in Rudduck, J. and Hopkins, D. (Eds.) (1985) *Research as a Basis for Teaching.* London: Heinemen.

Stenhouse, L. (1983) *Authority, Education and Emancipation.* London: Heinemann.

Suffolk Community Education (2002) *Youth Work Curriculum Statement.* Suffolk County Council.

Sunderland Youth Service (2005a) *Curriculum Development. A tool kit for youth work.* Sunderland City Council.

Sunderland Youth Service (2005b) *A Guide to Youth Work Performance Indicators.* Sunderland City Council.

Taylor, P.H. (1973) Purpose and Structure in the Curriculum. in Hooper, R. *The Curriculum: Context, Design and Development.* Edinburgh: OUP.

Taylor, P.H. and Richards, C.M. (1985) *An Introduction to Curriculum Studies.* 2nd edn. Berkshire: NFER-Nelson.

Thompson, N. (2001) *Anti Discriminatory Practice.* 3rd edn. Basingstoke: Palgrave.

Tiffany, G. (2001) Relationships and Learning. in Deer Richardson, L. and Wolfe, M. (Eds.) *Principles and Practice of Informal Education.* London: Routledge Falmer.

Tomlinson, D.R. and Trew, W. (2002) *Equalising Opportunities, Minimising Oppression.* London: Routledge.

Torbay Youth Service (2006) *Torbay Youth Work Curriculum Framework.* Torbay Met. Borough Council.

Tower Hamlets Youth Support Service (2004) *Youth Work Curriculum Framework . . . Making Effective Youth Work Possible.* London Borough of Tower Hamlets.

Turner, G. (2006) Review of Ford, K. et al. (2005) Leading and Managing Youth Work and Services for Young People. Leicester: NYA. *Youth and Policy*, 89: 100–2.

Turner, P. (2006) Why Does Youth Matter? *Youth and Policy*, 89: 49–53.

Tyler, R.W. (1949) *Basic Principles of Curriculum and Instruction.* London. University of Chicago Press.

United Nations (1989) *Convention of the Rights of the Child.* http://www.unicef.org/crc/

Van Vark (2005) I Want to Be like You. *Young People Now*, 9–15 Mar. 16–7.

Wade, H. and Badham, B. (2004) *Hear by Right: Standards for the Active Involvement of Children and Young People.* Leicester: NYA.

Wakefield Young People's Service (2006) *Young People's Service Curriculum.* City of Wakefield Met. District Council.

Wandsworth Youth Service (1999) *Youth Radio Development Report.* London Borough of Wandsworth.

Wandsworth Youth Service (2001) *Youth Service Curriculum Guidelines.* London borough of Wandsworth.

Wandsworth Youth Service (2003) *Fundamental F.M. Annual Report.* London Borough of Wandsworth.

Wenger, E. (1998a) *Communities of Practice, Learning, Meaning and Identity.* Cambridge: Cambridge University Press.

Wenger, E. (1998b) Communities of Practice: Learning as a Social System available online at http://www.co-i-l.com/coiUknowledge-garden/cop/lss.shtml

West Berkshire Culture and Youth Service (no date) *Youth Service Curriculum.* West Berkshire Council.

West Sussex Youth and Community Service (1989) *Curriculum Development Update: Consultative Draft.* West Sussex County Council.

West Sussex Youth Service (2000) *West Sussex Youth Service Curriculum* (issue 3). West Sussex County Council.

West Sussex Youth Service (2005) *West Sussex Youth Service Curriculum* (issue 5). West Sussex County Council.

Whitaker, D.S. (1989) *Using Groups to Help People.* London: Routledge.

White, P.J. (2005) The Value of Youth Work. *Young People Now,* 12–18 Jan. 16–7.

Williamson, H. (2003) Tolerance of Ideas Extends to Youth Work. *Young People Now,* 17–23 Sep. 11.

Williamson, H. (2004) Good Outcomes Can't Always be Measured. *Young People Now,* 24–30 Nov. 15.

Williamson, H. (2005) Challenging Practice: A Personal View on 'Youth Work' in Times of Changed Expectations. in Harrison, R. and Wise, C. *Working with Young People.* London: Sage/OUP.

Wiltshire County Council Youth Development Service (2005) *Learning for Life: A Youth Work Curriculum Framework.* Wiltshire County Council.

Wittgenstein, L. (1958a) *Blue and Brown Books.* Oxford: Blackwell.

Wittgenstein, L. (1958b) *Philosophical Investigations.* Oxfor-1d: Blackwell.

Wolff, J. (2003) *Karl Marx; Stanford Encyclopaedia of Philosophy.* http://www.seop.leeds.ac.uk/entries/marx/index.html

Woods, R. G. and Barrow, R. St C. (1975) *An Introduction to the Philosophy of Education.* London: Methuen.

Wylie, T. (1997) Developmental Youth Work 2000. in Ledgerwood, I. and Kendra, N. (Eds.) *The Challenge of the Future.* Lyme Regis: Russell House Publishing.

Wylie, T. (2006) Testing a Green Paper. *Youth and Policy,* 89: 64–9.

Wylie.T. (2001) Those That I Guard I do Not Love: A Memoir of HM Inspectorate in the Thatcher Era. in Gilchrist, R., Jeffs, T. and Spence, J. (Eds.) *Essays in the History of Youth and Community Work.* Leicester: Youth Work Press.

Wynn, J. and White, R. (1997) *Rethinking Youth.* London: Sage.

Young People Now (2005) *Funding: Trends and Spends Young People Now.* http://www.ypnmagazine.com/news/index.cfm?fuseaction=full_newsandID=8252

Young People Now News (2006) Minister Criticises Statutory Provision. *Young People Now,* 26th Aug.

Young, B. (2005) The Impact of Youth Matters on Youth Participation. *Youth and Policy,* 89: 70–4.

Young, K. (1999) *The Art of Youth Work.* Lyme Regis: Russell House Publishing.

Young, K. (2006) *The Art of Youth Work.* 2nd edn. Lyme Regis: Russell House Publishing.

Youth Bank (2006) http://www.youthbank.org.uk/

Index